The First Franciscan Woman

Margaret CARNEY, O.S.F.

The
First Franciscan Woman

Clare of Assisi & Her Form of Life

Franciscan Press
Quincy University
1800 College Avenue
Quincy, Illinois 62301-2699

Franciscan Press
Quincy University
1800 College Avenue
Quincy, Illinois 62301-2699.

Library of Congress Cataloging-in-Publication Data

Carney, Margaret.
    The First Franciscan Woman : Clare of Assisi and her Form of Life / Margaret Carney.
        p. cm.
    Includes bibliographical references.
    ISBN 0–8199–0962–9
        1. Clare, od Assisi, Saint, 1194–1253.   2. Christian saints—Italy—Assisi—Biography.   3. Assisi (Italy)—Biography.
    I. Title.
    BX4700.C6C37   1993
    271'.97302—dc20

                                       93–7917
                                        CIP

Cover design by John Sotirakis
Page layout by Jean François Godet-Calogeras

To
The Sisters of St. Francis
of the
Providence of God

Acknowledgements

My religious community is dedicated to the Providence of God. This providence is most often manifested in persons and in the course of developing this research many teachers, co-workers, and friends have enabled me to persevere towards this publication.

The faculties of the School of Theology of Duquesne University, the Franciscan Institute of St. Bonaventure University, and the Institute of Franciscan Spirituality of the Pontificium Athenaeum "Antonianum" guided my development in the fields of theology and the history of Franciscan spirituality. Particular mention needs to be made of Conrad Harkins, O.F.M., Maurice Sheehan, O.F.M. Cap., and Luigi Padovese, O.F.M. Cap., and George Worgul.

Serendipity often compliments scholarship in the formal sense and the adventures of this work were shared by a number of friends and colleagues who contributed linguistic skill, secretarial help and unflagging energies of encouragement. Sheila Carney, R.S.M., Nancy Celaschi, O.S.F., Leonora DiStefano, O.S.F., Alma Dufault, F.M.M., Aidan Mullaney, T.O.R., Raphael Pazzelli, T.O.R. and André Cirino, O.F.M., offered these providential supports.

My Roman sojourn was blessed by the hospitality of the School Sisters of St. Francis, the Franciscan Missionaries of Mary, and the Capuchin Collegio of San Lorenzo. All things—from

8

prayer to *pasta* to paper clips—were given in friendship and common devotion to our Franciscan renewal.

This book is based upon a dissertation which was completed in 1989 and published under the title *The Rule of St. Clare and the Feminine Incarnation of the Franciscan Evangelical Life.* I am indebted to Francisco Iglesias, O.F.M. Cap., for his critical evaluation of the potential of that research, to Optatus van Asseldonk, O.F.M. Cap., for the Franciscan equivalent of rabbinical wisdom and determination to address the lack of feminine presence in the field, to Regis Armstrong, O.F.M. Cap., who provided the tools for the research and the brotherly enthusiasm for each step taken in that direction.

Jean-François Godet-Calogeras redeemed the errors of my first attempts at a computerized text and continued the journey with me as architect of this published book. Roberta Agnes McKelvie, O.S.F., brought enormous resourcefulness to the preparation of this manuscript by perfecting its style and augmenting its documentation. Dr. Terry Riddell has been a gracious and accommodating editor as we collaborate to inaugurate the new Franciscan Press.

My small Franciscan sisterhood, to whom this work is dedicated, took a substantial risk in freeing me to pursue these studies. In spite of increasing concerns about financial and personnel limitations, my sisters shared my hope that I could make a special contribution by reclaiming the voice of so many women of our tradition rendered voiceless by the biases of the traditional histories at our disposal. Their love for our charism and their courage in pursuing the refounding of Franciscan life in our time is, indeed, a manifestation of Providence lifting the lowly and filling the hungry with good things. Sisters Virginia Pask and Marian Blodis led the community in the years in which this work began. I salute them here and I thank them. The members of my own Council, J. Lora Dambroski, Janet Gardner, Alma Pukel, Joanne Brazinski and Kathleen Bruzga know only too well the reasons for which I extend gratitude beyond telling to them.

Finally, my father, Edmund Earl Carney, should be credited with the educational result of his unfailing answer to every childhood question: "There is a book somewhere in this house with the answer to that. Look it up!" What follows results from a decade of "looking it up" in service to our shared future as friars, poor sisters and penitents who find in Clare our "leader, mother and teacher."

Margaret CARNEY, O.S.F.
Feast of St. Margaret of Cortona
May 16, 1992

TABLE OF CONTENTS

Introduction

THE FIRST FRANCISCAN WOMAN

Clare of Assisi, who was born in 1193 and died in 1253, was the most important woman who emerged within the unfolding history of the movement inspired by Francis of Assisi. She joined him in his search for a way to incarnate the powerful message of the Gospel of Christ in a situation of economic, social and ecclesiastical reformation. She has been revered through the centuries as his disciple, friend, and co-worker. In recent decades a resurgence of research into the origins of the Franciscan order has uncovered enormous quantities of information and insight concerning Francis. Only within the last five years has it become apparent that interest and concern have surfaced about providing a similar investigation of Clare's contribution. Clearly, the time has come to grasp the meaning of Clare and the entire feminine dimension of the Franciscan evangelical life. Wherever Franciscans gather, whether for academic convocations, centennial celebrations, or the events by which we continue to nourish our individual lives, the question of Clare, her sisters, and their role in our formation rises to meet us. After decades of incredibly rich discoveries of materials and methods for reclaiming the reality of Francis and the men who accompanied him, we are embarking upon the recovery of the "anima" of our charismatic roots.

The timeliness of this effort is supported by the relatively recent multiplication of scholarly publications of the writings and sources related to Clare.[1] We may think, for instance, of the appearance in recent years of the Spanish work of I. Omaechevarria, in French of D. Vorreux[2] and then that of M-F. Becker, J-F. Godet, and T. Matura. In the Italian language sector we recognize the studies provided by Sr. Chiara Augusta Lainati, and in Germany, those of Engelbert Grau.

With the publication of Regis J. Armstrong's *Clare of Assisi: Writings and Early Documents,* the English-language sector of the Franciscan family has been afforded a crucial tool that may help to reduce the gap which exists between Western Europe and English-speaking countries regarding adequate resources for the study of Clare's spirituality. This work coincides with a veritable explosion of interest and publication on the topic of medieval women. We have realized that it would take little effort to compile a substantial library of publications dealing with women from the Benedictine and Cistercian traditions, and the women who peopled that fascinating phenomenon known as the beguines. However, aside from an occasional appearance such as the Brookes' article in Derek Baker's *Medieval Women,* and Shank and Nichols' *Peaceweavers,* Clare and her many sisters among the varied expressions of feminine Franciscan life in the Middle Ages are notably absent in English-language scholarship. This absence impoverishes an appreciation of the diversity of medieval religious women's experiences on the one hand, and on the other indicates an inadequate appreciation on the part of the contemporary Franciscans of the historical role played by these women.

---

[1] Full bibliographic information for works cited here will appear in sections of the text in which they are used, unless otherwise noted.

[2] Damien Vorreux, O.F.M. *Sainte Claire d'Assise: Documents* (Paris: Éditions Franciscaines, 1983.)

It also raises a series of questions. How is it possible that after decades of renewed research and study on the part of Franciscan scholars around the world, so little is known of the early Franciscan women? Why is it that we in the English-speaking world found ourselves lacking basic tools—translations, commentaries, and studies needed to puruse this knowledge? Why is it that such prestigious gatherings as the annual Medieval Institute at Western Michigan University boasts dozens of offerings on medieval women, but women of the Franciscan era hardly rate a mention on the program compared with the number of papers on Benedictine women or the Beguines? Or—how is it possible that the incredible voluminous research on medieval women seems to have played little or no part in refining or revising our understanding of the early sisters? Even the excitement of expanding knowledge has been dampened by the repeated experience of reading pages devoted to the lives of early abbesses, mystics, wonder-workers, reformers and foundresses, only to discover that the first Franciscan women have rarely been given attention in the otherwise comprehensive research of modern medieval scholars.

These and similar questions began to confront me during the summer of 1986. At the invitation of Conrad Harkins, O.F.M., I taught a course on early Franciscan women at the Franciscan Institute of St. Bonaventure University. As I developed resources for the small group of students who shared that summer sojourn with me, I began to compare methods used for studying the many aspects of the history and spirituality of the Franciscan Order. I realized that the underlying assumptions of most work in the field was that all could be understood in light of the writings of Francis and his successors and in light of the experience and interpretations of the masculine branches of the Franciscan family. Clare was viewed most often simply in relationship to Francis, and her achievements were described principally in terms of how closely she approximated his language, his mode of life and his spirit. Little account was taken of how she was influenced by events after his death. (She survived him by twenty-seven years.) Rarely, if ever, was it imagined or suggested that *she* might have influenced *him* or the leaders of the community who lived between the time of Francis' death in 1226 and Clare's in 1253. Seldom was she described in the context of the many activities stirring among medieval women in their search for a perfect form of Christian life. Consequently, generations of Franciscans were absorbing images and interpretations of Clare that did not allude to the many activities among religious women of the time and the many leaders among them who consciously and—at times collaboratively—sought new models and missions for feminine aspirations. What would happen, I began to wonder, if we could place Clare within the framework of the history of the Friars Minor as it unfolded not only during the lifetime of Francis, but also in the years after his death, and also within the framework of the medieval women of central Italy in the late twelfth and early thirteenth centuries?

The decision to experiment with such a "reading" of Clare's story came gradually and with an encouragement from Regis Armstrong, O.F.M. Cap., then in the process of completing his own volume of research on the documents concerning Clare. Optatus van Asseldonk, O.F.M. Cap., President of the Institute of Franciscan Spirituality at the Antonianum also favored the project. Because of my own privileged experience of working on the text of the revised *Rule and Life of the Brothers and Sisters of the Third Order Regular* and my work among religious congregations during the renewal period of revision of constitutions and charism documents, I chose the *Rule of Clare* as the key text for this experiment. Some questioned the wisdom of limiting myself to this legislative text and omitting the more inspirational matters contained in her *Letters* and *Testament*. I found in the observations of contemporary writers in the field of the history of spirituality support for the general methodological approach. From my experience of studying the evolution of the *Rule* of Francis and my experiences of participation in rewriting the Third Order Regular Rule, I was convinced that this was the logical approach for this effort.

In the "Introduction" to her book, *Jesus as Mother: Studies in the Spirituality of the High Middle Ages,* Professor Caroline Walker Bynum summarizes some of the major shifts in emphasis in this field of study in recent decades. She states:

> Thirty or forty years ago, books on the history of medieval spirituality were surveys of various theories of the stages of the soul's ascent to contemplation or union. Recently the history of spirituality has come to mean something quite different: the study of how basic religious attitudes and values are conditioned by the society within which they occur. This new definition brings spirituality very close to what the school of French historians known as *annalistes* call *mentalité*; the 'history of spirituality' becomes almost a branch of social history, deeply influenced by the work of structural-functionalist anthropologists and of phenomenonologists of religion.[3]

She goes on to state that certain dominant trends have been studied within this social context: 1) the growth of affective spirituality in the Cistercians and, later, the Franciscans; 2) new patterns of study avoid emphasis on what characteristics separate various major religious groups (e.g., Dominicans, Benedictines, Franciscans) but seek instead to articulate common patterns arising from popular religiosity, both orthodox and heterodox; 3) while the experts acknowldege Grundmann's study of the beguines as one of the most important works of the century, a subsequent exploration of the feminine influence on

[3] Caroline Walker Bynum, *Jesus as Mother: Studies in the Spirituality of the High Middle Ages* (Berkeley: University of California Press, 1982), 3.

medieval spirituality has not kept pace with other areas of research; 4) the recent tendency to abandon the personal mystical literature of the period (treatises, scripture commentaries, sermons, visionary literature, hagiography, etc.) needs to be challenged by attempts to bring a fresh perspective to the reading of traditional materials. Professor Bynum concludes: "If we are ever to know what gave significance to life for even some of the medieval population, which aspects of reality they were rejecting and which they were affirming when they 'renounced the world'; where they felt themselves able to make choices, and what they felt to be the important differences in the roles open to them or imposed upon them, we must find ways of answering these questions from the works they actually wrote."[4] Armed with the documentation concerning what Clare "actually wrote" that Regis Armstrong has developed for us, it is possible to focus on a given text and hazard this type of analysis. The work of this book is the result of being able to use the basic tools of primary documents, the contextual analysis of an historical perspective, and the consciousness of employing a critical examination of the reality of the *women's* experience of these Franciscan events. Added to these factors is the unshakeable belief that what happened to these ancestors of ours matters. It is of real importance, and not simply the enthusiastic overflow of medievalists and theologians with an archeological bent. In that reality which we know as the Communion of Saints these persons exist in relationship to us. We draw a living inheritance from them, or else we are deceived when we speak of charism and tradition. It is as important to understand what we receive from them and what we do not as it is to hold in hand our own birth certificate or a parent's last will and testament.

I hand this exploration over to all who choose to share it with only one reservation. It is most important that we regard this as the first step in a journey that stretches out before us and which,

[4] Bynum, 6.

for the moment holds "horizons that fade forever and forever when we move" (Tennyson's "Ulysses"). We need many other studies, hypotheses, and intuitive searchings. We must establish Clare in her rightful place as a threshold figure among medieval women of spirit. She was the first woman to write a *Rule* sanctioned with pontifical approval. She dared to synthesize the evangelical ideals of Francis, the new forms of urban female religiosity, and the best wisdom of the monastic tradition to create a new and enduring order in the Church. She testified to Francis not only by the humility of her faithfulness, but by the authority of her leadership and formative ministry. She stands before us today still serving as "instruction and a lesson to others who learned the rule of living in this book of life" (Rev. 21:27) [*Bull of Canonization,* 10].

Chapter One

FRANCIS AND CLARE IN THE SOURCES

Francis and Clare of Assisi (a commune of central Italy) both enjoyed special graces as individuals and were mutually responsible for the development of the early Franciscan fraternity. Their relationship to their families, to one another, to their city, and to the Orders they founded has become a subject of endless fascination for experts and enthusiasts over the years. In what way did Francis and Clare share in a mutual gift of grace? Or to be more precise, in what way did they foster together an impulse of the Spirit manifested in definite structures in the church? In the development of this grace and of these structures, what elements were personal and unique to Francis? What elements were personal and unique to Clare? The purpose of answering these questions is the establishment of a just estimate of Clare's originality and responsibility for the development of the Franciscan charism during the critical first decades of the history of the Order. While few would argue that Clare was not, in her own right, a woman of great sanctity and fortitude, it is not always as clearly understood that she was also uniquely responsible for a certain historic unfolding of the Franciscan movement and its spirituality. When viewing Clare and analyzing her life, many tend to think of her in an auxiliary role to

Francis and the brothers. Should she be regarded as a most faithful disciple of Francis but with a notion of fidelity that is static and imitative? Or, rather, should she be understood in terms of the separate and significant responsibility she bore for the growth of the Franciscan vocation in the church during that span of twenty-seven years after the death of Francis in which she continued to govern, to write, and to legislate? Her achievement during these long years of leadership can be better appreciated when it is is placed within the context of understanding the nature of Clare's response to the invitation of Francis and, perhaps just as importantly, the nature of his invitation in itself.

In order to establish this appreciation, it is necessary to reconstruct from the early sources the history of the initial encounters of the two founders, the reception of Clare and the initiation of the Order of Poor Sisters. Then we must evaluate the gradual changes that occurred in Francis' relationship to the corporate group as well as the gradual assumption of responsibility and influence on the part of Clare.

Method for Use of Sources

The first question that arises is what selection is to be made among the early sources. Franciscans are indebted to Englebert Grau for his analysis of the current knowledge of the sources for the life of Clare.[1] With the affirmation that he offers regarding the primacy of the *Process of Canonization* as a fundamental document, this source becomes the starting point and a constant frame of reference.[2] The *Process* is, indeed, unique among the early Franciscan materials. Making use, as it does, of the sworn

---

[1] Englebert Grau, O.F.M., "Die Schriften der heiligen Klara und die Werke ihrer Biographen." *Movimento religioso femminile e francescanesimo nel secolo XIII* (Assisi: Società Internazionale di Studi Francescani, 1980) 195-238.
[2] Grau, 226-227.

testimony of persons who knew Clare and her family personally, it provides a record whose veracity is certain. Since it is a
legal testimony, it is also devoid of literary ornamentation and
theological speculations. Its very "ordinariness" inspires a sense
of confidence in the information it preserved.

If, with *Process* in hand, one looks into the *Legend of Clare,* it
becomes apparent that the author of the *Legend* made ex-
haustive use of the *Process*.[3] In a table published in 1920 by
Zefferino Lazzeri with his edition of the *Process,* one discovers
that while there are several instances in which the *Process*
contains more details than does the *Legend,* the *Legend* adds to
the material of the *Process* relatively few details of major significance, with the exception of information concerning the
miracles.[4] What is discovered in the *Legend,* of course, are
hagiographical additions that reveal what major lines of interpretation were first used to testify to the sanctity of Clare and to
interpret her life and miracles in a manner that combined
probity with edification and inspiration. In fact, due to the
massive amounts of common materials that can be compared
between documents, the reading of these two items simultaneously offers a splendid opportunity to watch the medieval
hagiographer at work.[5]

In addition to these two major sources, it is fruitful to examine
several other texts dating from the middle of the thirteenth
century onwards.[6] These remaining sources are regarded by
Grau as of secondary importance, since much of their content

[3] F. Pennacchi, ed. *Legenda sanctae Clarae virginis* (Assisi: Società
Internazionale di Studi Francescani, 1910).

[4] Z. Lazzeri, O.F.M., "Il processo di canonizzazione di santa Chiara d'Assisi,"
AFH 13 (1920) 403-507 (The table is found on pages 427-430). To be precise,
there are thirty-two details found in the *Process* which are not repeated in the
Legend, while the latter adds twenty items of information.

[5] See Armstrong, *Clare,* 184-187, for a thorough discussion of the question
of authorship of the *Legend*.

[6] Examples of such texts include : B. Bughetti, O.F.M., ed. "Legenda
versificata S. Clarae Assisiensis (saec. XIII)," *AFH* 5 (1912) 237-260; 459-481;

is dependent upon the *Process* and the *Legend*. [7] Sr. Chiara
Augusta Lainati has shown that for similar reasons they were not
included for publication in the *Fonte Francescane*, the Italian
publication of primary Franciscan sources.[8]

This raises the question of which sources for the life of Francis
should be utilized. Here lies a two-fold problem. The first
problem is that, obviously, these biographies have Francis and
the founding events of the Order of Friars Minor as their focus.
The material on Clare contained in them is clearly limited in
quantity. Secondly, the situation that dictated the writing of a
particular biography or story concerning Francis can be counted
upon to influence the way in which Clare's part in the drama of
Franciscan beginnings is depicted.

Trying to discover the story of the role of Clare in Franciscan
history *via* the sources for the life of Francis can yield only
partial success. Added to this difficulty is the very nature of the
biographical sources for Francis in themselves. All the complex
intricacies of "the Franciscan Question" arise. In an address
given in 1981, Edith Pasztor of the University of Rome summarized many aspects of the then-current "state-of-the-question"
and concluded her summary with a plea to her colleagues to
attempt a greater collaborative effort of communication regarding
works-in-progress.[9] She pointed to the research of the late
Raoul Manselli in establishing a method of form criticism that
obviates some of the difficulties involved in rigid adherence to
traditional labels of "official" or "non-official" for the biographies.
She also pointed to the dangers inherent in ascribing sources to

621-623; — Id. "Miraculum S. Clarae adhuc viventis in eius Legenda
praetermissum," *AFH* 5 (1912) 383-394; — M. Bihl, O.F.M. "Tres Legendae
minores S. Clarae Assisiensis (saec. XIII)," *AFH* 7 (1914) 32-54.

[7] Grau, 231-235.

[8] Chiara Augusta Lainati, O.S.C., "Le Fonti riguardanti il Secondo Ordine
Francescano delle Sorelle Povere di Santa Chiara." *Approccio storico-critico
alle Fonti Francescane* (Roma: Antonianum, 1979) 134-135.

[9] Edith Pasztor, "The Sources of Francis' Biographies," trans. Patrick
Colbourne, O.F.M. Cap., *Greyfriars Review* 1 (1987) 31-40.

the "Spiritual party" without noting more recent research that has exposed some erroneous thinking in these attributions of earlier decades. Rosalind B. Brooke, in describing what she calls "the most auspicious and distinguished contribution to the study of St. Francis to appear for many a year,"[10] lauds Manselli's work, *Nos qui cum eo fuimus,* as a major innovation in the study of Francis and the methods of his first biographers. While hailing Manselli's precision in following his own technique of *Formkritik,* Brooke points out that Manselli's avoidance of the use of the *Anonymous of Perugia,* the *Legend of the Three Companions,* or the *First Life* of Thomas of Celano must be taken into account. Brooke indirectly indicates the need to profit from Manselli's major work while augmenting it with attention to other areas, particularly the questions related to the dating of the *Anonymous* and the *Legend of the Three Companions,* and the relation of the Greccio letter to the sources.[11]

What is proposed in this work is the construction of a portrait of the relationship of Francis and Clare that depends upon the *Process* and the *Legend of Clare* on the one side, and an inclusive reading of the major biographies of Francis on the other. Therefore, the sources for Francis and Clare used will include the *Actus Beatus Francisci et sociorum ejus*[12] *(The Acts of Blessed Francis and His Companions);* the *Anonymus Perusinus*[13] *(The*

---

[10] Rosalind B. Brooke, "Recent Work on St. Francis of Assisi," *Analecta Bollandiana* 10 (1982) 653-676.

[11] Brooke, *Work,* 674-675.

[12] *Actus Beati Francisci et sociorum ejus,* ed. Paul Sabatier, (Paris: Fischbacher, 1902). — Marion Habig, O.F.M., ed., *St. Francis of Assisi : Writings and Early Biographies (English Omnibus of the Sources for the Life of St. Francis).* 4th rev. ed. (Chicago: Franciscan Herald Press, 1972) 1267-1350 (cited hereafter as *Omnibus).* The Little Flowers of St. Francis are often referred to by English-speaking persons as the "Fioretti." More precise terminology employed in scholarly articles is reflected in the title "Actus-Fioretti." This title indicates something of the complex textual history by which the Latin original became famous in its Italian version. See *Omnibus,* 1276-1292.

[13] L. DiFonzo, O.F.M. Conv., "L'Anonimo Perugino tra le fonti francescane del sec. XIII," *MF* 72 (1972) 117-483.. — Regis J. Armstrong, O.F.M.Cap., ed.

Anonymous of Perugia); the *Vita prima (First Life)* and the *Vita secunda (Second Life)* of Thomas of Celano;[14] the *Legenda Maior*[15] *(The Major Life);* the *Legenda Perusina or Compilatio Assisiensis)*[16] *(The Legend of Perugia or the Assisi Compilation),* the *Legenda trium Sociorum*[17] *(The Legend of the Three Companions);* and the *Speculum perfectionis (The Mirror of Perfection).*[18] Once these biographical sources have been examined, certain other texts from the writings and from external witnesses that relate in a particular manner to the factual event under consideration will be placed alongside them. (For example, in treating of the beginnings of Clare's life at San Damiano, the *Form of Life* given to Clare by Francis at that period will also be considered.) After pursuing the development of Clare's composition work, separate consideration will be given to certain sections of the *Actus-Fioretti* which have played a prominent role in coloring our understanding of the relationship of Francis and Clare.

A simple recitation of this plan, however, is hardly sufficient as a justification for adopting what may well appear an overly ambitious and confusing attempt to employ multiple texts simultaneously. Those familiar with the voluminous research

St. Clare of Assisi: Writings and Early Documents (New York: Paulist Press, 1988, sec. 41 b, c.

[14] Fr. Thomae de Celano: *Vita Prima S. Francisci. AF* X (1926-1941) 1-117. *Omnibus,* 227-355. — *Vita Secunda S. Francisci, AF* X (1926-1941) 127-268. *Omnibus,* 359-543.

[15] Doctoris Seraphici S. Bonaventurae: *Legenda Maior S. Francisci. AF* X (1926-1941) 555-652. —Ewert Cousins, trans. *Bonaventure* (New York: Paulist Press, 1978) 179-327.

[16] Rosalind B. Brooke, ed. and trans. *Scripta Leonis, Rufini et Angeli sociorum S. Francisci* (Oxford: Clarendon Press, 1970).

[17] T. Desbonnets, "Legenda Trium Sociorum," *AFH* 67 (1974) 38-144. *Omnibus,* 853-956.

[18] P. Sabatier, ed., *Speculum Perfectionis seu S. Francisci Assisiensis Legenda antiquissima autore fratre Leone* (Paris: Fischbacher, 1898). *Omnibus,* 1103-1265.

on the textual intricacies of these sources, and the questions of dating and authorship, will smile at the naïveté of such a proposal. It is, perhaps, this very wealth of scholarship that allows an attempt to offer such a reading. Whereas such a process would have certainly led to hopeless confusion a few decades ago, it can be attempted now precisely because an adequate critique of the materials lies at hand. A judicious use of these critical materials allows us to see each major biographical sources in a way which does not lose sight of what strengths it brings to the topic and what inadequacies it entails.

These sources will be studied with respect to the light they shed upon the chronological sequence of events in the lives of Francis and Clare. For this purpose the chronology for the life of St. Clare presented by Becker, Godet and Matura in their edition of her writings has been used.[19] Beginning with the first evidence of mutual influence between Clare and Francis, each event in this sequence will be traced in each source that speaks of it. (The absence of material in some sources will also prove instructive.) For each item in the chronology, information from all of the biographies listed above will be gathered.

In addition to developing a sequence of factual, chronological events, it will be necessary to consider the particular point of view each source contains. What spiritual or pedagogical motives inspired the composition of these works? Each of these biographical sources was inspired by a specific need or motive, ranging from papal decree (in the case of the *First Life* of Thomas of Celano) to formative pedagogy (in the case of the *Legenda Maior*).[20] In utilizing the biographies of Francis, the material they contain and any keys of interpretation that must be used in virtue of our knowledge of that biography's *Sitz im Leben*

[19] Marie-France Becker, Jean-François Godet, Thaddée Matura, *Claire d'Assise: Écrits*. Sources Chrétiennes 325 (Paris: Les Éditions du Cerf, 1985) 66-75.

[20] Regis J. Armstrong, O.F.M. Cap., "The Spiritual Theology of the *Legenda Maior* of Saint Bonaventure" (Ph.D. Dissertation, Fordham University, 1978).

will be noted. As a result, it will be demonstrated that, at times, the choice of material or the interpretation of material concerning Clare was influenced by factors operative when the biography was written. These same factors may have had little or no bearing on the original event. In certain instances the period of composition was a moment of highly charged meaning for the life of the evolving Order. The need to recapture a precise understanding of the words and the intentions of Francis moved more than one of the early companions or, subsequently their disciples, to engage in some writing activity. As Manselli has demonstrated, this determination—as evidenced in the pericopes that he studies from the various manuscripts attributed to the companions—enjoyed a kind of vocational fervor all its own.[21] The writers had a mission to fulfill. They were conscious of certain dangers that resulted from lack of proper evidence of the real Francis and his desires. This intensity and purposefulness informs their work. Their purposes must be clear in order to make proper use of their work in relation to other sources and to Clare's story.

Chronological Survey

San Damiano Prophecy to Clare's Conversion

The first indication found in which Francis intimated a knowledge of Clare's future role, although she herself is as yet unknown to him, comes in the form of the prophecy related in the *Second Life* of Thomas of Celano: "Most fervently he stirred up everyone for the work of that church and speaking in a loud voice in French, he prophesied before all that there would be a monastery there of holy virgins of Christ" (2 Cel 13). This material is augmented in the version presented in the *Legend of the*

---

[21] Raoul Manselli, *Nos qui cum eo fuimus; Contributo alla questione francescana* (Roma: Istituto Storico dei Cappuccini, 1980) 275-280.

Three Companions with a short encomium for the Poor Sisters which troubles to note the role of Gregory IX in providing "glorious institutions" and the subsequent confirmation of their life by the Apostolic See (*Legend of the Three Companions* VII: 24). In the *Second Life* (204) there is an allusion to the prophecy, while the *First Life* of Thomas of Celano makes no mention of it.

Clare would recall this moment in writing her *Testament*. She recalled it as a moment of prophecy regarding the vocational graces given to all those who became part of the company of Poor Sisters. "We can consider in this, therefore, the abundant kindness of God to us. Because of His mercy and love, He saw fit to speak these words through His saint about our *vocation and choice* through His saint" (TestCl 15).

This prophetic utterance of Francis, proclaimed even before he had a following of brothers, was transmitted orally for years and finally committed to writing toward the middle of the thirteenth century, while Clare was still living. It is worth noting that it was an important enough addition to the biographical materials on Francis for Thomas of Celano to include a double reference to it in his *Second Life*.

Early Life of Clare

The *Process* contains many testimonies concerning the evident holiness of Clare even prior to her encounters with Francis and the brothers. It is imperative to note that this document contains eye-witness accounts of persons who were members of her family household and/or blood relations. The testimony of these witnesses will be examined first; they relate what they knew of the spiritual gifts Clare evidently enjoyed from her earliest years.

One witness, Lady Bona de Guelfuccio of Assisi, a distant relative and neighbor, affirmed her belief that Clare "had been sanctified in her mother's womb," which came from observing her holiness both "before and after she had entered religion"

(Proc XVII: 1).[22] Bona described Clare's prudence in terms of staying "hidden" and avoiding public notice, "not wanting to be seen by those who passed in front of the house" (Proc XVII: 4). Bona also provided the precious detail that Clare sent alms to those who were working on Saint Mary of the Portiuncula, in addition to sending food to the poor (Proc XVII: 5, 1). Clare also had encouraged Lady Bona to make the pilgrimage to St. James in Campostella (Proc XVII: 6).

Another witness, Lord Ranieri de Bernardo of Assisi, whose wife was a relative of Clare (Proc XVIII: 2), echoed Bona's sentiments. His important contribution was admission of his own proposal of marriage which had been met not just with a refusal, but with Clare's admonition to him to despise the world (Proc XVIII: 2). He listed her good deeds as fasting, praying, and giving alms. Her conversations in the household were spiritual (Proc XVIII: 3).

Pietro de Damiano, a neighbor, estimated that at age seventeen Clare already had determined to live in virginity and poverty. Her inheritance was sold to be given to the poor, and all believed in her "good manner of life" (Proc XIX: 2).

Iovanni de Ventura, the watchman of the Favarone household, described Clare as being of "upright life and dress, as if she had been in a monastery for a long time" (Proc XX:2). He added that in spite of the elegance of the household, she saved food for the poor. In addition to fasting and prayer, he testified that she wore "a rough garment under her clothes" while "still in her father's house" (Proc XX: 1-4) .

Beatrice, the natural sister of Clare, remembered her life as being "from her childhood almost angelic" (Proc XII: 1). A very important assertion is contained in the record of Beatrice. Her testimony revealed that "after Saint Francis heard of the fame of her holiness" (Proc XII: 2), he preached to her. The "after"

---

[22] All references to the *Process* will be indicated within the text using the Roman numeral indicating the witness and the paragraph number of the citation.

validates the conclusion that Clare's reputation was indeed known beyond the confines of the Favarone household. It is also a detail of chronology that comes from the witness in closest relationship to Clare. Beatrice was a repository of privileged information because, as she herself attested, "she acted and talked with her as with her own sister" (Proc XII: 7).

Pacifica de Guelfuccio also corroborated this testimony from her years of experience as neighbor and relative. Clare's love of the poor and voluntary visitations to them (Proc I: 3-4), her life of piety and good works (Proc I: 1), her dedication to virginity (Proc I: 2), her reputation and the "great veneration" of "all the citizens" are cited (Proc I: 3). In recording the pilgrimages that she (Pacifica, that is) shared with her mother, Ortolana (Proc I: 4), Pacifica also revealed a glimpse of the maternal piety that may have inspired Clare's early aspirations. Pacifica was not only an intimate of the family, but after her entrance into San Damiano served Clare "almost day and night" (Proc I: 3), ranking as one who knew intimately the entire span of Clare's story .

What emerges in mosaic fashion when these fragments of testimony are arranged together is a portrait of a young woman who from childhood was seen as especially gifted in the things of the spirit. She was charitable to the poor in person and through intermediaries. She was respected for her purity of life and desire to avoid worldly gossip and encounters. She was openly known to be devoted to prayer, almsgiving, penitential practices, fasting. She was held in high regard for her spiritual qualities. While her family actively sought a suitable marriage, acquaintances and relations affirm (at least in hindsight) that her intentions towards a dedicated life had been visible even before the dramatic events of her Palm Sunday flight to join Francis and his brothers.

What is most striking in this mosaic is the pattern of practices ascribed to Clare at such an early period of her spiritual development. There was not simply a vague declamation of good intentions. She was seen as evolving a "form of life" even at this early stage. It was, in fact, a form of life consonant with the elements of lay penitential spirituality then in flower.[23] How else can such details as the desire to remain hidden, the choice of sober dress, the use of a penitential garment, the prayer, fasting, almsgiving and the consistent ministry to the poor be explained? Such was the young woman soon to meet the same Francis who had alternately shocked and gladdened Assisi with his decision to challenge its mores and institutions (1 Cel 11; 23). Such was the young woman to whom Francis would turn to fulfill the prophecy made in the Spirit some years earlier, for whom he had undertaken the radical renovation of the church of San Damiano, transforming the repaired edifice into a structure of "living stones" (1Pet 2: 5).

Response to Francis' First Preaching

Clare was twelve years of age when Francis rebuilt San Damiano. When she was fifteen, he returned to the Spoleto Valley with the *Primitive Rule* which Innocent III had approved verbally, and with the preaching mandate that accompanied it (1 Cel 33). It is estimated that their first meeting occurred in 1211, when she was about seventeen years of age. During these five years, what impression had the young Franciscan movement made upon Clare? Given the notoriety which Francis had attained in his early conversion activity in Assisi (AP 17; *Legend of the Three Companions* 35) and the growing fame and positive regard the friars slowly achieved after their return from Rome (cf. 1 Cel 36, *Legend of the Three Companions* 54) it is difficult to believe that Clare could remain unaware of the phenomenon blossoming on the edges of the commune in which her family held such a powerful social position.

The *Anonymous of Perugia* provides the first indication of the milieu created by the early preaching activity of the friars and

---

[23] See André Vauchez, "L'Idéal de sainteté dans le mouvement féminin franciscain aux XIIIe et XIVe siècles." *MRFF*, 322-323 and Bertulf Van Leeuwen, O.F.M., "Clare: Abbess of Penitents," *Greyfriars Review* 4 (1990) 73-81.

the effects which most likely included Clare in their general wake.[24] In reading the account of the early ventures of the friars, one is immediately struck by the aspect of what today would be called "vocation recruitment" evident in these early missions. The author cites the text of Matthew 10: 34-35[25] as the preaching theme and continues: "In the same way many women, virgins and those not having husbands, after hearing their preaching, came to them with sorrowful hearts and said: 'What shall we do? We cannot be with you. Tell us, therefore, how we can save our souls.' For this reason they [the friars] established monasteries of recluses for doing penance in every city in which they could. They also appointed one of the brothers to be their visitator and corrector" (AP 41 b, c). This material is incorporated into the *Legend of the Three Companions* in the fourteenth chapter. That source states that "not only men, but also women and unmarried virgins were fired by the brothers' preaching, and, on their advice, entered the prescribed convents to do penance..."(*Legend of the Three Companions* XIV: 60). Rather interestingly, Bonaventure introduced Clare into the *Legenda Maior* through this same perspective, by describing the broad phenomenon of the friars' preaching impact. First, he described the growth in the numbers of those who accepted a life of penance and then, within this ambit, stated: "Young women, too, were drawn to perpetual celibacy, among whom was the maiden Clare, who was especially dear to God" (LM IV: 6). If, indeed, the recollections preserved in the *Anonymous of Perugia* and subsequently in the *Legend of the Three Companions* and the *Legenda Maior* represent a very early strata of recollection of the beginnings of the fraternity, then the description of the feminine vocational response to the friars' preaching provides

[24] Armstrong, *Clare*, 261.
[25] "Do not suppose that I have come to bring peace to the earth: it is not peace I have come to bring, but a sword. For I have come to set *a man against his father, a daughter against her mother, a daughter-in-law against her mother-in-law.*"

an important context for the meetings of Francis and Clare.[26] Current consensus regarding the relationship of these sources allows one to accept these citations as a key to understanding the environment in which Clare and Francis seek out one another's company to treat of the things of the Lord.[27]

First Encounters

It is the *Process* which presents the nature of the first meetings of Francis and Clare. As previously indicated, Clare's sister Beatrice revealed that Francis had already heard of Clare before their first meeting (Proc XII: 2). Interest in the account of Bona de Guelfuccio is fired by the fact that she accompanied Clare on these visits. Accompanied by Bona, Clare went many times to meet Francis and she feared discovery of these encounters by her parents (Proc XVII: 3). The content of these meetings is described by Bona as "preaching" about "converting to Jesus Christ" (Proc XVII: 3). Francis, too, was accompanied, apparently by Brother Philip, for Bona tells us that he also preached to Clare on the same theme (Proc XVII: 3-4). Amata, the niece of Clare, speaks of the "exhortation and preaching of Saint Francis" (Proc IV: 2) while Pacifica uses the term "admonition" (Proc I: 2). Lord Ugolino de Pietro Girardone testifies that it was "public knowledge" that Clare entered religion "at the preaching of Saint Francis and his admonition" (Proc XVI: 3, 6), and Filippa and Cecilia repeat similar thoughts (Proc III: 1; VI: 1).

Is it possible to discover further content in the "admonition" or "exhortation" referred to by the witnesses? An attempt at comparison between the raw material of the *Process* and the re-working of that material in the *Legend of Clare* can be made. The *Legend* attributed the discernment that brought Clare and Fran-

---

[26] See Lorenzo Di Fonzo, OFM Conv., "L'Anonimo Perugino tra le fonti francescane del sec XIII," *MF* 72 (1972) 117-483. Even with the discussions of the problem of dating which surround this source, it is obviously one of the **early** sources.

[27] Brooke, *Work*, 675.

cis together to "the Father of spirits" (cf. Heb 12: 9). The author portrayed each of the saints as responding in different ways to these divine promptings, but implied Francis had a more active interest in the prospect of meeting Clare than is evident in the simple narratives of the *Process*. Francis is depicted as "longing for spoil," wanting to "wrest" Clare from the world and "win" her for Christ. The frequency of their visits, however, is ascribed to Clare's eagerness to hear the words of Francis which "seemed to her to be on fire" (LegCl 5). Whereas the remembrance of Bona simply states that Francis urged the "conversion" to Christ upon Clare, the *Legend's* author has Francis encourage her to "despise the world" and its "deceptive" beauty. The same author then introduces bridal imagery and the theme of spiritual espousal as he enlarges his description: "He whispered in her ears / of a sweet espousal with Christ, / persuading her to preserve the pearl of her virginal purity / for that blessed Spouse Whom Love made man /" (LegCl 5).[28]

Then an important passage follows which attempts a description of the inner transformation taking place in Clare after she received guidance from Francis: "Immediately an insight into the eternal joys was opened to her / at whose vision the world itself would become worthless / with whose desire she would begin to melt, [and] / for whose love she would begin to yearn for heavenly nuptials"(LegCl 6).[29] This "insight" is translated into a determination to live in virginity, which is couched in terms of rejection of "allurements of the flesh" in favor of "marriage with the great King" (LegCl 6). The author then summarizes the effect of this early guidance: "Then she committed herself thoroughly to the counsel of Francis, placing him, after God, as the guide of her journey"(LegCl 6). The goal of this journey is Christ, and Clare's efforts to "gain Christ" are identified *via* the words of

[28] Armstrong, *Clare*, 193-94. Clare, however, does use this mode of expression in her letters. See, for example 1LAg 19-30.

[29] This text appears to parallel that of LTS 7-8 in which Francis, at an early stage of conversion, is similarly moved with inner sweetness and in which a marriage metaphor is used to express his experience. See also 2 Cel 7.

Paul in Philippians 3: 8.[30] That these events represented a radical change in Clare's spiritual perception and experience of grace are further attested to by words she spoke as her death approached. In her final days, when the chaplain admonished her to accept her sufferings in patience, she replied: "...in a very unrestrained voice: 'After I once came to know the grace of my Lord Jesus Christ through his servant Francis, no pain has been bothersome, no penance too severe, no weakness, dearly beloved brother, has been hard'" (LegCl 44).

Palm Sunday

It is the *Legend* which contains the specific description of the turning point at which Clare decided to act upon the counsel of Francis. "The Solemnity of the Day of the Palms was at hand when the young girl went with a fervent heart to the man of God asking [him] about her conversion and how it should be carried out" (LegCl 7). Francis had instructed her in specific detail to dress in her finery and join the townspeople in the cathedral. The narrative that follows (which has no parallel in the *Process* excepting the detail of Clare's opening of the barred door, XIII: 1) raises as many questions as it answers. What was the precise meaning of the bishop's gesture in carrying the palm to her? Why did she not leave her family home by the usual door? Who accompanied her? How did she manage to get through the guarded city walls and go to the Portiuncula without detection or interference? The *Legend* leaves the questions unanswered, yet briefly and beautifully describes the scene of Clare's investiture, having placed her flight in the liturgical light of the banishment of Jesus beyond the city walls celebrated in Holy Week (LegCl 7).[31]

---

[30] "Her soul...received whatever he said of the good Jesus with a warm heart. She...considered as almost dung everything acclaimed by the world in order that she might be able to gain Christ (cf. Phil 3:8)" (LegCl 6).

[31] The author speaks of her flight as "leaving the camp" — a citation of Heb 13:13: "Let us, then, go to him outside the camp and share his shame. For there is no permanent city here on earth; we are looking for the city that is to come."

The first witness in the *Process*, Beatrice, also underscored the alacrity with which Clare followed the counsel of Francis, reporting that "she went to serve God as soon as she was able" (Proc XII: 2). Beatrice added the detail that Clare sold her inheritance and gave it to the poor (Proc XII: 2-3). This permits one to infer that Francis followed the same pattern in advising Clare about her entrance into his company as he had in the case of Bernard (1 Cel 24; 2 Cel 15; AP 10-11; *Legend of the Three Companions* 30). The narration continues, Francis "gave her the tonsure before the altar in the church of the Virgin Mary, called the Portiuncula, and then sent her to the church of San Paolo de Abbadesse" (Proc XII: 4). This testimony was repeated by Ugolino (Proc XVI: 6), Bona (Proc XVII: 6), Ranieri (Proc XVIII: 3), and Iovanni (Proc XX: 6). Interestingly, while five witnesses in the process state that it was Francis who tonsured her, the *Legend* depicts the scene more communally and states that "the brothers...received the virgin Clare with torches" and that she then had "her hair shorn by the hands of the brothers" (LegCl 8).

The *Process* (XII: 4) added the detail that Francis next led Clare to the church of San Paolo, with the *Legend* indicating that this was a temporary exigency (LegCl 8). Neither the three witnesses who gave information concerning Clare's struggle with her parents in San Paolo (Proc XX: 4; XVIII: 3; XX: 6) nor the author of the *Legend* (LegCl 9) indicated that Francis was present or took any role in this confrontation. In fact, the *Legend* presents the miniature drama as a trial that proved the mettle of Clare and which did not lessen her growth in hope and love. It was Beatrice who provided the information that her sister's transfer to Sant' Angelo de Panzo was made in the company of Francis, Philip and Bernard (Proc XII: 5). Interestingly, the dramatic story of the flight of Agnes to Sant' Angelo and the second violent encounter between Clare and her relatives was not recounted in the *Process*. The *Legend* did not place it in chronological sequence as part of the story of Clare's conversion, but rather treated it as a part of the section on the power of her prayer (LegCl 24-26). Once again, Clare endured this threat and that to her beloved sister independently of any obvious intervention by Francis. This absence is important in that it indicates that while Clare sought spiritual direction from Francis, she was thoroughly capable on her own of taking initiatives that had serious social and legal consequences. She responded to the questions of her own property and her family obligations in her own right.

The final stage of her pilgrimage to San Damiano is also treated sparingly. The *Process* says only that "she stayed for a little time" at Sant' Angelo (Proc XII: 5) and then went "to San Damiano" (Proc XX: 7). The *Legend* states that the move was necessary because "her soul was not at rest" (LegCl 10). The *Legend* then adds lyric passages which celebrate this fact while providing several layers of analogy or metaphor regarding the foundation of San Damiano and the vocation of Clare. Celano had, in fact, already described the same event in the earlier biographies of Francis (1 Cel 19-20; 2 Cel 204).

Clare entered into the confines of San Damiano accompanied only by Agnes. Her reputation quickly spread and, as it did, the number of members of her new sisterhood increased (LegCl 10). That her influence was limited to women is negated by the statement of Iovanni: "Then she went to the place of San Damiano where she became mother and teacher of the Order of San Damiano, and she begot there many sons and daughters in the Lord Jesus Christ, as is seen today" (Proc XX: 7). In her *Testament,* Clare affirmed the awe experienced by Francis when he had witnessed the heroic dedication of the Poor Sisters to their Gospel mission. The *Legend* enlarges upon this also: "The ardor of young men was no less moved to enter the struggle / and was provoked to spurn the allurements of the flesh/ through the strong example of the more fragile flesh"(LegCl 10). This leads to the belief that other young recruits to Francis' fraternity found inspiration and courage in contemplating the Poor Sisters' efforts to live the Gospel.

Clare was formally installed as the abbess after three years, according to Pacifica, who was present when Francis insisted upon it (Proc I: 6). What can be assumed about the years that intervened between her arrival at the monastery and her assumption of formal governance in accord with church legislation?[32] What information from the sources allows additional fragments to be inserted into this mosaic, providing a glimpse of something of the development of the Order of Poor Sisters? Or, more significantly, which facts reveal something about the way in which Francis and Clare continued to strive together "in order to know Christ" (Phil 3: 10)?

First Years at San Damiano: 1212-1215

An important witness to the nature of Francis' instruction of Clare and her sisters exists in the *Form of Life*. Esser states that this writing of Francis was preserved in the sixth chapter of the *Rule of Clare* and is consequently found inserted within the original bull of Innocent IV preserved in the Proto-Monastery in Assisi. As for the time of composition of the *Form of Life* he states: "It is surely correct to assign the date of composition of this *opusculum* to the beginning of Clare's religious life."[33] Gregory IX also refers to this simple rule of life in his letter to Agnes of Prague of May 11, 1238.[34] It is preserved by Clare and is composed of a single sentence:

> Since by divine inspiration you have made
> yourselves daughters and servants of the most

[32] The Lateran decree forbidding the foundation of new religious orders required some measures to be taken since Clare, unlike Francis, had no oral or written approval for her form of life.

[33] Caietanus Esser, OFM, ed. *Opuscula Sancti Patris Francisci Assisiensis*, Bibliotheca Franciscana Ascetica Medii Aevi XII (Grottaferrata: Collegii S. Bonaventurae ad Claras Aquas, 1978) 162.

[34] *BF* I , 242-244.

high King, the heavenly Father, and have taken
the Holy Spirit as your spouse, choosing to live
according to the perfection of the holy Gospel,
I resolve and promise for myself and for my
brothers always to have the same loving care
and special solicitude for you as [I have] for
them.[35]

Three features of this brief instruction immediately strike the
reader. The first is the Trinitarian foundation for the life of the
Poor Sisters. The second is that the term "spouse" is used in
relation to the Holy Spirit, a relationship that is also proposed in
Francis' *Letter to the Faithful* I: 8. This attribution casts an interesting light upon the direction given by Francis and recounted
in the *Legend* in sections 5-7, in which bridal imagery is used to
pose a relationship with Christ analogous to and superior to an
earthly betrothal. The third is that the term that Francis used to
describe his relationship to the brothers and to the sisters is one
of *curam diligentem et sollicitudinem specialem:* loving care
and special solicitude. This care is pledged in words of solemn
promise *("I resolve and promise")* and involves not only the
personal fidelity of Francis to the relationship but the continuing
fidelity of the brothers corporately as well.[36]
    In order to pursue further the question of the nature of this
curam diligentem in the mind and heart of Francis, it is necessary
to move forward chronologically, to consider his language in
the *Later Rule* (6: 8). There, when speaking of the quality of the
love that must exist among the brothers, he admonished: "Et
secure manifestet unus alteri necessitatem suam, quia, si mater
nutrit et *diligit* filium suum (cfr. 1 Thess 2, 7) carnalem, quanto
diligentius debet quis *diligere* et nutrire fratrem suum
spiritualem?"(And let each one confidently make known his

---

[35] Regis J. Armstrong, O.F.M. Cap. and Ignatius C. Brady, O.F.M. *Francis and Clare: The Complete Works* (New York: Paulist Press, 1982) 44.
[36] Armstrong-Brady, *Works*, 44-45.

need to the other, for if a mother has such care and *love* for her son born according to the flesh (cf. 1 Thess 2:7), should not someone *love* and *care for* his brother according to the Spirit even more diligently?"[37] This expression of love or esteem that is implied in Francis' use of *diligo* contains the image of a maternal solicitude expressed in feeding or nourishing the other person. Examination of further implications of Francis' choice of language in this primitive *Form of Life* for Clare and her companions will be presented in Chapter Five.

With additional investigation into other sources, one finds little concerning these early years at San Damiano, and yet this "little" should not be passed over without comment. Celano, writing his *First Life* some fourteen years after Clare began living at San Damiano, delighted in playing upon the image of the "living stones." Noting that Clare's conversion took place six years after that of Francis, he likened her to the foundation of the reconstructed chapel: "...the Lady Clare...the most precious and firmest stone of the whole structure..." (1 Cel 18). In his *Second Life* he recalled that "after the virgins of Christ began to come together in that place...they professed the greatest perfection in observing the highest poverty and in adorning themselves with all virtues" (2 Cel 204). When Clare recalled these early years, however, she evoked a portrait that contains more of the hard edges of reality: "When the Blessed Father saw that we had no fear of poverty, hard work, suffering, shame, or the contempt of the world, but that, instead, we regarded such things as great delights, moved by compassion he wrote a form of life..." (RegCl 6: 2). Again in her *Testament*, she repeated this memory, with the addition that Francis' amazement was augmented by the fact that "we were physically weak and frail" (TestCl 27-29). Nevertheless, Francis turned to Clare for help; this is attested to by a section found in the *Legenda Maior*. He asked Sylvester and Clare for help in discerning whether he should live as a hermit or give himself to the task of preaching.

[37] Italics added.

"He also asked the holy virgin Clare to consult with the purest and simplest of the virgins living under her rule and to pray herself with the other sisters in order to seek the Lord's will in this matter" (LM XII: 2). Because Bonaventure was not following a strict chronology, he did not indicate the time of this request.[38] What is more singular is that Francis, through the brothers, received the joint replies of Clare and her sisters and of Sylvester as the will of God. The friars returned and told him "God's will as they had received it" and he immediately took to the roads to "carry out the divine command" (LM XII: 2). The confidence of Francis in the prayer and discernment of Clare was unequivocal.

The only event that can be firmly dated within this period is Clare's assumption of the office of abbess sometime between 1215 and 1216 (Proc I: 6; LegCl 12). Beyond this, a number of items indicate continuing communication between Francis and Clare. For example, there are the stories of Francis sending Brother Stephen to be cured of a mental illness by Clare (Proc II: 15; LegCl 32) and the information that she frequently prayed the Office of the Passion that Francis had composed (LegCl 30), but these do not submit to easy chronological identification.

It appears that sometime in this early period Francis made efforts to temper the severity of Clare's penances; there is evidence as well that this concern was shared by the sisters of the monastery as stated in the *Process*. Francis—accompanied by the bishop of Assisi—intervened to force Clare to eat enough to sustain bodily health (Proc I: 8; II: 8).[39] The presence of the bishop in this scene alerts one to the probability that Clare most likely was resisting the prudential advice of Francis and her sisters. He clearly felt constrained to bring some higher author-

---

[38] *Actus-Fioretti* 16 says "at the beginning of his conversion..." which indicates an early time frame for this request for Clare's discernment.

[39] For comments on the bishop's role at this time see Jean-François Godet, "Progetto evangelico di Chiara oggi," *Vita Minorum* 56 (1985) 222. For comments concerning the role of food in Francis' and Clare's asceticism, see Caroline Walker Bynum, *Holy Feast and Holy Fast* (Berkeley: University of California Press, 1987) 94-102.

ity to bear upon the situation. It would appear that such involvement pre-dates the appointment of Hugolino as Cardinal Protector. It also heightens awareness of the role of the bishop in the early organization of the sisterhood, which had begun with the conferral of the palm branch, most likely continued in the donation of San Damiano, and was now being acted upon in a pastoral confrontation. Another very interesting record in the *Process* indicated that Francis once recommended five women as candidates to the monastery. One of these, however, was judged not suitable by Clare. The sister recalling the events, Cecilia—who had herself entered because of the exhortations of Clare and the preaching of Philip, (Proc VI: 1)—stated that Clare was placed under considerable pressure to accept even this woman. She did so reluctantly, and in the end, her judgment was vindicated when the candidate left the community a short time later. Cecilia affirmed that this took place while Francis was still living (Proc VI: 15). So it can also be surmised that while each had supreme confidence in the special spiritual gifts of the other, there was nothing magical or fatalistic about their consultations.

It also seems possible to develop an entire discussion on the theme of the material contained in the *Process* and in the *Legend of Clare* which bears witness to the constant and pervasive influence of Francis upon Clare. (This means a kind of influence which is manifested in a continuous stream of events or records, not one which can simply be assigned to individual instances.) It is impossible to read many of the details of the activity of Clare without discerning therein a response to the preaching and intentions of Francis. This response is neither mechanical nor mimetic. Clare appears to possess a talent for translating themes found in the writings of Francis into concrete, incarnate activities and norms for decisions. A single example here should suffice to indicate a larger pattern. Francis in his *Letter to Clerics, Letter to the Custodians* and *Letter to the Entire Order,* advances the

Eucharistic reforms sought by Lateran IV.[40] In one place, he specifically urges: "The chalices, corporals, appointments of the altar, and everything which pertains to the sacrifice, must be of precious material" (EpCust I, 3) and in other texts (2 Cel 201e, LP 80b and SP 65e) Francis wanted to send the friars out with ciboria and host irons. The *Process* makes numerous references to the work of spinning and sewing that Clare performed (Proc I: 11; II: 12; VI: 14; IX: 9) in order to prepare sets of altar linens to be distributed in local churches. This kind of symbiosis of thought and missionary intent can be found repeatedly. To launch such a study would move too far afield from the topic of this current work. However, there is plentiful evidence that such a study would handsomely reward efforts to identify those secondary levels of correspondence between the preaching and genius of Francis and the intuitive grasp and concrete realizations of Clare.

Consideration of this early period must refer to a final document, the famous letter of Jacques de Vitry written from Genoa in 1216.[41] In the letter, de Vitry mentioned neither Clare nor Francis by name, but gave a general account of the groups he had encountered during his travels in Umbria, whose titles are the "Lesser Brothers" and "Lesser Sisters." He depicted them as working daily to "capture souls." In fact, his assessment of the influence of their evangelization parallels the description found in *Anonymous of Perugia* 41b. His description of the women states: "The women live near the cities in various hospices. They accept nothing but live from the work of their hands. In fact, they are very much offended and disturbed because they are honored by the clergy and laity more than they deserve."[42] The indication in this report is that both groups of the early Franciscan movement were equally well-known. The women were seen as part of the group with separate but equally important functions

[40] Armstrong-Brady, *Works*, 49, 52, 55.
[41] Armstrong, *Clare*, 245-246.
[42] Armstrong, *Clare*, 246.

and values to offer. It is also very important that the Franciscan women were already so highly regarded just four years after Clare came to San Damiano. The early experiences of "contempt" referred to in Clare's words above—and the spiritual consolation they created—seem to be a thing of the past by 1216. It is also clear that de Vitry witnessed plural manifestations of the groups, for he speaks of "hospices." This would seem to corroborate the words of the *Process* and *Legend* which indicate the rapid spread of Clare's influence.

However, at approximately the same time that de Vitry recorded his impressions, changes were at work in the structure of the church's response to this phenomenon and in the structure of Francis' relationship to Clare and her sisters. These changes indicate a point of division in the story of these beginnings. For within the year preceding the de Vitry account, Clare had been named abbess, and in another year Cardinal Hugolino would assume a commanding presence in shaping the development of the form of life of the Poor Sisters. Jacques de Vitry's letter preserves a cameo image of these first Franciscan women in the springtime of their foundation.

The "Middle Years": 1215-1220

In examining the years between 1215 and the return of Francis from the Holy Land in summer of 1220, one finds little that gives explicit evidence of contact between Francis and Clare. Yet within this five year period major changes that must have required deliberation and discernment took place in both branches of the Order. Clare requested and received the *Privilege of Poverty* from Innocent III prior to his death in July, 1216. This was one of the actions which was a unique testimony to her unity with Francis' vision. Then followed the period in which Hugolino became cardinal protector, legislated a new rule of life, and introduced Cistercian visitors. The next mention of Francis refers to his return from the Holy Land and his reaction to the initiative taken by Philip—having a friar named visitator to San Damiano. Jordan of Giano's *Chronicle* also tells of Philip's success in having obtained certain papal privileges to facilitate his work among the monasteries of Poor Sisters.[43] Francis had the privileges revoked. Philip had been closely associated with Clare and her monastery from the beginning of her conversion, and it is difficult to imagine that the reaction of Francis would not have had some repercussions there. This is one of the interesting but mysterious intersections of the relationship of Francis and Clare.

The "Later Years": 1221-1224

In this segment of time, seen as "later years" in the life of Francis, there is no strict evidence in the sources of actual collaboration between Francis and Clare. However, one only has to consider the monumental task Francis undertook in the composition of a *Rule* for the friars to realize that this was a period during which decisions of great moment for both foundations were made. In the *Earlier Rule* (XII), Francis addressed the question of suspicious relations with women and imposed limitations for those exercising sacramental offices or providing spiritual direction for them. When this material was transferred into the *Later Rule* (XI), a single sentence enjoined chaste behavior with women. But to this was added a strict prohibition against going into monasteries of nuns without the required permission of the Apostolic See. When one also considers the publication in 1220 of *Cum secundum consilium* with its requirement of a novitiate,[44] and the explicit regulations in the *Earlier Rule* (13) for the punishment of fornication, it may be concluded that Francis was being forced to deal with one of the consequences of the rapid expansion of the brotherhood during a period in which training in religious discipline had not advanced to the required level.

[43] L. Oliger. "De origine regularum ordinis sanctae Clarae," *AFH* 5 (1912) 181-209; 413-447.
[44] *BF* I, 6.

While there is no evidence to suggest an exact date for them, it is here that it would be appropriate to treat of four segments of the *Second Life* by Thomas of Celano that speak simultaneously of Francis' rapport with San Damiano and the problem of training the brothers by "word and example."[45] The first two (2 Cel 204-205) are entitled "How Francis wanted his brothers to deal with the Poor Sisters." The first segment (204) begins with a laudatory introduction which links the Order to the inspiration of the Holy Spirit and extols the poverty and virtues of the sisters. Then a shift occurs: "Though their father gradually withdrew his bodily presence from them, he nevertheless gave them his affection in the Holy Spirit by caring for them." The next words echo Clare's *Testament* (27-28) in recalling the privations the sisters had embraced; this is followed by a summary of the *Form of Life* with its promise of continual care. To this is added a rather important note, however: "...he emphatically commanded that it should always be so, saying that *one and the same spirit* had led the brothers and the poor ladies out of the world." Then, in 2 Cel 205 there follows a dialogue in which the brothers question the reduced number of his visits to San Damiano. Francis' answer is a strong affirmation of affection: "Do not believe, dearest brothers, that I do not love them perfectly." He insists that his conduct is motivated solely by the necessity of giving example. This segment of the *Second Life* concludes with Francis' counsel about the kind of brother who may be sent as a minister to the Poor Sisters: "I do not want anyone to offer himself of his own accord to visit them, but I command that unwilling and most reluctant brothers be appointed to take care of them, provided they be spiritual men, proved by a worthy and long religious life." This exposition is followed in 2 Cel 206 with two examples of brothers punished by Francis for visiting monasteries for reasons of simple personal affection for relatives living therein. Finally, in 2 Cel 207 Francis applied these restrictions to himself. The story is re-

[45] Adm 7: 4, TestCl 5.

counted that his vicar had asked him "repeatedly" to preach to the sisters at San Damiano. Francis reluctantly agreed. The touching detail is included that the sisters came to hear the sermon "though no less to see their father"—almost as if to heighten the dramatic effect of what followed. Francis then gave his symbolic sermon of being sprinkled with ashes and reciting the *Miserere*. The sisters, one is led to believe, clearly understood that "they should regard themselves as ashes and that there was nothing in his heart concerning them but what was fitting this consideration." The moral was then drawn by Celano that his visits to the sisters were "forced upon him and rare," and that the brothers should behave likewise keeping guard "against the snare laid out for them" (2 Cel 207).

If this last sentence seems to have moved far from the protestations of love found in 2 Cel 204, perhaps there are additional indications in three other sections (2 Cel 112, 113, 114) about the dilemma Francis faced. These treat of the more general topic of conduct toward women. In the sources being examined, 2 Cel 112 contains the strongest negative statement regarding Francis and women.[46] It also includes his famous protest that he could recognize only two women by sight. And yet this harsh description, in which women are described in terms of "honeyed poison" and "importunate loquaciousness," is followed by the assurance that he "taught by wonderful and brief words" those women who had demonstrated "an urgency of holy devotion." (It should also be noted that this section ends with an apostrophe by Celano in which he eagerly echoes the pejorative attitude toward the "impediment" that women constitute. "Rightly so, Father, for looking upon them makes no one holy. Rightly so, I say, for they provide no profit but only great loss, at least of time. They are an impediment to those who would walk the difficult way and who want to look up to the

---

[46] A number of other negative statements attributed to Francis by Brother Stephen and recorded by Thomas of Pavia also deserve study, but they are beyond the scope of this investigation. They are found in *AFH* 12 (1919) 382-384.

face that is *full of graces*.) Elsewhere in *Second Life* (113), there is a delicate parable in which Francis teaches prudent mortification of the sense of sight in the pursuit of chastity. It is noteworthy that in this small *exemplum*, with its overtones of the troubadour lyrics, the source of the difficulty is not imputed to the woman, but to the weakness of the male messenger. In fact, the entire tone of this tiny account is in stark contrast to the preceding text. Then *Second Life* (114) makes a specific application with an actual instance of Francis' refusal to look directly at the women to whom he is preaching. He cautions against looking upon a bride of Christ and cautions against any dealing with women other than those required by pastoral responsibility. Celano has juxtaposed one set of stories reflecting Francis' teaching with regard to the discipline of chastity to be observed in all dealings with women (2 Cel 112-113), with another group of stories (2 Cel 204-207) that seems truly ambivalent in the attempt to combine faithfulness to the Poor Sisters with punitive reactions to friars who presumed to serve them without permission.

What factors are at work influencing this portrait of Francis' relations with Clare and her sisters? While 2 Cel 204 has parallels in other sources (LP 45; SP 90; 2 Cel 13) sections 205-207 do not. (Likewise 2 Cel 112-114 are taken up again by Bonaventure, *Legenda Maior* V: 5, and in *Legend of Perugia* 96 and *Mirror of Perfection* 86 and 95.) These items enter into the biographies, therefore, with the publication of Celano's *Second Life* in 1247. The context in which these materials were collected for addition to the biography of Francis is critical. Among other events taking place in the Order, the question of the relationship of the friars with the Poor Sisters was by no means a dead issue at this point. When *Quo elongati* had been promulgated in 1230 with its prohibition against the brothers serving as preachers,[47] Clare rebelled. If the Poor Sisters were to be deprived of the friars'

---

[47] *Quo elongati*, ed. H. Grundmann, *AFH* 54 (1961) 20-25. The same question arose during the generalate of Haymo of Faversham, 1240-1244.

preaching ministry, they would also do without the food brought
to San Damiano by the friar-questors. Some sixteen years later,
almost simultaneously with the publication of Celano's second
biography and its collection of new materials from the early
companions, came the *Rule of Innocent IV*, which included
specifications on the relationship of the friars to the Poor
Sisters.[48] Such explicit links had not been present in the *Rule of
Hugolino* under which the Poor Sisters and other monasteries
had been operating. That the brothers were by no means in
agreement regarding the nature of their obligations to the sisters
is clear.[49] In addition, the Order of Friars Minor was struggling
with its own concerns regarding the observance of poverty as
reflected in the papal decisions of the period and the beginnings
of formal commentaries upon the *Rule*. [50]

Is it possible to conclude that the choice of materials found in
Celano's *Second Life* (204-207) represents an attempt to answer
a question that was very much present to the brothers in the
middle years of the thirteenth century—namely, how obligated
were they to the care of the Poor Sisters? In the attempt to answer
the question, the companions and friars who responded to the
appeal of Crescentius in 1244 (for new materials about Francis)
remembered those stories that treat of Francis' instructions on
the matter of women. The "teachings" were recalled and put in
writing under the pressure of finding historic models for contemporary dilemmas.[51] (How often do we not engage in the
same exercise?) In light of this discussion, it seems there might
have been more than an acceptable amount of pressure concerning the friars' service to the monasteries. One way of
responding might have been to bring forth the warnings of

[48] Armstrong, *Clare*, 110, note 4.

[49] Oliger, 421-427.

[50] M.D. Lambert, *Franciscan Poverty* (London: Church Historical Society,
1961). See Chapter Three below for further specifications of Lambert's
analysis of this period.

[51] Further development of Innocent's program to give the friars jurisdiction
over all monasteries of the Poor Sisters will be treated in Chapter Two.

Francis concerning women. Nevertheless, what is quite fascinating is the degree to which some were still insisting (twenty years after the death of Francis) on the very intention which he had made explicit in both the *Form of Life* and the *Last Will,* that is, the obligation to care for the sisters, while at the same time exercising maximum caution lest this obligation become a license to engage in questionable relationships. What cannot be overestimated is the profound sense of fidelity to this relationship that continued to inspire the biographers of Francis, particularly Celano and the contributors to the *Legend of Perugia,* at a time when a compromise might have been struck and all but the most negative statements about the sisters purged from the stories.

The "Final Years": 1224-1226

In these final years of the life of Francis, Clare contracted the serious illnesses that would beset her for the remainder of her life. The chronology for her life places this at approximately the same time as the reception of the Stigmata by Francis.[52] Indeed, from this point on the communication between Francis and Clare and her sisters takes place within the ambit of the declining health of Francis and the urgency on both sides of the enclosure of San Damiano to have some final experiences of communication and friendship. In the last year of his life, Francis stayed in a hut "near San Damiano" during a time of excruciating suffering and spiritual oppression (LP 42-44; SP 90). Triumphing though grace over his temptations of spirit, he wrote the *Canticle of Brother Sun* with its magnificent interplay of masculine and feminine symbolism. Having finished this masterwork, inspired by news of the grief and concern of the sisters for him, he wrote another song especially for them (LP 45). In contrast to the sentiments recorded in *Second Life* (204)—or perhaps in a kind of odd harmony with them—one reads his final feelings. "Since he could not go in person to visit and console them, he

---

[52] *Écrits,* 71.

had his companions bring them what he had composed for them…When he thought of them, his spirit was always moved to pity because he knew that from the beginning of their conversion they had led and were still leading an austere life…" (LP 45).

The *Canticle of Exhortation* he then sent them expresses tender emotions illumined by faith in their vocation and the reward that awaits them. The language is familiar, colloquial. "Listen, little poor ones, I beg you through great love…each one will be crowned queen in heaven…"(CantExh).[53] Once more the particular source in which this pericope is found must be considered; this is some of the material gathered from the early companions. Celano did not choose to include in the *Second Life* the background of this song for the Poor Sisters, although 2 Cel 204 does parallel the material. It falls to the *Legend of Perugia* (or the *Assisi Compilation*) to preserve the warmth and particularity of detail of this incident. Given the determination of the *Legend of Perugia's* author to preserve details revealing the complexity and intensity of Francis' personality, this story holds particular interest. Here is a record drawn from recollections of those who most closely portray the Francis remembered by his friends as "a real, even if very unusual, religious leader trying to face the human problems of life."[54] Here is a precious testimony of the depth of attachment that existed at the last between Francis and his companions and Clare and her companions.

According to the *Second Life* (204), Francis, when close to death, "emphatically commanded" that the sisters always be entitled to help and counsel; this command seems based on his conviction that the origin of the vocation of the brothers and

---

[53] Armstrong, *Clare*, 250-251. A summary of the findings on this Umbrian dialect composition can be found in Desbonnet's "Introduction " in T. Desbonnets, T. Matura, J-F. Godet, D. Vorreux, eds. and trans. *François d'Assise: Écrits*. Sources Chrétiennes 285 (Paris: Les Éditions du Cerf and Les Éditions Franciscaines, 1981) 46-47.

[54] Rosalind B. Brooke, "Recent Work on St. Francis of Assisi," *Analecta Bollandiana* 10 (1982) 671.

sisters is one. However, just as the final days of Francis began to be counted, the friendship of Clare emerged from within the collective concern of the Poor Sisters. The *Legend of Perugia* contains the poignant narration: Clare, ill and feeling herself in danger of death, "wept in bitterness of spirit and could not be consoled" (LP 109; cf. SP 108). This is the only instance in the sources that portrays Clare in such emotional and spiritual extremity.[55] In her anguish she sends word to Francis through one of the brothers: she has one simple human longing—to see him before her death. Receiving the news, Francis "is moved with pity" (LP 109). He "pondered" what she desired and—as he had done on other occasions—sent a letter. For him, this symbolizes the desire to be personally present to the recipient.[56] The letter contained an absolution and a blessing. He also sent an inspired verbal reassurance that she would indeed see him before her death and be consoled. Her "seeing him" consisted of the viewing of Francis' body as it was being translated to the church of San Giorgio for burial.

In the sixth chapter of her *Rule*, Clare preserved the tenor of a letter from Francis which is also contained in the *Opuscula* as the *Last Will*. [57] While this may not be identical with the letter sent by Francis at this time, it does provide insight into some of his last wishes for the community of San Damiano. It is a simple but significant directive insisting that the "life and poverty of Jesus Christ" are the goal of his vocation and that of the sisters. They must guard against being taught or advised by "anyone" to depart from this. Seen in light of the activity of Hugolino to regulate and provide financial stability for the many convents of the Spoleto valley during these years, this final message is more

---

[55] Only in the description of the attack of the Saracens (LegCl XIV:22) is Clare described in tears, and nowhere else is she described as experiencing "bitterness of spirit."

[56] Examples can be found in EpFid II, 3; EpCust II, 6-7; EpMin 21.

[57] RegCl VI: 3; Esser, *Opuscula* 318.

than a simple homiletic exhortation.[58] It is a plea for fidelity to the charism endangered not so much by enemies as by the beneficent intentions of friends.

The account of the funeral of Francis contained in *First Life* (116-117) combined several classic elements modeled on early hagiographic sources.[59] However, there is agreement with it in the *Legend of Perugia* (109); the description of the iron grating of the enclosure being removed and the additional details that "the friars took the holy body from the bed and held him at the window in their arms for a good hour."[60] Celano described the sisters kissing "his radiant hands" and Bonaventure included Clare and her sisters as witnesses to the Stigmata based on this information (LM XIII: 8). This particular segment of an otherwise triumphal procession to San Giorgio relates the contagion of grief "shared by all, so much so that hardly anyone could keep from weeping..." (1 Cel 117). This last hour of earthly contact between Clare and Francis ended in a combination of consolation and affliction. Celano concluded somberly: "When he had been taken away, the door which will hardly ever be opened for so great a sorrow, was closed (Mt 25: 10) to them." On the other side of that door Clare was left to live out twenty-seven years in pursuit of their shared vocation without "her comforter in soul and body" (LP 109).

Two Accounts: A Parable and a Dream

Before summarizing these findings concerning the shared vocation of Francis and Clare, it is essential to give special consideration to two further accounts from the early sources.

[58] Mario Sensi, "Incarcerate e Recluse in Umbria nei Secoli XIII e XIV: Un Bizzocaggio Centro-Italiano," *Il Movimento religioso femminile in Umbria nei secoli XIII-XIV* (Regione dell'Umbria: "La Nuova Italia" Editrice, 1984) 94-96.

[59] Armstrong, *Clare*, 258-259, n. 15.

[60] *Scripta Leonis*, 281. *Omnibus* LP 109 (1085) says "for at least a minute." *Omnibus* SP 108 (1247) says "for a long while."

The first will be *Fioretti* 15, the story of the meal shared by
Francis and Clare; the second will be the Clare's dream about
Francis, related by Sr. Philippa in the *Process*.

Actus-Fioretti 15

The foregoing analysis of the sources of information about
Clare and Francis avoided the use of the materials contained in
the *Actus-Fioretti*. This avoidance reflects a common tendency
to classify the *Actus-Fioretti* as a romanticized exercise in fourteenth century piety or polemic. Such an avoidance results,
however, in the danger of ignoring both the strength of oral
tradition that is generally acknowledged to serve as its base as
well as its tremendous popular impact that has generated many
conscious and unconscious impressions and images of Francis
and his early companions.[61] Of the five incidents involving Clare
in *Actus-Fioretti*, items 16, 19, and 35 have counterparts in early
sources. A fourth item, the miracle of the sign of the cross on the
bread, is a story of an event that occurred after Francis' death.
Therefore, only chapter 15, "How St. Clare Ate a Meal with St.
Francis," will be addressed.

First, it should be noted that this particular story comes from
the early strata of material. Its historicity has been opposed by
Pascal Robinson, but has also been affirmed, at least in part, by
Cuthbert.[62] The chapter ends with details concerning Agnes'
mission to Florence and the fear of the sisters that Francis would
ask Clare to leave San Damiano for service in another monastery. It is certain that sisters of San Damiano were sent to provide
government and formation for other monasteries, and this
concluding observation in Chapter 15 adds to the sense of the
story being rooted in an identifiable time.[63] But the story pre-

[61] Raphael Brown. "Introduction" to the *Little Flowers of St. Francis. Omnibus*, 1282-1283.

[62] See note 1 (Chapter 15), *Omnibus*, 1517.

[63] *Omnibus* , 1517.

sents an opportunity to share the wonder of the *cittadini* of the
area near the Portiuncula who, thinking their woods were on
fire, arrived in "the Place" to discover Francis, Clare and their
companions rapt in a mutual ecstatic experience. There are two
interpretive possibilities: 1) the tale is true but the "fire" is
embellishment;[64] 2) the tale is a parable meant to convey a
lesson in story form. Assuming—if only for the sake of enlarging
the argument—the second approach, one is led to ask how this
story survived and why. What value did it represent in this
collection? Edith Pasztor has pointed out how critical it is to
provide a proper sense of the dating of the *Actus*.[65] Brown, for
example in his Introduction,[66] dates the work after 1327; Pasztor,
suggests dates between 1313 and 1318. In any event, its composition is contemporaneous with (or very close to) the period
during which the disruptions caused by the Spiritual party and
the investigations of theologians within the order and the bulls
of John XXII bring a definitive end to the early contours of the
Franciscan dream. And yet here, rising from the embers of
inquisitorial fires, are collections of stories that breathe the early
simplicity and ingenuousness of the movement. If the oral
tradition from which this story comes is, indeed, based upon an
actual event of those early years which has been glossed with
details of a more imaginative or allegorical nature, then one
must be grateful for the preservation of the tale and meditate
upon its implications. If the account is not based upon fact but
is presented in a kind of verisimilitude, one can hazard the
opinion that it represents what Mircea Eliade describes as the
myth of return to a primitive Eden-state.[67] Is this story preserved

[64] Cuthbert of Brighton, O.F.M. Cap., "A disputed story concerning St. Clare,"
AFH 6 (1913) 670.

[65] E. Pasztor, unpublished lecture, University of Rome, January, 1988.

[66] See note 61.

[67] Mircea Eliade, *Myths, Dreams and Mysteries,* trans. Philip Mariet (Glasgow:
Harvil Press, 1960). Chapters III and IV deal with the "nostalgia for Paradise"
and accompanying mystic phenomena in primitive traditions. Eliade describes the symbolism of the garden, mastery of animals, and the fire
surrounding the Garden of Paradise (65-710). Eliade believes that this "nostalgia" was "victorious" in Francis.

in order to keep alive a memory of a brief moment in the egalitarian beginnings of the Franciscan movement? Is it a recollection of a time before clericalization and claustration had severed relationships and pared them to a legal minimum? Is it, in fact, more a parable-prophecy of the future, a story intended to preserve an image of an Eden-state in which man and woman walk in the garden, hold converse with God, and in which as a sign of Yahweh's presence fire burns but does not consume? Was there hidden within the heritage of history and hagiography of the first Franciscan century a myth of radical optimism that recalled an original, liminal moment? In the very preservation, might not the early companions have sustained the hope that such a goal, the goal of return to Eden-Portiuncula, was worth the suffering present everywhere at that time in the crisis-ridden order?[68] Current developments in the study of Franciscan texts allow a re-reading of this story, with its powerfully evocative symbols and its heretofore unexamined historical levels of meaning.

The Dream

There remains a final section of the *Process* which requires a special treatment, the story recounted by Sr. Philippa of the Clare's dream in which she is nursed by Francis as a child at its mother's breast. While the full account is contained in Philippa's testimony, there is added reference to it by two other witnesses, Cecilia and Amata (Proc VI: 13; IV: 16). Because this account is unique in the sources for Clare and Francis it is recounted here in full:

> The Lady Clare also related how once, in a
> vision, it seemed to her that she brought a bowl

[68] Timothy Johnson, O.F.M. Conv., "Liminality and the Religious Experience of Saint Francis of Assisi," *The Cord* (January 1985) 19-27. In this article Johnson applies anthropologist Victor Turner's concepts of the stages of the formation of a community to the early Franciscans.

of hot water to saint Francis along with a towel
for drying his hands. She was climbing a very
high stairs, but was going so quickly, almost as
though she were going on level ground. When
she reached saint Francis, the saint bared his
breast and said to the Lady Clare: 'Come, take
and drink.' After she had sucked from it, the
saint admonished her to imbibe once again, and
after she did, what she had tasted was so sweet
and delightful that she in no way could describe
it.
After she had imbibed, that nipple or mouth of
the breast from which the milk comes, remained
between the lips of the blessed Clare. After she
took what remained in her mouth in her hands,
it seemed to her that it was gold so clear and
bright that everything was seen in it as in a
mirror. (Proc III: 29)

In a search for the roots of the images presented in this dream
one should return first of all to the *Form of Life,* recalling that
Francis promised to Clare and her sisters a relationship characterized by "loving care and solicitude" (FormViv 2). This same
expression is found in the *Later Rule* (6: 8), where Francis asks
about the kind of care one should have for his brother in the
Spirit. Francis employed here an image of maternal nurture. In
this passage the citation from Thessalonians refers to Paul
reminding his audience that "...we could have insisted on our
own importance as apostles of Christ. On the contrary, while we
were among you we were as gentle as any nursing mother
fondling her little ones"(1 Thess 2:7). Nor is this the only
instance in which Francis characterizes himself in maternal
imagery. He addressed Leo "as a mother" (EpLeo 2) and the
brothers sent to live in hermitages were to be "mothers" to their
companions (RegErm 1, 2, 4). Likewise, the biographies are rich
in instances in which this maternal relationship of Francis to the

brothers is signified. When he takes the primitive community to Rome, he is the "poor woman in the desert" (1 Cel 16b; 2 Cel 16b; *Legend of the Three Companions* 50; LM III, 10). Later, when encountering difficulties with his responsibilities, he is a small hen whose wings are too short to protect her brood (2 Cel 24a; *Legend of the Three Companions* 63b).[69]

In searching further for the source of this image that recurs so often in the thought of Francis and becomes so powerfully present to Clare in her dream, one encounters the monastic writers of the twelfth century. Particular credit must be given to Professor Caroline Walker Bynum for her summary of this theme in *Jesus as Mother: Studies in the Spirituality of the High Middle Ages*. In the fourth chapter ("Jesus as Mother, Abbot as Mother: Some Themes in Twelfth-Century Cistercian Writing") she provides a rich study of the rise of the image of the abbot as a mother and even offers several instances of the image of the nursing abbot-mother from the literature of the period. In particular, she cites Bernard of Clairveaux's *Sermons* on the *Song of Songs*, citing such passages as the following: "Learn that you must be mothers to those in your care, not masters *[domini];* ...Be gentle, avoid harshness, do not resort to blows, expose your breasts: let your bosoms expand with milk not swell with passion..."[70] Bynum explains:

> Breasts, to Bernard, are a symbol of the pouring out towards others of affectivity or of instruction and almost invariably suggest to him a discussion of the duties of prelates or abbots. Bernard not only develops an elaborate picture of the abbot (he usually has himself in mind) as mother, contrasting *mater* to *magister* or *dominus* and

[69] The friars, in turn, are seen as women who are sterile when their preaching does not proceed from prayer, while the humble brothers are the fruitful mother figures (2Cel 164 b; LP 71 c; LM VIII, 2; SP 72 b).

[70] Bynum, 148.

stating repeatedly that a mother is one who
cannot fail to love her child; he also frequently
attributes maternal characteristics, especially
suckling with milk, to the abbot when he refers
to him as father.[71]

It is impossible to do justice here to the additional research on
the feminization of religious language of this period and the
search among the Cistercian writers for new images of authority
that are included in this invaluable chapter of Bynum's work. It
is enough to say that she provides evidence that the image of
Francis nursing Clare does not rise from a purely private and
unique relationship, but rather from a widely disseminated font
of twelfth century spirituality.[72] Given the fact that Cistercian
writers were so prominent in the propagation of this imagery
and that Cistercian visitors were appointed to San Damiano, the
conjecture can be made that these very images may well have
been presented in homiletic form within the monastery. (Recall
that both the *Process* and *Legend of Clare* recount that Clare
distinguished among sermons, enjoying those of the learned in
the arts, as well as those of the more simple preachers [LegCl
37]).

This dream will undoubtedly continue to fascinate students of
Franciscan life and literature and will continue to admit of
varying levels of interpretation.[73] For purposes of this study, it
is important to affirm that in itself the dream is less mysterious

---

[71] Bynum, 115-116.

[72] This statement does not imply a lack of appreciation for the deep personal
and affective bond that existed between Francis and Clare. Rather, it is
important to understand such material in the sources in terms of their cultural
or anthropological context as well as the inter-subjectivity they indicate.

[73] See, for example, the excellent study of Marco Bartoli, "Analisi storica e
interpretazione psico-analitica di una visione di S. Chiara di Assisi," *AFH* 73
(1980) 449-472, as well as pages 180-198 in his work *Chiara d'Assisi* (Rome:
Istituto Storico dei Cappucini, 1989).

to our twentieth-century eyes when it is viewed in light of the language of Francis himself. This language must, in turn, be viewed against the background of religious language and developments in affective spirituality that spilled over into the thirteenth century from the streams of the twelfth.[74] These reflections are not intended to minimize the importance of this dream as a key to the inner relational world of Francis and Clare. In fact, its value as such a key is enhanced when one considers that apparently it was not a biographical fact known to all of the sisters. It was fully shared only by Philippa. It is very significant that the three women who possess knowledge of it, Philippa, Cecilia and Amata all testify that they were specifically encouraged by Clare to join her in religion (III: 1; IV: 1; VI: 1). From the beginning, Clare shared her spiritual insight with these three. The dream is known to them. What is more surprising is the fact that evidence verified by sworn testimony, which so clearly underscores the spiritual intimacy and delicacy of affection between Clare and Francis, should be so little known, in contrast with the *Fioretti* chapter discussed above. This might be explained by the fact that until recently the *Process* has been so little utilized as a source. It might also be ascribed to a certain modern reticence that is puzzled, if not dismayed, by a description of such intimacy. What this testimony provides is a unique confirmation that there did indeed exist a relationship between Francis and Clare at once public and personal, characterized by a profound inner unity. Rather than marking them as two people who were beyond "mortals," it places them within a long procession of great religious figures who contributed generation after generation to the process of spiritual development in a world where "male and female he created them" (Gen 1: 27).

[74] Bynum, 166-169.

Summary Observations

What conclusions about the nature of the shared vocation of Francis and Clare and about the relationship that grew in response to this charismatic gift can be drawn?

1. The relationship between Clare and Francis was the relationship of equals. Clare had already achieved a reputation for holiness prior to her first meetings with Francis. Francis respected her ability to govern her community and deferred to her judgment in certain matters. Clare, on her part, likewise saw Francis as an essential presence in her vocational story, but both retained and exercised independent judgement and responsibility.

2. The work of Clare and Francis in establishing a new way of evangelical life was a work of shared suffering, hardship, teaching, prayer, discernment, and success. At the same time, it must be acknowledged that the relative silence of the sources on the actual events involving them both between 1213-1224 presents a serious obstacle to making an accurate assessment of their shared labors.

3. The evangelical liberty of spirit that apparently characterized the earliest years of the brotherhood and sisterhood gradually gave way to concerns for discipline, ecclesiastical approval, and the structural adjustments that this entailed. As a result, a gradual physical separation occurred, occasioned by the clarification of regulations for enclosure on the one side, and the need to rectify abuses among the friars on the other.

4. The sources covering the final years of Francis' life reveal a consistency of intention regarding his conviction that the vocation and rights of the sisters were equal to those of the brothers. Among his final gestures of personal concern and affection

were special communications directed to Clare and her companions.

5. The language, imagery and symbolism used to characterize the relationship of Francis to Clare and her sisters was rooted in the great literature of medieval monasticism, not only in the tradition of the troubadour lyrics.[75] It was language that revealed an inclusiveness of many persons who shared a common experience of prophetic awareness and work. It was language that revealed the affectivity forged by an evangelical chastity. This chastity, while not lived without cost, was their fundamental option, an option that infused and transformed their human relationship.

6. The relationship of Clare and Francis was, above all, a relationship that demonstrated the presence of Christ as Grace: "These are they who believe in his name—who were begotten not by blood, nor by carnal desire, nor by man's willing it, but by God" (Jn 1: 13).

[75] For a full development of this idea, see F.X. Cheriyapattaparambil, O.F.M. Cap., *Troubadour Influence in the Life and Writings of the Man-Saint of Assisi* (Rome: Antonianum, 1985).

Chapter Two

THE RULE OF CLARE

The Formation of the *Rule*[1]

The Form of Life *(1212-1215)*

Having examined the story of Francis and Clare as their earliest biographies present it, it is now possible to examine one specific activity by which Clare witnessed her solidarity with Francis: the *Rule*. The story of the *Rule of Clare,* confirmed by Innocent IV just two days before her death in 1253, begins with her entrance into San Damiano in 1212. The information she shares in her own *Rule* and her *Testament* reveals that at the

---

[1] A list of principal works dealing with the *Rule of Clare* is given in *Écrits,* 36, and in C. A. Lainati, "Le fonti riguardanti il secondo ordine Francescano delle Sorelle Povere di Santa Chiara," *Forma Sororum* 23 (1986) 131-145, 196-220. Among these texts we cite the following: D. Ciccarelli, "Contributi all recensione degli scritti di S. Chiara," *MF* 79 (1979) 356-360; J. Garrido, *La forma de vida de Santa Clara* (Aranzazu: Aldecoa Diego de Siloe, 1979); J-F. Godet, "Progetto evangelico di Chiara oggi," *Vita Minorum* 56 (1985) 198-301; E. Grau, cited in Chapter One, Note 1; L. Iriarte, *La regola di santa Chiara* (Milano: Biblioteca Francescana Provinciale, 1976); C. A. Lainati, "La Regola francescana e il II Ordine," *Vita Minorum* 44 (1973) 227-249; Id. "La clôture de sainte Claire et des premières Clarisses dans la législation canonique et dans la pratique," *Laurentianum* 14 (1973) 223-250 (English trans. in *The Cord,* Jan. 1978, 4-15

beginning Francis provided a *Form of Life* for the Poor Sisters. While the actual text of this *Form of Life* no longer survives, there is a section of it preserved in Chapter VI of the *Rule* of Clare: "Because by divine inspiration you have made yourselves daughters and servants of the Most High King, the heavenly Father, and have taken the Holy Spirit as your Spouse, choosing to live according to the perfection of the Holy Gospel, I resolve and promise for myself and for my brothers to always have that same loving care and solicitude for you as [I have] for them" (RegCl 6: 3).

Clare likewise refers to this primitive text in her *Testament:* "Afterwards he wrote a form of life for us, especially that we always persevere in holy poverty. While he was living he was not content to encourage us with many words and examples to the love of holy poverty and its observance, but he gave us many writings that, after his death, we would in no way turn away from it, as the Son of God never wished to abandon this holy poverty while He lived in the world" (TestCl 33-35). Another witness to the existence and nature of the rule is found in the letter of Gregory IX to Agnes of Prague.[2] In 1238 Gregory recalls this rule in the following words: "Blessed Francis gave them, as new-born children, not solid food but rather a milk-drink, a formula of life, which seemed to be suitable for them."[3] Further on, in his eagerness to convince Agnes of Prague that she is not obliged to the observance of this primitive rule, he writes: "You are in no way held to that Rule since it was not approved by the Apostolic See."[4]

and Feb. 1978, 47-60); L. Oliger, "De origine Regularum Ordinis S. Clarae," AFH V (1912) 181-209 and 413-447; I. Omaechevarría, *Escritos de Santa Clara y documentos contemporaneos* (Madrid: Biblioteca de Autores Cristianos, 1970); Id. "La 'Regola' e le Regole dell'Ordine di S.Chiara," *Forma Sororum* 14 (1977) 165-175, 213-222, continued in 15 (1978) 141-153; Peter van Leeuwen, "Clare's Rule," *Greyfriars Review* 1 (September, 1987) 65-76.

[2] *Angelis gaudium, BF* I, 242-244.

[3] *Angelis gaudium BF* I, 242-244.

[4] *Angelis gaudium, BF* I, 242-244.

Aside from this fragmentary reference to the *Form of Life* received from Francis which Clare preserved in her *Rule,* there is minimal written information regarding the manner in which the writings of Francis served the continuing formation of the sisterhood at San Damiano. Nevertheless, Chiara Augusta Lainati believes that many of the written and oral teachings of Francis are preserved in the *Rule* of Clare and not "lost" as is often assumed.[5] Clare's third letter to Agnes of Prague contains a summary of specific instructions that Francis provided regarding fasts and the observance of feast days (3LAg 29-41). Similarly, Lainati is certain that the *Rule for Hermitages* played a role in developing Clare's *Form of Life.*[6] Nor is it difficult to see, as proposed in Chapter One, many activities of the Poor Sisters recorded in the *Process* and *Legend* which seem to mirror the written teachings of Francis. Consequently, this earliest version of the *Rule* includes only the material preserved by Clare in the 1253 text. Clare's correspondence with Agnes contains one clear summary of Francis' instructions and Gregory's correspondence with the same abbess reveals his official—and negative—evaluation of this primitive rule.

The Privilege of Poverty (1216)

The first major turning point in the story of this *Rule's* evolution occurs in 1215 with Canon 13 of Lateran IV. The canon included the following statements: "Lest too great a diversity of religious orders lead to grave confusion in the Church of God, we strictly forbid anyone in the future to found a new order, but whoever should wish to enter an order, let him choose one already approved. Similarly, he who should wish to found a new monastery, must accept a rule already approved."[7] The

[5] Lainati, *Fonti,* 143.

[6] Lainati, *Regola,* 232.

[7] Constitution 13 (Ne nimia...monasteriis praesidere). *Disciplinary Decrees of the General Councils Text, Translations, and Commentary,* H.J. Schroeder, O.P. (New York: Herder, 1937) 255.

68

CHAPTER 2

sources echo the first impact of this legislation when Francis prevailed upon Clare to accept the title of abbess (LegCl 12; Proc I: 6). It is certain that at this period Francis insisted that Clare assume the title of Abbess. It is possible that he was concerned about the absence of an approved proposal for the community at San Damiano. The friars could avoid being assigned one of the older rules because of the oral approval granted them by Innocent III in 1209. Clare and Francis, confronted with the absence of any legal foundation for the primitive *Form of Life,* were trying to create a base for the continued existence of San Damiano using a formula that would meet with Church approval.

Clare was then confronted with a major problem, that of preserving a commitment to absolute poverty that was essential to her Franciscan vocation. In a bold gesture she appealed directly to Innocent III for a papal exemption from the usages of traditional monasticism which allowed for ownership of goods, and, indeed, required such ownership. The exemption was called the *Privilege of Poverty.*

Written in Innocent's own hand sometime between the end of the Lateran Council and his death on July 16, 1216,[8] the text of the *Privilege* which survives is not the original document, but a re-confirmation given by Gregory IX in 1228.[9] It is based upon the original privilege conceded by Innocent and marks the beginning of Clare's long process of developing legislation that would give juridical form to the Gospel inspiration to which she and her sisters were pledged. It also demonstrates the remarkable determination of Innocent III to protect the fledgling community. It was his final contribution to stabilizing and protecting the Franciscan movement. As Brenda Bolton has observed: "All previous approved rules had been based on the presupposition that, although individuals were without property, houses would have to maintain themselves by sufficient income from corporate possessions. So this privilege represented for Clare a

[8] See Armstrong's summary of the textual tradition of the *Privilege* , 83.
[9] Armstrong, *Clare*, 103-104.

guarantee that her community could not be obliged to adopt an existing rule. It seemed that Innocent had, therefore, helped her to create an entirely new form of convent community, which maintained itself on alms and the profits of manual labor in the same way as the Franciscans."[10] This attempt to be self-supporting without ownership of property became the core of life for Clare's foundation. The most important words of the *Privilege* assured her that "No one can compel you to receive possessions."[11]

The Rule of Hugolino (1219)

The next stage of development centers on the appointment of Hugolino as Papal Legate for Lombardy and Tuscany in 1217.[12] Honorius III, after hearing reports from his legate about the phenomenon of new convents of women springing up in these areas, instructed Hugolino in August, 1218, to exempt these convents from local diocesan jurisdiction, thus taking all of these small foundations directly under the wing of the Apostolic See.[13] In the further discharge of this order, Hugolino composed a rule, or constitutions, whose principal tenets were exemption from local bishops and observance of the Benedictine rule.[14] The prescriptions of this rule, especially those dealing with enclosure, silence, fasting and mortification, were influenced by the more austere Cistercian spirituality which at this period

[10] Brenda Bolton, "Mulieres Sanctae." *Women in Medieval Society,* ed. Susan Mosher Stuard (Philadephia: University of Pennsylvania Press, 1976) 154. (Originally published in *Studies in Church History* 10 [London: Basil Blackwell, 1973]).

[11] "The Privilege of Poverty of Pope Innocent III," in Armstrong, *Clare*, 84.

[12] "Gregory IX," *New Catholic Encyclopedia* VI 775-777. See also, Robert C. Figueira "Legatus apostolicae sedis: the Pope's 'alter ego' According to Thirteenth Century Canon Law," *Studi Medievali* 27 (1986) 527-574.

[13] Armstrong, *Clare*, 85-86. See below, Chapter Five: "The Rise of Urban Religious Forms" for a fuller treatment of this situation.

[14] Oliger, 193-209.

was the favored expression of ecclesial reform.[15] This rule was given to Clare and her sisters, as well as other religious groups of women in Hugolino's jurisdiction, in 1219. In accepting it, she did not renounce the spiritual counsels of the *Form of Life* and she retained the *Privilege of Poverty*.

It is important to remember that this legal collage of the Benedictine Rule, the Hugolinian Rule and the *Privilege of Poverty* granted by Innocent III and the *Form of Life* was valid only for San Damiano and a small number of monasteries that distinctly adopted this monastery's program.[16] Many other monasteries of women whose association with Clare and the friars was not incorporated into a legally binding arrangement were not able to preserve the specific Franciscan content of their observance with these legal protections.[17] It is essential to understand the complex phenomenon of the proliferation of these monasteries, the lack of clearly specified responsibilities of the friars in their regard, and the fact that Francis and the brothers were increasingly occupied with their own internal development and missionary journeys.[18] The fact that the questions continued concerning the combination of obligations is illustrated by the 1228 renewal of Clare's *Privilege of Poverty* by Gregory IX when his efforts to dissuade Clare from this risky option failed (Proc I: 13).[19]

[15] Van Leeuwen, 67-68.

[16] See Lazaro Iriarte, O.F.M. Cap., "Clare of Assisi: Her Place in Female Hagiography." *Greyfriars Review* 3 (August, 1989) 173-206 for an assessment of Hugolino's role at this time.

[17] See Roberto Rusconi, "L'espansione del Francescanesimo femminile nel secolo XIII." *MRFF*, 264-313. Section 1 of this article treats of some of the convents established and the various forms of relationships among them (270-284).

[18] Lainati, *Regola*, 234-235.

[19] Godet makes the interesting observation that Clare did **not** seek a renewal of the privilege from Honorius III, implying that her experiences with Hugolino gave her reasons for concern that may not have existed with his predecessor. See Godet, *Progetto*, 226.

The text of Hugolino's *Rule* consists of fourteen sections.[20] The contents may be summarized as follows: (1) the form and manner of living; (2) the need for rules and laws; (3) the *Rule of St. Benedict;* (4) obligation to remain enclosed; explanation of life required prior to entrance; (5) Divine Office; (6) silence and the parlor; (7) fasting; (8) care of the sick; (9) clothing, bedding, tonsure; (10) entrance into the monastery; (11) the chaplain; the grille; (12) the visitator; (13) the portress and the key; (14) obligation of the *Rule.* The document consists principally of defining obligations. At times it is exhortatory (e.g., 3, 8, 14) and at other times it is stern and commanding (e.g., 2, 4, 10).

Scholars differ in their assessment of the actual role played by the Benedictine legislation in the formation of Hugolino's *Rule.* Chiara Augusta Lainati stresses the fact that it formed merely a juridical base for the more important prescriptions of Hugolino. The oldest manuscript of Hugolino's *Rule* (Pamplona, 1228)[21] makes no mention of the *Rule of St. Benedict,* a fact which she takes to indicate that Hugolino recognized the Franciscan base for the life of San Damiano. She goes on to assert that the legislation of Hugolino contributes to an organic development of what she identifies as the true Franciscan line of development as opposed to the later "Urbanistic" development which began with the *Rule of Innocent IV.* She explains: "On the one hand there exists and is developed a line of thought which goes directly to St. Francis and St. Clare. This line of thought stems from the primitive little rule and the 'oral and written counsels' of St. Francis; it passes through the Rule of '19 [*Rule of Hugolino*] side by side with the *Privilege of Poverty.* Finally, it passes through the *Later Rule,* becoming focused in the definitive *Rule of St. Clare* ..."[22]

Meanwhile, Godet reflects upon the positive values represented by the choice of the Benedictine Rule as a base, seeing

---

[20] Armstrong , *Clare,* 87-96.

[21] See Omaechavarría, 216.

[22] Lainati, *Regola,* 236.

in this option a reflection of Clare's desire to preserve a model of evangelical life represented in the monastic tradition of disciples gathered around the person of Jesus, thus offering a life of witness within the Church. Given the other Rules available, he feels that the Benedictine model mirrored most closely the ideals Clare and Francis sought to express through San Damiano.[23] The influence of this juridic necessity had far-reaching effects, as is attested to by the fact that in the eighteenth century the Bollandists inscribed Clare among the saints of the Benedictine order. This evoked the necessity of a thorough study of the origins her *Rule,* which prompted the 1912 work of Oliger. In a study of the *Rule of Clare* published at the turn of the century, Ernest Gilliat-Smith observed that there were many elements in the Benedictine observance of medieval convents that would have served Clare's purposes well.[24] Writing from within the Benedictine tradition, he notes that this *Rule* was "large, elastic, mild, leaving as it does, so much to the discretion of local superiors."[25] He also points out that the fourth chapter lists works of mercy that were to be performed from within the cloister in an expression of charity that was not limited to those within the monastery. Hospitality and providing shelter were offered without weakening the discipline of the monastery. Material detachment was expected. A monk or nun could leave the cloister with permission in cases of necessity. These comments from a writer whose goal was to describe Clare's association with the Benedictine tradition serve as a warning against too quickly dismissing the role that this tradition played in her ultimate endeavors.

There is even reason to believe that Clare may have benefitted by the Benedictine Rule's attitude toward the common good. Terrence Kardong, in his *Commentary on Benedict's Rule,* writes that Benedict carefully combined an element from the

[23] Godet, *Progetto*, 223.

[24] Ernest Gilliat-Smith, *St. Clare of Assisi: Her Life and Legislation* (London and Toronto: I.M. Dent & Sons, Limited, 1914) 138-148.

[25] Gilliat-Smith, 69.

Rule of Augustine with Acts 4: 32: "First he [Benedict] transposes...'Let all things be in common' now precedes 'Let no one call anything his own.' His purpose is clearly calculated. He wants the common life and common goods to provide a milieu in which the individual can practise [sic] personal dispossession."[26] Kardong points out that Chapter 34 of Benedict's *Rule* is "strictly communal in concern. It is aimed at mutual generosity against selfishness."[27] Clare could not have missed the significance of these concepts, and supplied what Kardong admits Benedict missed, "the kenosis of Jesus as a motivation for the ascetical dispossession he [Benedict] teaches"[28] in Chapter 33 of the rule. With the added element of kenosis, it was only a short step to move beyond the "all things held in common" concept of the Benedictine Rule to the "living without anything of one's own" found in RegCl 1: 2. It is possible to add the kenotic motivation found in Clare's *Testament:* "out of love of the God Who was placed poor in the crib, lived poor in the world, and remained naked on the cross" (TestCl 45) and discover one of the adaptions of the Benedictine life that served Clare well.

Perhaps the strong warnings of Francis to his brothers that they avoid adopting Benedictine practices (e.g., his refusal to allow the title of "prior" in Reg NB 6: 3 and his violent rejection of the suggestion that the *Rule of Benedict* be adopted at a stormy period in the Order's beginnings described in LP, 114) have created an aversion, at least for some, to acknowledging any indebtedness to this same tradition in the evolution of the Franciscan experiment. It is equally possible that in the contemporary experience of reshaping the structures of religious life, that some apostolic congregations actively resist the monasticization of institutes founded precisely to create an alternative to the monastic model. Both of these facts suggest that there might be unnecessary reluctance to give a positive

[26] Terrence Kardong, O.S.B., *Commentary on Benedict's Rule* (Wilmington: Michael Glazier, 1986) 14.

[27] Kardong, 16.

[28] Kardong, 16.

view of Clare's reliance upon the Benedictine tradition for
insight, custom and actual documentation. There may also be
hesitation to give positive value to the role of the Benedictine
influence upon her if one does not sufficiently appreciate the
shift that has recently taken place in studies of the history of
spirituality. Caroline Walker Bynum describes this change:

> Furthermore, in direct and intended contrast to
> earlier histories of spirituality, the new schol-
> arship avoids the question of the particular
> characteristics of religious orders (e.g.,
> Franciscan as opposed to Dominicans,
> Cistercians in contrast to old-style Benedictines),
> attempting instead to set out those features that
> characterize many groups, including the het-
> erodox.... It sees the most pressing issues of the
> period as matters not of doctrine but of practice
> or what we might call lifestyle, particularly the
> question of what "true poverty" is and of how
> "evangelism" (which comes increasingly to mean
> preaching) is to be carried out.[29]

If, then. one is to appreciate the manner in which Clare
appropriated aspects of the monastic tradition, one needs to
disabuse oneself of imagining the ongoing mutations of religious life-styles as activities in which one version of religious life
comes to a definitive end and another version is attempted
without any reference by subsequent pioneers to positive and
negative values of preceding founders.

While it is clear that the actual verbal dependence upon the
Rule of Benedict in the text of Clare is minor in comparison with
her complete dependence upon Francis' *Rule* texts, it is equally
clear that Clare had used Benedictine—or more generically,
monastic—customs and wisdom in the governance of her

[29] Bynum, 4.

community. Hers is, in fact, a synthesis of the evangelical content of Francis' proposal with the conventual customs of more ancient religious orders. This synthesis overcame many of the difficulties the friars themselves fell heir to in the decades after the death of their leader. It is, in an ironic way, most unfortunate that the friars appeared to have paid so little official attention to how she managed to apply Franciscan norms to a stable community living in a fixed dwelling, thus requiring clear directives for the sharing of goods, assignments of labor, descriptions of officers' roles, regulations of elections and discipline for infractions. Perhaps a more attentive observance on their part of the manner in which she dealt with the evolving questions of the communitarian experience of the Franciscan movement would have prevented many a schism in the early fraternity.

The Rule of Innocent IV (1247)

The years between Hugolino's and Innocent's *Rules* were eventful for the Poor Sisters and their Abbess. Monasteries continued to be founded in Italy and in other countries. Francis was enrolled in the calendar of the saints. A procession of visitators came and went. Gregory IX died. Records indicate a good many questions arose and a constant exchange of documentation seems to have kept the papal chancery busy.[30] Innocent IV, confronted by constant demands from both friars and sisters for arbitration, began to deal with Franciscan problems of observance in peremptory ways.[31] He initiated an active program to force both of the mendicant orders to assume jurisdiction of the convents of women associated with them. Grundmann examines this program in detail and concludes that

[30] See, for example, Williel R. Thomson, "Checklist of Papal Letters relating to the Three Orders of St. Francis: Innocent III— Alexander IV," *AFH* 64 (1971) 367-580.

[31] "Innocent IV," *New Catholic Encyclopedia* VI, 524-525; Leonardo Pisanu, O.F.M. *Innocenzo IV e i Francescani (1243-1254)*. Studi e Testi Francescani,

the Friars Minor were more successful in avoiding an absolute obligation of responsibility for the sisters than were their Dominican counterparts.[32] But it is precisely as part of this attempt of Innocent to place the pastoral and economic problems of the sisters on the shoulders of the friars that his *Rule* must be read.

Innocent IV's first legislation for women's monasteries was a re-confirmation in 1245 of the existing Hugolinian *Rule*.[33] This was followed by a second text, composed by him, that both obliged the Friars to take administrative responsibility for the convents and which gave great latitude in the jurisdiction over property. Innocent's *Rule* is much longer than that of Hugolino. Its contents may be summarized as follows: (1) form of life; enclosure; explanation of life; (2) Divine Office; (3) silence; the parlor; (4) fasting; care of the sick; (5) clothing; common dormitory; (6) entrance into the monastery; (7) the chaplain and the grille; (8) the visitator; (9) door, enclosure, and portress; (10) extern sisters; (11) receiving and retaining possessions; (12) obligation of the rule.

The major elements of this text are the newly specified relationship with the Franciscan Order; the *Later Rule,* and the *Privilege of Poverty.* At first glance this appears as an improvement, but it is drastic in its reduction of the autonomy of the monasteries. Ironically, the eleventh section is in direct contradiction to the *Later Rule,* in permitting procurators.[34] This text also contains a veritable explosion of legislative details.

---

41 (Roma: Edizione Francescane, 1968). See especially 201-205 on relationship of the friars with the Poor Sisters and the conclusions, 279-289.

[32] Herbert Grundmann, *Movimenti religiosi nel medioevo,* trans. Maria Ausserhofer e Lea Nicolet Santini (Bologna: Società editrice il Mulino, 1974). See Chapter V, "L'inserimento del movimento religioso femminile negli Ordini mendicanti," 193-293.

[33] *BF* I, 394. Armstrong, *Clare* , 109-124.

[34] Recall R. Brooke's description of Innocent as "extraordinarily callous and cavalier in [his] treatment of the Franciscan conscience," as witnessed in his act of placing the papal treasury in the Sacro Convento in Assisi for safekeeping in 1243. Rosalind B. Brooke, *Early Franciscan Government* (Cambridge: University Press, 1959) 265.

They show that a very strict interpretation of monastic dress, conduct, and claustration was in the ascendancy.

Chiara Augusta Lainati regards this text as giving rise to what she calls a "curial" line of legislation that culminates in the *Rule of Urban IV* in 1263. She does not see this text as making any positive contribution to Clare's final redaction of her *Rule*.[35] Godet, on the other hand, while acknowledging the insuperable problem of Innocent's refusal of the *Privilege of Poverty*, credits him with the encouragement of juridical ties between the friars and the sisters by the various prescriptions of his legislation.[36]

Perhaps the question is not primarily one of textual dependence. Reviewing Clare's text shows little reliance on Innocent IV for actual language. Even those instances in which Clare does adapt concepts from her ecclesiastical superiors demonstrate her ability to use the material in a thoughtful and original way. The real contribution which came from Innocent's work on a Rule of his own was to inadvertently signal a critical shift in curial policy that galvanized Clare into action. Having seen the text of Innocent's *Rule*, Clare could no longer assume that the observance in San Damiano would be secure in the future. New papal interventions could weaken her program in fundamental ways. Placed side-by-side both the *Rule of Hugolino* and the *Rule of Innocent* took away as much as they gave in support of her project. Clare was undeniably compelled to prepare her own version of the "Rule and Life" of the Poor Sisters.

[35] Lainati, *Regola,* 236-240.
[36] Godet, *Progetto,* 227.

The Rule of Clare

Clare Writes her own Rule

It is obvious that Clare was not attempting to compose a thoroughly original document, but a synthetic text that drew upon all that went before it: the *Form of Life*, the *Privilege of Poverty*, the *Rules* of Benedict, Hugolino, Francis and Innocent IV. Since the *Rule of Clare* speaks of the consultation of the sisters in weekly chapters (RegCl 4: 15-18) it may be supposed that the accumulated wisdom of the community was involved in the retention or addition of elements.[37] Based upon her correspondence with Agnes and Ermentrude, it can also be supposed that Clare also knew of the experiences and wishes of her sister abbesses and their communities and took these into account. Also, since the *Last Will* of Francis promised the continuing solicitude of the friars for San Damiano, and since the *Rule of Innocent* prescribed certain specific acts of jurisdiction on the part of the Minister General, it may also be supposed that Clare had access to the minister (John of Parma at this time) either in person, or through other friars. Another detail of the *Legend* fraught with implications is the news that present at Clare's deathbed were Juniper, Angelo and Leo.[38] This presence of the most intimate companions of Francis at the point at which she completed composing her own *Rule* indicates a sustained dialogue among the early companions and champions of a primitive observance. Further, the actual form of the Bull of approval testifies to stages of curial advisement as she worked on the text.[39]

---

[37] A further proof of this involvement of the community in reaching and ratifying important decisions is found in the "Mandate of 1238" which bears the signatures of so many of them. Armstrong, *Clare*,107-108.

[38] More about the significance of the companions' relationship to Clare will be discussed in Chapter Three.

[39] See Armstrong, *Clare*, regarding role of Raynaldus, 256.

The final stages in the drama of Clare's legislative triumph unfolded around her in her last days. Englebert Grau has admirably summarized the events that most likely occurred in these eleventh hour deliberations.[40] First he recalls that the text had already been approved on September 16, 1252 by the Cardinal Protector, Raynaldus with the canonical brief *Quia vos*. The original Bull, *Solet annuere,* preserved in the Proto-Monastery of Santa Chiara in Assisi shows this text with the signature of the Cardinal contained intact. Above this text on the same parchment there is in Innocent's own handwriting the notation "*Ad instar fiat S.* " ("to be done as it is"), and on the bottom, again in the pope's hand, "*Ex causis manifestis michi et protectori mon[asterii] fiat ad instar*" ("It will be done according to the petition for reasons known to me and the protector of the monastery.").[41]

These notations were necessary because ordinary procedures were suspended in the approval of this document. The normal process involved the pope initialing a request with the first letter of his baptismal name—in this case "S" for Sinibaldus. This signature and the papal seal caused the chancery to prepare the bull which was then signed by a cardinal. In this instance, however, the written request was waived. Clare was very close to death and Innocent was responding to an oral petition made by Clare during one of his final visits to her.[42] Although Innocent verified in his own handwriting that he was dispensing with the usual procedures, he nonetheless took care that the document was in proper legal form. Then, from his residence, he sent the text bearing his seal to the dying abbess. Before the text was committed to safe-keeping another hand added the precious notation: "Blessed Clare touched and kissed this many, many times out of devotion."[43]

---

[40] Grau, 210-211.

[41] See *Écrits*, 20.

[42] Such a visit was made sometime between August 1-8, 1253.

[43] *Hanc beata Clara tetigit et obsculata (!) est pro devotione pluribus et pluribus vicinis.* See *Écrits*, 21.

So ends the lengthy story of canons, counsels, cardinal protectors and "the labyrinthine ways" reflected in the saga of Clare's *Rule*. It would be a mistake, however, to imagine this drama as simply an inspiring page depicting one woman's charismatic tenacity. Indeed the full import of Clare's determination could not have been realized until our own era. Within a decade after her death, this text, for which she worked so diligently, had been set aside in favor of a new solution from Pope Urban IV.[44] Consequently, the full value of Clare's conceptualization of her form of life remained literally and metaphorically buried for many of her followers for centuries. The physical rediscovery of the text has been joined to the re-discovery of its theological and spiritual vitality in the wake of the Second Vatican Council.

Sources, Language and Structure of the Text

In speaking of the divine commission which he believed to be his, Francis insisted upon the originality of his *Rule*. He would not consider adapting his *Rule* to fit the patterns of older rules, and he struggled with the friars and with the curia to overcome arguments that he do so (LP 114; 1Cel 32, 33; LTS 63). Clare, however, while insisting that she was acting in fidelity to his teaching, made no attempt to argue that her *Rule* was original. Her actions consistently reminded curial officials that she was simply carrying out the provisions of the form of life and teachings of Francis. Due to the ambiguous legal situation in which she found herself in the post-Lateran years, her main line of defense was an appeal to the authority of Francis' written and oral teaching (e.g., RegCl 1: 3; 6: 1; TestCl 7). Clare was determined not be placed at any distance, legal or attitudinal, from the program of Francis. "The Son of God has been made for us *the Way*, which our blessed father Francis, His true lover

---

[44] Oliger, 439-444. For a fascinating narration of the re-discovery of the *Rule of Clare*, see Sr. Mary Clare, P.C.C., "The Finding of the body of Saint Clare, " *The Cord*, 35 (September, 1985) 247-253.

and imitator, has shown and taught us by word and example"
(TestCl 5). Her argument was that she was simply following the
path Francis had indicated. However, in following this way,
which required "obedience and reverence" to the Pope, Clare
also incorporated elements that came from the Roman curia, in
addition to those elements which grew out of her experience.

As a result, the text itself does not immediately convey a sense
of originality. One could, in fact, be tempted to assert the
opposite opinion. The language often seems awkward and
labored where Clare tried to assimilate preceding versions of
Hugolino's *Rule* or Innocent's *Rule*. She added original material
that is sometimes merely factual or, at other times, spontaneous
and full of personal feeling.[45] It is also historically significant that
in the composition and confirmation of this text, Clare became
the first woman to write for a feminine religious order legislation
that achieved the status of a papally approved rule of life.[46] She
thereby becomes a threshold figure in the history of religious
life among women.

It has often been observed that Clare writes in a Latin style
superior to that of Francis.[47] This suggests either the possibility
of a secretarial hand at work on the text or the fact that Clare's
noble status had given her excellent educational opportunities
and the possibility of developing such skill, or both. In reading
the text, one is also struck by the manner in which Clare moved
from language that is clearly legislative and juridically precise to
language that is full of identification with personally treasured
values and realities. For example Chapter II contains her clear
exposition of requirements for entrance into the sisterhood:

[45] *Écrits*, 42.

[46] Peter Dronke, *Women Writers of the Middle Ages: A Critical Study of Texts
from Perpetua (d. 203) to Marguerite Porete (d. 1310).* (Cambridge: Cambridge University Press, 1984) 320-332.

[47] See *Écrits* for comments on language and style for all of Clare's writings,
33-35.

> And if she believes all these things and is willing
> to profess them faithfully and to observe them
> steadfastly to the end; and if she has no husband,
> or if she has [a husband] who has already entered
> religious life with the authority of the Bishop of
> the diocese and has already made a vow of
> continence; and if there is no impediment to her
> observance of this life, such as advanced age or
> ill-health or mental weakness, let the tenor of
> our life be thoroughly explained to her (RegCl
> 2: 4-6).

Note the contrast in language when this is followed at the conclusion of the chapter by a plea to the sisters to persevere in the use of poor clothing. One suspects a fear on Clare's part that this norm is weakening. Whatever the situation, she gave free reign to deep feelings of concern: "I admonish, beg, and exhort my sisters to always wear cheap garments out of love of the most holy and beloved Child Who was wrapped in such poor little swaddling clothes and laid in a manger and of His most holy Mother" (RegCl 2: 24).

Even when Clare reproduced the most juridical aspects of previous rules, she recast certain provisions in language that indicates the importance of articulating legal norms in a spirit of prudence. For example, she wrote to Agnes of Prague: "I beg you, therefore, dearly beloved, to refrain wisely and prudently from an indiscreet and impossible austerity in the fasting that you have undertaken. And I beg you in the Lord to praise the Lord by your very life, to offer the Lord your *reasonable service* and your *sacrifice* always *seasoned with salt.*" (3LAg 40-41).

Modern texts divide the *Rule* into twelve chapters, although this division did not exist in the original Bull. This structure was added later in an obvious attempt to make the text conform in appearance to that of the *Later Rule*. But this chapter arrangement results in an artificial grouping of elements and can mislead the reader into perceiving relationships where none originally existed.[48] These twelve chapters are arranged in the following order: (1) the Form of Life of the Poor Sisters; (2) those who wish to accept this life and how they are to be received; (3) the Divine Office, fasting, confession and communion; (4) the election and office of the abbess; the Chapter, officials, and discreets; (5) silence, the parlor and the grille; (6) the lack of possessions; (7) the manner of working; (8) the sisters' not acquiring anything as their own; begging alms; the sick sisters; (9) the penance to be imposed on the sisters who sin; the sisters who serve outside the monastery; (10) the admonition and correction of the sisters; (11) the custody of the enclosure; (12) the visitator, the chaplain, and the cardinal protector.

Relationship of Clare's Text to Francis' Rule

Before reviewing some of the contemporary approaches to the analysis of Clare's *Rule,* it is helpful to reflect upon the manner in which Clare employed the sources she received from Francis himself, especially his *Rule.*[49] When studying her document, it becomes clear that her utilization of Francis' texts was not a question of expediency nor of simple imitation. The manner in which Clare based her own work upon Francis' shows her deep conviction of having a responsibility to witness to their mutual charism. In the first chapter Clare made a clear declaration that Francis instituted the Poor Sisters (RegCl 1: 1). Francis, in turn had received the life of the Gospel (RegB 1: 1) by divine inspiration, as he stated in his *Testament* (14). Francis submitted this expression of divine inspiration to the Church for verification, and promised "obedience and reverence" to the Pope (RegNB 1: 3; RegB 1: 2). Clare, in turn, did the same; she

---

[48] *Écrits* , 21

[49] This comparison was facilitated by an unpublished table of comparisons between the texts of the *Rule of St. Benedict,* the *Rules* of Hugolino and Innocent, the *Testaments* of Francis and Clare and the *Rule (Earlier* and *Later)* of Francis and the *Rule of Clare.* The table was made available through the generosity of Jean-François Godet.

promised voluntary obedience to Francis (RegCl 1: 4). In light of the prohibition in the *Earlier Rule* concerning receiving women into obedience (RegNB 12: 4), this firm assertion of Clare's takes on new light. She was not narrating a neutral fact. Francis' decision to receive her and her sisters in 1212 represented a unique moment in the development of the Order. Her entrance was exactly like that of the early brothers. By beginning and ending the first chapter of her *Rule* in this way, Clare is reminding her readers that Francis' relationship with her and her sisters was a deliberate choice with spiritual and canonical consequences.

In the second chapter she, like Francis in the *Earlier Rule*, describes the new candidate for the Order as one moved "by divine inspiration" (RegCl 2: 1). This is the inspiration she recalls in her *Testament* (24-26). This inspiration has yielded in Clare a special "reading" of the Gospel. For this reason the formative process is one of explaining "the tenor of our life, " a phrase for which she found the precedent in the *Earlier Rule* (2: 3). In describing the manner of receiving and educating new members, she clearly keeps Chapter 2 of both texts of Francis before her eyes: she warns that superiors may not become involved in the financial affairs of candidates (RegCl 2: 10-12; RegNB 2: 5; RegB 2: 7-10). When Francis treats of the situation of the member following profession he warns that the friars must not "wander outside obedience" (RegNB 2: 10; RegB 2: 12-13). In the same place in her text (RegCl 12) Clare enjoins the cloister but states the cases of prudence in which a sister may leave the monastery. At the conclusion of his second chapter, Francis warns the friars not to judge those who live and dress well (RegNB 2: 14-15; RegB 2: 17). In the same place Clare pleads with her sisters to continue to to dress poorly for the sake of the Christ Child (RegCl 2: 25). Although a repetition of values is present, the specific applications differ. Clare does not merely echo Francis, she interprets him according the lessons of her own lived experience.

The third chapter, which deals with the recitation of the Office and fasting indicates something of the liturgical development that had taken place since the time of Francis. He had legislated liturgical uses based on those of the Roman curia (RegNB 3: 3-4; RegB 3: 1-4). In 1253, Clare legislates recitation according to the usages of the Friars Minor, which had become normative for the Church.[50] She also states that the office should be read without being sung. This implies a concern to avoid a division among those who are literate and capable of performing this extended liturgical service, and the serving sisters. It may also imply a desire to avoid being obliged to a classical monastic conception of Office as the primary form of labor, as opposed to ordinary manual labor. In dealing with the regulation of fasting, Clare gives a simple outline in a position equivalent to Francis' Gospel-based counsel that the brothers eat what is set before them (RegNB 3: 11-13; RegB 3: 5-8,14; RegCl 3: 8-11; cf. 3LAg 32-37). A comparison with the fasting regulations in the texts of Innocent and Hugolino demonstrates her prudence and liberality. Clare also mandates that confession be offered twelve times and the reception of holy Eucharist seven times in the year. This is a careful prescription of her desire to lead "a truly catholic life." She also provides that the Mass be **inside** the enclosure when these seven special feasts are celebrated. She seems in this way to desire a unity expressed liturgically similar to that described by Francis in the *Letter to the Order* (30-33).

When she deals with the election of the abbess in the fourth chapter Clare is able to offer more precision on these points than had Francis in describing governmental decisions of this type (RegNB 4; RegB 8: 1-5). She repeats her description of the abbess contained in her *Testament* (63-66). As Francis qualified the minister as "servant" (RegNB 4: 2; RegB 8: 1) she offers a qualification of title ("abbess and mother," RegCl 4: 7), but she adopts the Scriptural citation about rendering an account for those entrusted to her (Mt 12: 36) from the *Rule of Benedict* (64).

---

[50] Brooke, *Government*, 283.

In the fifth chapter which deals with silence and introduces the first specific forms of material enclosure, she seems to have been more influenced by the *Rule for Hermitages*. The *Rules* of Hugolino and Innocent impose continual silence. Clare, on the other hand, adopts a pattern of silence of specific times and places. Francis recognizes silence as related to fraternal charity: "And all the brothers should beware that they do not slander or engage in disputes (cf. 2Tim 2: 14); rather they should strive to keep silence whenever God gives them [this] grace."(RegNB 11: 2) But Clare allows speech when needed to serve the sick and for meeting the needs of all: "They may speak discreetly at all times, however, in the infirmary for the recreation and service of the sick."(RegCl 5:3) Here is another example of a different material regulation, but a spirit very much in harmony with that of Francis.

Francis wrote the *Testament* after he wrote the *Rule* and the relationship of the two texts has been a troublesome question through the centuries. Clare, however, wrote her *Rule* **after** she wrote her *Testament*. [51] Chapter Six of her *Rule* presents an interesting phenomenon. Clare incorporated, almost literally, some thirty-one verses of her *Testament* in this Chapter. She also used material contained in her letters (1LAg 17-19; 2LAg 17; 4LAg 18-22). She did not reproduce the text from either *Rule* of the friars here, but rather the texts specifically given to her sisterhood by Francis, the *Form of Life* (3-4) and the *Last Will* (7-9). It is a marvelous synthesis in which she clearly departs from all previous texts and speaks her own "credo" firmly rooted in the original primitive *Form of Life* given by Francis when the Poor Sisters were founded. Here only the voices of Francis and Clare address us from the parchment.[52] Continuing the de-

---

[51] In *François d'Assise: Écrits*, pp. 27, 31-33, Desbonnets indicates that the *Testament* of Clare is one of her last writings, "in the same time as the *Rule*," but it is not possible to be more definite than that. He writes: "The *Testament* is a cry of fidelity. It is written towards the end of a life of combat whose issue is not clearly certain." This implies a time **before** the *Rule*.

[52] See Chapter Three for the development of this point.

scription of the life of the poor in Chapter Seven, Clare draws material directly from the *Earlier Rule* (VII: 3,6,7,11 and V: 2), the *Testament* (20-21) and the *Exhortation to the Poor Ladies* (4). She adds the *proviso* of assigning work in chapter, guarding thereby the spirit of sisterliness and minority. Chapter Eight is a hymn on the "sine proprio" (with nothing of one's own) theme in the writings of Francis. Antecedents for verses one to six are found in the *Earlier Rule* (VII: 8,13; IX: 3-8), the *Later Rule* (VI: 1-6), Francis' *Testament* (22, 24) and the *Exhortation to the Poor Ladies* (1, 6). Verse 11 has its counterparts in the *Earlier Rule* (VIII: 3,6,7) and the *Later Rule* (IV: 1,3; V: 3) in which Francis prohibits money. In regard to the use of money, Clare plainly demonstrated her ability to prescind from the legislation of Francis when there was just cause. "If, however, money is sent the Abbess, with the advice of the discreets, may provide for the needs of the Sister" (Reg Cl 8:11). The final segment on the care of the sick may be compared to Clare's own sentiments in her *Testament* (63) and several passages in which Francis speaks of the needs of the sick (RegNB 10: 1; 9: 10-11 and RegB 4: 2; 6: 8-9).

The material dealing with correction and mutual reconciliation in Clare's ninth chapter draws from several parts of the texts of Francis. First, Clare deals with reconciliation in a community without priest-members. (This could account for her prescription of confession on an apparently monthly basis in the third chapter.) She distinguishes between ordinary and extraordinary correction and penance, but she draws upon the same foundation as Francis in counseling charity towards the offender. Verses 1-11 of Chapter Nine of Clare's *Rule* is based upon parallel passages found in RegNB 5: 5-8; 11: 1-4 and 21: 5-6 and in RegB 7: 1-3. The second half of Chapter Nine concerns the conduct of extern sisters. In parallel texts in the RegNB (11: 1-3 and 7-9) and RegB (12: 1-4) Francis concerned himself with the conduct of the friars when they "go through the world," and their specific conduct in relation to religious women.

In the tenth chapter Clare describes the concept of servanthood required of the abbess in the accomplishment of her duties. She solemnly warns the sisters to guard against pride, avarice, and other divisive vices, and exhorts them to patience in persecution. The entire chapter is modeled very closely on the tenth chapter of the *Later Rule*. Segments can be found in the *Earlier Rule* as well (e.g., 4: 2-3; 5: 2; 17: 19 ; 9: 14; 22: 26; 11: 1-8 and 16: 12, 21). The comparison demonstrates how well Francis synthesized his material on these points in his second redaction and how Clare was able to profit from this summary.

In the eleventh chapter there are minimal points of reference to Francis with the exception of parallel ideals concerning observance of enclosure in the *Rule for Hermitages* and Francis' prohibition concerning women's monasteries referred to above. In this chapter Clare is drawing principally from the lengthy and detailed prescriptions of Hugolino and Innocent. Finally, in the twelfth chapter she repeats the submission to the church, the request for a cardinal protector and the concluding declaration of intent to live in the Catholic faith, following the poverty and humility of Christ—to which she adds "and His most holy mother" (RegCl 12:13).

In this document which transmits and stabilizes her understanding of vocation and charism, Clare is in full concord with Francis. She utilizes his articulation as often as possible, but she does not hesitate to adapt or suppress that which does not pertain to life at San Damiano.

Approaches to Analysis of the Rule

There appear to be three general approaches to the study of the structure of Clare's *Rule*. One concentrates on identifying the manner in which Clare works within the framework created by the *Later Rule* of the Friars Minor. A significant amount of work has been done by various authors in demonstrating how

Clare used or edited the material in the *Later Rule*. [53] An article by Peter van Leeuwen in *Greyfriars Review* concludes with such an outline.[54] He divides Clare's text into fourteen headings. Under these headings he lists the items found in Clare's text and the corresponding chapters or verses from the *Later Rule*. By using such devices one is able to appreciate both Clare's determination to use as much as possible of the work of Francis as well as the manner in which Clare adapts her sources to the exigencies of her own situation.

A second approach to the analysis of the *Rule* is that taken by Jean-François Godet in his presentation in *Vita Minorum* in Spring, 1985. In this publication Godet presented a version of the text in which there are no internal divisions; the entire *Rule* is presented in units of individual thought. This presentation is a major contribution to understanding the text in a manner liberated from the traditional "architecture" of the twelve chapters. Taking his cue from the acknowledgement that the twelve chapter divisions were not in the original text, Godet moves "inside" the text to explore how one idea leads to another, and uncovers an internal logic that is analogous to that of the *Later Rule*. He maintains that Clare's *Rule* contains three basic divisions. He states:

> The first part contains the definition of the identity of those for whom the *Rule* is intended; there are some sentences which determine the essential traits which characterize the community, its purpose, and its form of life. It is the nucleus of the whole *Rule*, which will then be developed more in other parts. What does it

---

[53] Often a text provides this information by way of notes *(Fonti Francescane)* or typographical devices that enable the reader to identify the origins of the various elements visually *(Écrits)*. The edition of I. Boccali, *Textus Opuscolorum S. Francisci et S. Clarae Assisiensium* (Assisi: S. Mariae Angelorum, 1976) provides numerous references in marginal notes.

[54] Van Leeuwen, 73-74.

mean to be a Poor Clare, what is the essence of
their project of life, is it life of community or
solitude, in what relationship do they stand with
each other, and in what type of relation?

The second part is concerned with the conditions
for entrance and living of the evangelical life
and the consequences of this choice. In modern
terms, we would refer to this as "formation," or
more properly, initial formation.

The third part—the longest—is concerned with
the development, in the Middle Ages they would
have said "the exposition," of the contents of the
life: how time and space are utilized, that is, in
what way the Poor Clare inserts herself into the
two dimensions proper to being human.[55]

Godet further specifies that in this third part Clare basically
treats of two factors, time and space. The manner in which time
is used in prayer, in work, in the rhythms of the ordinary day is
an element reflected in many prescriptions of the *Rule*. The space
that is occupied—delimited deliberately—also characterizes
certain choices about how the Poor Sisters wish to organize
their existence. By prescinding from the myriad details of the
Clare's *Rule* and concentrating on larger patterns of human
concern, Godet enables a contemporary reader to re-read the
Rule with a greater appreciation of its value as an expression of
a manner of life.[56]

A third approach to the reading of the text might be termed an
exegetical or hermeneutical approach. In this mode the commentator identifies a pattern of instruction or exposition that is
rooted in the text but which is discerned more by an intuitive
reading than by a linear, logical progression. Such analysis
recognizes that a reader brings to the text an inner sensitivity

[55] Godet, *Progetto*, 237.
[56] Godet, *Progetto*, 237-238.

that allows other lights (from Scriptural study, for example) to suggest ways of understanding Clare's language or intention. This kind of study definitely moves into a realm of more creative analysis, whose values supplement the more ordinary methods of interpretation. For example, Javier Garrido studies the *Rule* as a series of concentric circles whose centers are exhortations.[57] He believes that the *Rule* is a paranetic text that finds its biblical roots in the prophetic preaching and in Deuteronomy. It is a call to obedience in faith to the covenant, although the manner in which Clare uses the exhortation in her *Rule* differs from that of Francis. Garrido states: "It consists in an exhortation to recall the history of God, the first vocation, the primitive form. This style belongs also to the more particular manner of biblical legislation. Deuteronomy, for example, arose as legislation essentially by remembering the first Alliance of Sinai."[58]

Many studies of the *Rule* exist which take an historical-pastoral approach and are designed to assist the Poor Sisters today who wish to understand, but, above all, to live the *Rule of Clare*. Such would be the case in the commentary of Iriarte,[59] a work that combines historical background and a sensitive exposition that explores fundamental values and solutions for contemporary problems.

A Reflection on the Nature of Clare's Rule

Given the varied methods of analysis examined above, further interpretation seems prudent. Does the experience of the constant reading and reflection involved in this research offer

[57] Javier Garrido, O.F.M. *La forma de vida de Santa Clara* (Aranzazu: Aldecoa Diego de Siloe, 1979). The schema suggested by Garrido for the structure is as follows: Solemn introduction and synthesis—Chapter I; First exhortation—II: 19-24; Second exhortation—IV: 8-14; Memorial Exhortation—VI; Hymn to poverty—VII: 1-11; Great exhortation—VIII: 12-21; Concluding program—XII: 12-13, 178-180.

[58] Garrido, 83.

[59] See note 1, this chapter.

any additional insights into the nature of the text? Two possibilities emerge. The first is an experience of the text as a structure not unlike the structure of the enclosure itself. To the extent that the enclosure implies and requires some structures of separation from the world (whether material means such as walls, doors, grilles or behaviors such as silence or limited visits with others), the text can also show in itself something of this spatial, physical protection of a "pearl of great price." It would seem that Clare, in placing the text before her own eyes, presented this experience of enclosure by placing the heart of the *Rule* clearly and unequivocally in the physical center of the text. This becomes rather evident when one evaluates the text according to Godet's presentation of numbered lines corresponding to units of thought.[60] The material corresponding to the first five chapters account for two hundred and ninety-six lines of text. The material corresponding to Chapters VI-VIII accounts for one hundred and sixty-four lines. The material corresponding to Chapters IX-XII accounts for two hundred and sixteen lines. There is, therefore, a remarkable proportionality of length and density of text to the inner theological and spiritual logic it expresses. On either side of a central declaration of intent are arranged the structures which support the sisters' intentions. In Chapters I-V Clare delineates the identity of the Order, the means of admission, the daily program of prayer and discipline, and the internal governmental structures. The three chapters in the center (VI-VIII) express most clearly and ardently the identification of Clare and the Poor Sisters with Francis and the Friars Minor. In Chapters IX-XII she provides for additional structures of correction and canonical provisions of enclosure and visitation. Lastly, she describes the bond of relationship to Friars and the Church.

This scrutiny of the physical and spatial composition of the text in relation to the thought patterns and spiritual vision that comprise it leads to a second interpretation. The biographical

---

[60] Godet, *Progetto*, 201-221.

sources for Clare speak often of her constant occupation with needle-work. Recall Pacifica's testimony in the canonization process:

> She also said that when she was so sick that she could not get up from bed, she had herself raised to sit up and be supported with some cushions behind her back. She spun [thread] so from her work she made corporals and altar linens for almost all the churches of the plains and hills around Assisi. Asked how she knew these things, she replied that she saw her spinning. When the cloth was made and the sisters had sewn it, it was hand-delivered by the brothers to those churches and given to the priests who came there." (Proc I: 6).

The witness Cecilia tells of her making the corporals and silk-covered boxes to hold them (VI: 14).[61] Preserved in the Proto-monastery today is an alb that tradition holds was made by Clare for Francis. (It is, in fact, an enduring tradition even today among the women of Assisi, this devotion to the artistic needlework that enhances the garments or items of household linen that are always on display in countless shop windows.) Knowing Clare's constant application to her spinning and needle-work, it is not difficult to imagine that the labor of redacting the *Rule* was not a separate and unrelated exercise, but the application in language of her skill in spinning and embroidering. It is important to understand that the spinning and sewing described in the sources was neither an ascetical exercise nor a hobby. It was a form of labor by which the Poor Sisters might earn their daily bread and share the lot of poor working women.

---

[61] See Proc II: 12; IX: 9; LegCl 28.

Likewise, the *Rule* was not a literary exercise undertaken to provide for self-expression. It was work. It was Clare's last effort to protect the charism that she and Francis had so carefully planted and tended (TestCl 37-52).

In her *Rule* Clare spun a basic fabric from the raw material of the Gospel. Yet this same material, this evangelical imperative, is binding on every Christian. Clare, as Francis had before her, traced upon this fabric a design that was particular and new. In order to achieve this design, she took up several kinds and colors of thread.

In the center of the design, the point to which the eye of the beholder is immediately drawn, she employed the threads that are most precious and unique. In the center she concentrated the textures and colors that most demonstrated the beauty and originality of the new design of this Franciscan evangelical life as it was lived among and by women at that moment.

Close to the center, but distinct in placement and pattern, she employed still other threads, often borrowed from the work of Francis and, at times, from Benedict. Sometimes these threads were so closely intertwined with her own that it becomes impossible to distinguish one from the other.

Still further from the center she provided a border that enclosed or hedged it about. Here she used threads that seem very different in color and texture. They are, perhaps a bit more somber and heavy to the touch. They represent the limits of the design. They provide at once contrast and definition, the balance of the new and bright with the old and tested stuffs of which the history of religious life is woven. Here she placed those threads borrowed from Innocent and Hugolino. They linked the new and creative center with the traditional designs of the monastic texts and canonical norms.[62]

---

[62] It is important to consider, in this regard, the fact that the guilds that supervised such crafts as spinning and weaving imposed certain rules of production upon their members. In this regard, Clare's handiwork is like the work of her contemporaries in these guilds. It is comprised of a combination

To the skilled observer the needle-work Clare accomplished on the fabric of Gospel intentions manifests a creative epiphany, a new moment in the historic procession of the art form. The raw material, the finished fabric, the embroidered design emerged as expressions of the vocation which she held so dear: "With what eagerness and fervor of mind and body, therefore, must we keep the commandments of our God and Father, so that, with the help of the Lord, we may return to Him an increase of His *talent!*... Therefore, if we live according to the form mentioned above, we shall *leave* others a noble *example* and gain, with very little effort, *the prize* of eternal happiness" (TestCl 18, 23). Using the talents which had sustained her sisters and her brothers throughout her life, Clare wove a text, designed a new pattern, as she had so many times produced a thing of beauty in cloth and thread to hold the blessed Eucharist. Like those corporals, sent in silken boxes throughout Umbria, this work of her hands and heart has supported the communion of her sisters through the ages. In this, she is certainly deserving of "full devotion and immense honor" (BC 3).

Summary Observations

1. From 1212 until 1252 Clare maintained faithfulness to the primitive *Form of Life* given to her and the Poor Sisters by Francis. With the passage of years she, together with her sisters, added to this nucleus the teachings and writings which they had received from Francis. While modern readers lack detailed information about how she incorporated his counsels into her written program, the sources give enough evidence of ways in which she consciously invoked the authority of his teaching and

of personal talent and standard rules of the trade that had to be observed for the work to be validated. See Chapter Three for additional references on this point.

governing functions. There also exists ample evidence of the ways in which she, though living an enclosed life, sought to mirror the program of Francis and the brothers to the greatest possible extent, but often in ways notable for creativity.

2. Clare's actual written *Rule* text owes its primary inspiration to the *Rule* of Francis, as is obvious when textual comparisons are made. Her use of his *Rule* neither prevents her from making insightful adaptations to the Poor Sisters' situation, nor does it absolve her from incorporating other elements deemed necessary for canonical or prudential reasons.

3. An adequate understanding of the content of the *Rule* requires an understanding of the prior texts of Hugolino and Innocent IV. In addition, one must study the program of church policy regarding religious women in the years following Lateran IV. Awareness of this background puts one in a better position to appreciate both Clare's originality and the historical limitations of her situation, and avoids the danger of "canonizing" historically conditioned elements or giving them equal weight with fundamental evangelical charisms.

4. There is no contemporaneous description of the actual writing of Clare's *Rule*. However, it can be ascertained from its contents, and from both the *Process* and the *Legend,* that Clare consulted with her sisters within San Damiano and with other leaders in other monasteries, with the Friars, and with concerned members of the hierarchy.

5. The structure of the text is capable of supporting various types of analysis. Recent critical editions have made the text available in such forms that additional attempts to provide hermeneutical keys can be anticipated. Many studies have been done with a primary interest in pastoral formative service to the members of the Second Order. Additional research conducted along linguistic and historical-critical lines can add much to an

appreciation of the *Rule*. It is extremely important to promote study that recovers the text as a primary source of general Franciscan spirituality.

Chapter Three

CLARE'S INCARNATION OF GOSPEL POVERTY

Women and Property in the Middle Ages

This chapter, as well as those that follow, will attempt the creation of an analytical "triptych" in which Clare's *Rule* will be the central subject, but will be enlightened and commented upon by means of two adjoining sections. Each of the next three chapters will open with a section that provides a brief survey of the situation of medieval women in relationship to one of the four themes under consideration in Clare's *Rule*. Examination of the vast body of historical research available concerning the economic, social and canonical situation of medieval women discloses important factors that weighed heavily in the choices Clare exercised with regard to the *Rule* and life at San Damiano. The second section of these three chapters will deal with how those themes reflect the historical development of the Friars Minor for the period between the death of Francis and the death of Clare. Francis and Clare repeatedly insisted that a close bond of "care and solicitude" must link the two branches of the Franciscan family. Significant insights emerge from the search for indications of how the friars' continuing efforts to be faithful to Francis' ideals, or their inability to carry them forward in their original forms, may have affected Clare's thought and behavior. Creating such "triptychs" as a method of examining Clare's definitions of 1) poverty, 2) mutual love, and 3) governance and canonical status, develops an understanding of Clare in terms of the realities she encountered in her day-to-day existence. It is necessary as well to bring balance to the hagiographic tendency to view her as an idealized figure, detached from the controversies of her times. This alternative analysis provides a sharper perspective on how she arrived at certain decisions, and reveals more clearly her attitudes, her fears, and her hopes. It also provides a clear picture of the magnitude of her choices by placing them in the context of being aided—or hindered—by the ideals and practices of her contemporaries among religious women and among the friars.

Modern scholarly journals provide evidence of vast efforts currently being made to develop an inter-disciplinary understanding of medieval women.[1] The results of this contemporary research touch this writer's main concern—the *Rule* and life of Clare and her companions. The following limited explorations may afford new ways of reflecting upon the early Franciscan sources.[2]

[1] See, for example, Francis Oakley, *The Medieval Experience: Foundations of Western Cultural Singularity* (Toronto: University of Toronto Press, 1988); the bibliography on medieval Italy, provided by Stuard in *Women in Medieval History and Historiography* (Philadelphia: University of Pennsylvania Press, 1987) 145-159; M. Bartoli, "Donna e Società nel Tardo Medioevo: Guida Bibliografica," *Cultura e Scuola* 73 (1980) 81-88; Carolly Erickson and Katherine Casey, "Women in the Middle Ages: A Working Bibliography," *Medieval Studies* 37 (1975) 340-359.

[2] Such efforts to contextualize the story of medieval religious women in the Benedictine and Cistercian tradition has already received much attention. See, for example, pp. vii-xi of the "Foreword" in John A. Nichols and Lillian Thomas Shank, eds. *Medieval Religious Women, Volume One: Distant Echoes* (Kalamazoo: Cistercian Publications, Inc., 1984).

Economic Ferment and Religious Fervor

In her important study of the role of women in the religious movements of the Middle Ages, "Mulieres Sanctae," Brenda Bolton writes:

> The early thirteenth century was an extraordinary period in the history of piety. Throughout Europe, and especially in urban communities, lay men and women were seized by a new religious fervor which could be satisfied neither by the new orders nor by the secular clergy. Lay groups proliferated, proclaiming the absolute and literal value of the gospels and practicing a new life-style, the *vita apostolica.* This religious feeling led to the formation, on the eve of the fourth Lateran council, of numerous orders of "poor men" and, shortly afterwards, to the foundation of the mendicant orders. From this novel interpretation of evangelical life women by no means wished to be excluded and many female groups sprang simultaneously into being in areas as far distant as Flanders and Italy.[3]

To the extent that these men and women were involved in movements which incorporated a commitment to material poverty as an essential characteristic, it is important to know what aspects of their own economic condition they were enhancing or rejecting in making this option. Were these movements drawn from classes that hoped for practical economic betterment, or were they seeking some common utopian comfort by their dedication? Or, to the extent that these movements attracted recruits from upper economic levels, what sort of

---

[3] Bolton, "Mulieres Sanctae," 141.

renunciation of economic achievement was required by hold-ing membership in one of these groups? These questions are posed with a clear awareness that there is a risk taken in attributing religious affiliation primarily to economic factors. Herbert Grundmann, as cited by Bolton, warns that one may not simplistically assert that these movements were movements in which the poor protested against the rich. Rather, he sees them as movements in which those who prospered renounced their goods for an evangelical ideal. He recalls that these movements originated as a protest against the failures of religious leaders to live the Gospel ideals. However, this protest against the hypocrisy of clerics and prelates was gradually strengthened and given direction by the commercial prosperity of Lombardy, Southern France and Flanders, by groups such as the Waldensians, Humiliati, and others. The renunciation of goods voluntarily assumed by members of these groups, then, reflected a reaction against goods acquired unjustly as well as against the failure of the Church to witness to the primitive Christian community's message. Bolton believes, in fact, that religious motivation and not social tension was the primary factor influencing the women of Italy (Lombardy and Umbria) who would have been numbered among the first Poor Sisters. She states:

> Here the religious factor seems to have been of prime importance. The religious poverty movement appeared to represent a reaction to landed wealth or newly acquired urban pros-perity among those circles best placed to par-ticipate. Perhaps they felt that competition to achieve status was irreconcilable with their interpretation of the Gospel. These women, whether Beguines or Poor Clares, wished not only to be poor but to live with the poor. Against the natural order of society they deliberately chose to deny their noble or rich background and turned instead to a way of life scorned by

those they had known. It seems likely that poverty and chastity represented for these women a personal and social *renovatio*—a spiritual renewal through the adoption of a new life-style—the *vita apostolica*. [4]

Medieval Women in the Economic Sector

Who were these women of "landed wealth or newly acquired prosperity"? Married women of the nobility often enjoyed some measure of economic power as the result of a husband's long absences at war or participation in the Crusades. When a widow inherited a fief, she also inherited the managerial powers that went with it. A woman's right to this type of inheritance was granted in most Western European countries.[5] Records detailing the business enterprises of such married women tell of their negotiating debts, collecting rents, leasing land, maintaining buildings, marketing produce, and defending (sometimes with armed retainers) the rights of the absent husband. A husband's absence or premature death, however, were not the sole occasions for noble women to exercise some authority. Even when the husband was presiding over his fief, the wife had duties that included supervision of the servants and management of certain budgetary concerns of the estate. She also had considerable social obligations and was expected to be well versed in the formalities of entertaining knights and observance of the correct social forms, such as the seating of guests at banquets.[6] This economic and social prestige came at a price, however: the actual or attempted control of marriage arrangements by feudal

[4] Bolton, "Mulieres Sanctae," 147. It would be helpful to recall the injunction of Bynum cited in the Introduction regarding the dangers of adopting a one-sided sociological approach to the sources for the history of spirituality, *Jesus as Mother*, "Introduction," 3-8.

[5] Shulamith Shahar. *The Fourth Estate: A History of Women in the Middle Ages* (London: Methuen, 1983) 126-131.

[6] Shahar, 150.

lords. Marriages were arranged as forms of economic control and consolidation; often the bride and the dower (or, in the case of widows, the fief) brought to the marriage figured as a reward for loyal service.[7]

Shulamith Shahar points out that the political and economic motives that operated in the marriage plans of noble families were often found among wealthy and middle-class urban populations as well. The chief difference in the actual fulfillment of these arrangements for the nobility was the right of the feudal lord to intervene. Selection of a mate for a feudal heiress or widow involved considerations of the husband's obligatory military service to the lord; many alliances were formed in which the woman's happiness was of minor importance compared to the overriding economic and military goals.[8]

If such were the opportunities and restrictions of women of the nobility, what might be the experience of women in the developing urban populations? A major restriction in the rights of urban women was their exclusion from government of the communes or towns.[9] Nevertheless, this lack of power was ameliorated somewhat by the fact that women enjoyed considerable status in urban economies. Shahar writes:

> One could scarcely envisage production in the
> medieval town or its internal commerce without
> the activities of women. Their role in labour—
> and there are those who regard it as one of the

[7] Shahar, 133-138. See also Paul LaChance, O.F.M. *The Spiritual Journey of the Blessed Angela of Foligno According to the Memorial of Frater A.* (Roma: Pontificium Athenaeum Antonianum, 1984) 51-55.

[8] Shahar 131-132. It should be noted that Herlihy, whose work we will cite below, holds that this was more true of the early Middle Ages and that church reforms did much to curb this resurgence of patriarchal absolutism.

[9] Bartoli "Donna..." 81-82. See especially note 7. See also Shahar, 175 and Diane Owen Hughes. "Invisible Madonnas? The Italian Historiographical Tradition and the Women of Medieval Italy," *Women in Medieval History and Historiography*, 25-57.

manifestations of the new urban ethos—was
particularly prominent, and won them some
place in the guilds of artisans and the petty
merchants, despite the restriction imposed on
them. The guild which became the ecclesiastical corporation—the university—was closed
to them.[10]

Marriage and Inheritance

Another major limitation on the status of women can be
discovered in the Italian communes. Here, unlike other parts of
Europe, a daughter's right to inherit was drastically curtailed.
Daughters who married were given no part of their inheritance,
or their dowry was deducted from it. A daughter sent to a
convent could be settled with a smaller dowry. These restrictions
reflected a fear of dispersal of property should a daughter marry
someone outside the commune. While the feudal lord's power
over marriages was missing in the new urban societies, the
"new" urban nobility still determined marriage plans along
political, class and economic lines. It must also be recalled that
these marriages were more significant as the union of two
houses than as the union of two persons. The marriage was
often an occasion for establishing new political bonds or can-
celling old feuds.[11]

The research of David Herlihy regarding family and household patterns of the Middle Ages contains some valuable indications of the kinds of familial organization that would have
influenced the life of Clare, daughter of Favarone di Offreducio.[12]
Herlihy demonstrates that the power of the feudal lord described
above was not permitted to continue into the high Middle Ages
without opposition on the part of the Church. This contestation

---

[10] Shahar, 175.

[11] Bartoli "Donna…" 84-85.

[12] David Herlihy, *Medieval Households* (Cambridge, Mass.: Harvard University Press, 1985) chapter 4 , 79-111.

was based upon the principle that such human interference by the feudal lord might result in conflict with God's claims upon individuals. Herlihy believes that the Church was acting to curb a resurgence of patriarchal absolutism in medieval families. Historians have traced the reaction to this ecclesial effort in the rise in the eleventh and twelfth centuries of agnatic lineage or patrilineage as expressions of this patriarchal domination. Herlihy describes this arrangement:

> The agnatic lineage differs from the old bilateral kindred (the *cognatio)* in several significant ways. It is organized around the agnatic line of descent, and becomes a kind of fellowship of males, stretched backwards and forwards over time. Women no longer serve as the nodules through which pass the surest kinship ties. The daughter is treated as a marginal member of her father's lineage....Women also lose the claim to a full (or at least a fair) share with their brothers in the family patrimony. Their fathers and brothers arrange for their marriages and provide the dowries that the changing terms of marriage now require.[13]

In northern Italy the *consorteria* emerged as a prevalent model of agnatic lineage derived from Roman, Lombard and Frankish legal systems that ensured equality among male heirs. Great families preserved property in common by creating a kind of corporation that made collective decisions concerning its own management. Since these corporations often possessed a fortified tower, they were also known as "tower societies."[14]

[13] Herlihy, 82.

[14] It is interesting to recall here the document preserved in the Cathedral archives of Assisi in which Clare's grandfather declares that his family will not construct any walls or towers that will impede the beauty of the new cathedral. See note 17.

Members of these *consorteria* were recruited principally from the line of agnate relatives. At times, formal contracts defined the memberships in inner circles extended to those who were not blood kin. While the *consorteria* continued to hold common property, the memberships could be rearranged over time with suitable contracts. It was from such great households of *consorteria* that the commercial revolution of the Middle Ages took its impetus.[15]

When researchers turn to the communal archives of Assisi in search of information concerning Clare's family, it is to descriptions of such a powerful consortium that they are led.[16] Additionally, the *Process* testimony from Pietro di Damiano indicates that there were seven knights in Clare's family (XIX: 1) and Lord Ranieri testifies to the fact that she came from one of Assisi's most noble families (XVIII: 4). Ioanni di Ventura (XX: 2) affirms this. In such a family the role of the woman was one of providing a standard of honor and gentility. Especially upon the occasion of their weddings, women carried forward the family's claims to honor and status. Any breach in the social contracts surrounding betrothal and marriage could not only blot a family reputation, it could also lead to civic havoc if a vendetta resulted.[17]

By the late Middle Ages a plurality of women over men in European society and the declining values of women's position in both noble classes and communal labor markets created more pressures on heretofore acceptable marriage practices. Such demographic pressures gave added value to such factors as physical appearance, wealth and social connections.[18] Women tended to marry at a young age—fifteen was not uncommon for urban marriages. Certainly by the the age of eighteen (Clare's

[15] Herlihy, 89-92.

[16] Arnaldo Fortini, *Francis of Assisi*, trans. Helen Moak (New York: Crossroad Publishing Co., 1981) 327-329. See also the description of Clare's eleventh century ancestors in Chapter 2, 63-73.

[17] Hughes, 7-10. See also Fortini-Moak, 345, note h.

[18] Herlihy, 100-101.

age when she left home) a young woman was expected to be "settled." On the other hand, males tended to marry later, often creating a generational gap between husband and wife and contributing to the large number of young widows in the population.[19]

Clare's Rejection of Marriage

In light of these realities, what can be said of Clare's rejection of marriage? At the time of her flight to the Portiuncula Clare was eighteen, both a suitable age for marriage and the age of legal independence. She exercised the right to sell her portion of inheritance, but a clear date or chronology for this action cannot be determined (XIX: 2). While this sale would have had great significance, there is no indication of her family's reaction to this decision. Although plans for her marriage were surely being made (XVIII: 2), she managed to avoid making any promises to accept a suitor while she searched for her true calling (XVII: 3). She possessed physical beauty (XVIII: 2) as well as powerful social connections (XX: 2) that placed her in an enviable position. Her marriage would surely have been one arranged so as to promote the interests of the *consorteria* headed by her uncle Monaldo. Her meetings with Francis were held in secret because of her fear of discovery by her relatives (XVII: 3).

Yet there is also evidence that her sensitivities were, if not actually opposed to her family's wealthy entitlements, at least enlarged to include the world of the poor and marginalized. Very little is known about the years of exile in Perugia.[20] Did her childhood experience of the violence of class struggle create a radical questioning of the wealth that excited such envy and hatred? In any event, Clare's decision not to marry struck a fateful blow to the family's plans. The very drama which she and

[19] Herlihy, 103-111.
[20] Some indications concerning this experience are reflected in Nesta de Robeck, *St. Clare of Assisi* (Milwaukee: The Bruce Publishing Co., 1951) 19-25; Fortini-Moak, 333-337.

Francis created to mark her Palm Sunday "flight" seems predicated upon a recognition of the social impact of her rejection of her position.[21] The encounter between Clare and her relatives at San Paolo of Bastia opens a window onto the rage characteristic of offended status (LegCl 4: 9). Clare, by her adroit use of canonical privilege and by the sale of her inheritance, had made it clear that she would not cooperate in the family's plans for its own aggrandizement (XX: 4-6; XVIII: 3). Given the austere life she had already led within her home, her relatives might have been in some measure prepared for Clare's action (LegCl II: 4). Rather, it is the response to her sister Agnes' flight that demonstrates the full impact of the social implications resulting from the these two departures (LegCl XVI: 24-26). The physical violence by which Monaldo and his cohorts abused Agnes reveals a pride wounded beyond reason. The description of these events in the *Legend of Clare* very plainly reveals the great personal risk and heavy social censure entailed in Clare's and Agnes' rejection of the authority of the *consorteria* over their lives.[22]

[21] Peter Brown, *The Cult of the Saints* (London: SCM Press, Ltd., 1983) 43. Brown here treats of the social function of Christian processions and pilgrimages. Palm Sunday was an occasion on which social barriers between the sexes were relaxed as young women of marriageable age processed in their finery and young men joined the procession as much to see them as to perform Christian cultic duties. While Brown's sources describe this as lasting at least until the eleventh century, it is not difficult to imagine that such cultural layers of meaning were exploited by Francis when he directed Clare to participate "dressed and adorned" (LegCl 70) and then to leave that very night to begin her life of poverty and minority.

[22] LegCl 24-26: "…one of the knights in a fierce mood ran towards her and, without sparing blows and kicks, tried to drag her away by her hair, while the others pushed her and lifted her in their arms….While the violent robbers were dragging the young girl along the slope of the mountain, ripping her clothes and strewing the path with the hair [they had] torn out…."

Economic Security
and Medieval Religious Women

After Clare's rejection of social affluence she encounterd yet another form of contention. After abandoning the world of social privilege to live within the sphere of poverty, she faced the ironic necessity of struggling against ecclesiastical power that sought to guarantee the economic security and privileges of medieval monasteries. Without denying that many medieval monasteries struggled incessantly against penury, it can also safely be asserted that it was not uncommon for women's monasteries, as well as those of their male counterparts, to be centers of prosperity. Jean Leclercq points out that from the early Middle Ages forward, monasteries in Western Europe often functioned as familial institutions in which women who were either widowed or unable to marry lived out their days. As extensions of family identity these monasteries were financially secure, and their governance often was controlled by their patrons in order to conserve the interests of the family.[23] This pattern gave rise to a series of problems and abuses. The recruitment of monastic vocations was limited to the nobility and since the choice of monastic life was often a consequence of limited opportunities for marriage or independent economic existence, the quality of religious observance sometimes suffered.[24] A related abuse occurred when the "donation" for the member who was enrolled as a solution to family need was made in such a manner as to render it an act of simony. The canonical problems this engendered lasted until the council of Trent.[25]

In the eleventh and twelfth centuries monastic possibilities grew with the rise of the new orders and with the advent of

---

[23] J. Leclercq, "Il monachesimo femminile nei secoli XII e XIII." *MRFF*, 63-99.

[24] Leclercq, 79-83.

[25] Leclercq, 87-89. See note 42.

double or twin monasteries. These new foundations often included women who did not come from upper levels of society. The women's economic security was assured by the close cooperation, or even by a kind of symbiotic union, with monasteries of monks.[26] This is not the place to enter into a thorough study of the forms and financial arrangements of these new religious ventures. Suffice it to say that until the early thirteenth century, monastic communities of women received their subsistence and security (both economic and ecclesiastical) by dependence upon family or male branches of their orders.[27] At the close of the twelfth century, however the first stirrings surface of a phenomenon which took the institutional church unaware. Inspired by the poverty movements and formed by the social fluidity of the new urban realities, small groups of women sought a religious life without the traditional trappings of endowment, enclosure and aggregation with existing masculine orders.[28] Cardinal Hugolino became one of the key figures in the development of church policy regarding this phenomenon. When he received faculties from Honorius III to regulate the canonical status of these groups of women in central Italy,[29] a key component of his policy was the establishment of permanent means of income for each foundation. Sensi writes: "The stable points of the policy of Cardinal Hugolino were precisely reclusion and the privilege of exemption; when he became Pope, he added the obligation that every foundation have a patrimony or dowry sufficient for support of the community. And his new preoccupation was to furnish for the mon-

---

[26] Leclercq, 66-73.

[27] See Noreen Hunt, "Enclosure," *Cistercian Studies* XXI (1986) 51-63 and *Cistercian Studies* XXII (1987) 126-151.

[28] Mario Sensi, "Incarcerate e recluse in Umbria nei secoli XIII e XIV: un bizzocaggio centro-italiano" *MRFU* , 87-121.

[29] See the Letter of Pope Honorius III to Cardinal Hugolino (1217), Armstrong, *Clare*, 85. Also see David Flood, "Cardinal Hugolino on Legation," *Haversack* Vol. 11, No. 2 (Dec., 1987) 3-9, 24.

asteries which lived according to the *forma vitae* which he had
given, possessions and fixed rents."[30]

He goes on to point out that Clare avoided being obliged to
accept this arrangement because of the *Privilege of Poverty*
given by Innocent III in 1216, for San Damiano and those few
monasteries which were able to model their regimes upon hers.
The continuing struggle of Clare for freedom from property and
fixed income lasted far longer than her first campaign for
freedom from familial obligation and expectation.

The first panel of the triptych is now in view. The "world" in
which Clare lived included the world of economic development
and the passive and symbolic roles held in that world by women
of noble lineage. In spite of attempts by the church to protect
freedom of vocation, the choice of marriage or monastery often
rested upon family might and means as much as upon grace and
holy desires. In glancing briefly at the monastic realities of her
time, one sees that economic and canonical practice conspired
to both protect and delimit the women who sought lives of
seclusion.

The Order of Friars Minor and the Poverty Controversies

During the years in which the quiet gestation of Clare's *Rule*
was taking place, what legislation or developments shaped the
experience of the Friars Minor in their efforts to observe the
Later Rule? How were these developments communicated to
Clare? To what extent did the experiences of the Friars Minor
become matter for her consideration and action? Obviously
these are questions that, for the most part, do not have conclu-
sive or documented answers at this stage in the study of Clare.
Nonetheless, a careful attempt to reconstruct the dual paths

---

[30] Sensi, *MRFU*, 96-97. By reclusion is meant a kind of separated, solitary life,
not implying full strict, monastic enclosure.

which the Poor Sisters and the Friars Minor travelled allows some hypothetical responses. The century after the death of Francis can be viewed as a long, labyrinthine series of efforts on the part of the Order to reconcile its own expansion and ecclesial role with the ideals preserved in the biographies of Francis and in the texts of his own writings, pre-eminently, the *Rule*.[31] Entire forests have been despoiled and oceans of ink drained dry in the efforts of historians, apologists and antagonists to verify the truth of their conflicting interpretations of these events. What follows below is an ecologically defensible study of those events which must be taken into account if one is to understand both the genesis and the content of Clare's *Rule,* especially in regard to evangelical poverty.

Interpretation by the Papacy: Quo elongati

M. D. Lambert in his book *Franciscan Poverty* has admirably summarized many of the aspects of this question surrounding the evolution of the meaning of poverty.[32] His third chapter, "The Development of the Observance," treats the questions that engaged the attention of the friars in the early period following

[31] Notable studies of the origins and interpretation of the *Rule* include: Ignatius Brady, ed. *The Marrow of the Gospel* (Chicago: Franciscan Herald Press, 1958); Martino Conti, O.F.M. *Lettura biblica della Regola francescana* (Roma: Ed. Antonianum, 1977); Dino Dozzi, O.F.M. Cap. *Haec Est Vita Evangelii Jesu Christi: Il Vangelo come vita nella "regola non bollata:" di Francesco d'Assisi* (Roma: Pontificio Istituto Biblico, 1987); C. Esser, O.F.M., *The Rule and Testament of St. Francis* (Chicago: Franciscan Herald Press, 1978) and "The Definitive Rule of the Friars Minor," *Round Table of Franciscan Research* 34 (1969) 4-67; David Flood O.F.M. and Thaddée Matura, O.F.M., *The Birth of a Movement* (Chicago: Franciscan Herald Press, 1975) 13-54.

[32] M.D. Lambert, *Franciscan Poverty* (London: Church Historical Society, 1961). Lambert's work is chosen as a foundation for this section because of his lucid explanation of the various papal interpretations of the *Rule*. It should be noted, however, that recent research would require some criticism of his use of labels for the various "parties" among the friars and particularly for some of his assertions about the Spirituals.

the death of Francis. Contemporaneous apostolic developments were central to the problem. A combined need for trained
clerics and the exemption of friars from the control of local
clergy and bishops contributed to a vast expansion of the Order.
In the wake of Lateran IV, buildings suitable for the pursuit of
studies were also needed.[33] As the friars grappled with these
realities, it quickly became apparent that this demand for a
multiplicity of resources raised questions of ownership previously unknown in the Order. Could the friars merely use goods
and properties without owning them? If the friars did not own
these material things, who did? Gradually, two camps emerged.
The "conventual" party placed apostolic effectiveness as the
chief value to be preserved and saw the necessity of re-inter-
preting the *Later Rule* in this light. The "observant" party held
poverty as the central value of the Order and required that any
apostolic initiative be measured against its relationship to this
observance.[34] Unable to achieve consensus on how to satisfy
both emerging schools of thought, the Order had recourse to
the papacy. Issued in 1230, in response to requests from the
Order, the Bull *Quo elongati* gave the first official interpretation
of the limits of observance in matters of ownership for the
friars.[35] Gregory IX, in what Lambert calls a "moderate canonist's
solution," declared that the *Testament* was void of legal force
and that the friars were bound only to such counsels of the
Gospel as were specifically set down in the *Later Rule*.[36] In order

---

[33] Lateran IV Canon 10 (*De praedicatoribus*), Canon 21 (*De confessione
facienda*) and Canon 27 (*De instructione ordinandorum*) required a program
of education for all who sought the preaching ministry. Canon 10 linked
preaching with hearing confessions; Canon 21 required annual confessions
and Canon 27 required bishops to provide for the education in the divine
office and administration of the sacraments. The friars, in order to fulfill their
preaching mission, had to abide by these regulations.

[34] Lambert, *Poverty*, 68-69. Lambert feels that the withdrawal of Francis from
administrative control during his lifetime set in motion this dual track of
interpretation.

[35] "Quo elongati," ed. H. Grundmann, *AFH* 54 (1961) 20-25.

[36] Lambert, *Poverty*, 82.

to help the brothers deal with the problem of receiving money, he established the office of the *nuntius*, a person who would act as an agent of the almsgiver in procuring what was intended for the brethren. The *nuntius* was then bound to give any excess money to the *amicus spiritualis* (provided for by Francis in RegB 4: 2), who supplied the ordinary necessities of the brothers, especially the sick. In *Quo elongati* Gregory IX in effect inaugurated an experimental system of administration of temporal goods. In this system the friars did not have ownership, but they did have "use." They themselves remained wholly responsible for maintaining some standard of poverty, since Gregory had not ordered what **must** be done, but only what **was permitted**. Maintenance of this standard would prove to be fraught with tensions, since the pontiff had blocked the return to the *Testament* as an authoritative document. From this point on in Franciscan history the brothers walked "on razor's edge" since the quality of their observance depended on their own daily behavior and the consistency of the decisions of superiors. Given such a situation, the normal course proved to be a desire on the part of superiors for wider powers to simplify the governmental machinery created by the Gregorian system. The crucial question—not satisfactorily answered in this effort—was whether or not the friars were bound to renounce complete dominion over property and goods.[37]

Interpretation by the Order:
Exposition of the Four Masters

While *Quo elongati* was issued during the generalate of John Parenti, two years later Elias returned for his second, ill-fated term as Minister General. Without engaging in the debate on

[37] Here Lambert cites the position of Ehrle regarding *Quo elongati*. He also states his conviction that Clare understood the obligation to be renunciation of all dominion. Clare also makes no distinction regarding moveable goods. In this regard Lambert refers to Joergensen-Sloane 136-137 and 185-191.

Elias' responsibility for a movement away from strict poverty, one can note that during the years of his administration the Order surely moved toward secure accommodations that allowed a life of study and exemptions that enabled the friars to prepare for their place in the life of the church.[38] The building programs in which they engaged strained their resources and the generosity of their benefactors. More exemptions allowed practices such as receiving money intended as moral restitution to be used for such purposes as the building of the studium at Bologna.[39] One must not, however, place disproportionate blame on Elias' excessive ambitions, since such activity reflected a trend among the friars who were, in general, seeking more financial discretion, and because, in reality, "there was no considerable body of Franciscan legislation before 1239."[40]

By the time of Elias' deposition and the election of Haymo of Faversham conditions in the Order had changed. Rosalind Brooke affirms that by this time Dominican influence could be seen at work in the decisions of the Friars Minor.[41] The internal

[38] Interpretations of these events often focus on the motives of one or another key figure in early Franciscan history. The following observations of Conrad Harkins, O.F.M. serve to provide another optic: "The Order gradually finds that to be faithful to its apostolic preaching mission...it must become educated and clerical. Nor should one conceive that education and ordination were imposed on the Order by some alien spirit. The same spirit which moved the Fourth Lateran moved within the Order. Friars became educated and ordained because they sought education and ordination. The young men pouring into the Order at Paris, Oxford, Bologna saw the Order as providentially sent to provide the preachers the bishops of the Church were calling forth. The friars would go forth in the poverty of the Apostles to bring a second springtime to the Church. What begins in 1215 is no less than a profound change within the Order, which would be regarded by some as an evolution and by others as a perversion" (unpublished lecture notes, 1984).

[39] Lambert, *Poverty,* 91.

[40] Brooke, *Government,* 294, note 1.

[41] Brooke, *Government,* 293-296. This is a table of comparisons regarding connections between the Dominican constitutions and the Franciscan Constitutions of Narbonne, 1260. One idea which Haymo sought to adopt was that of a chapter of Definitors. Brooke writes: "It seems...that the two Orders kept

administration of the Order was often by-passed in the form of papal interventions communicated directly to provincial levels. While Haymo was known for a personally poor life style, he appeared to favor modifications that would simplify certain aspects of life for the brotherhood.[42] It was during his term, moreover, that the Order made its first attempt to give a systematic internal response to the myriad questions on the observance of their *Rule*. This took the form of the first mandated commentary: *The Exposition of the Four Masters*. [43]

The *Exposition*, the work of Alexander of Hales, John of La Rochelle, Robert of Bascia and Odo Rigaldus, was undertaken by order of the 1241 Chapter of Definitors.[44] It is a juridical and academic work which clearly favored a strict interpretation of the *Rule* according to the presumed "intentions" of Francis himself. While it failed to touch the details of the mundane material questions of daily life, the *Exposition* clearly warned against allowing the *nuntius* to function as a banker, distinguishing between the Franciscan call to perfect poverty *(paupertas perfecta)* and the imperfect poverty *(paupertas imperfecta)* of other Orders.[45] Its authors held that: "'Perfect' poverty...depends on God's providence so completely that it does not even retain the necessities of life for itself. This is the poverty of mendicancy, which the friars themselves are bound to observe. This high ideal demands two things of the friars. In the first place, since they are pilgrims and strangers, the friars are

---

fairly constantly in touch and from time to time took note of each other's legislation." (226) She also says that the "majority of borrowings" were in the areas of governance. (227)

[42] Lambert, *Poverty,* 93-94.

[43] Livarius Oliger, O.F.M., ed., *Expositio Quator Magistrorum Super Regulam Fratrum Minorum (1241-1242)* (Roma: Edizioni di "Storia e Letteratura", 1950).

[44] The definitors were the members of the "governing council" of the friars, advisors to the Minister General.

[45] Duane V. Lapsanski, *Evangelical Perfection: An Historical Examination of the Concept in the Early Franciscan Sources* (St. Bonaventure, N.Y.: The Franciscan Institute, 1977) 172-176.

not to have any fixed possessions. Secondly, they are to exercise only the use of things and are to go begging for alms...."[46] The Masters quote the ruling of Pope Gregory IX that the friars are not to have the possession of anything whatever, neither as individuals nor as a group, but that they may have the use of movable items. They then raise the additional problem, not solved by the pope, as to who has the possession of these movable items.

Ordinem vestrum *and* Quanto studiosus

However laudable the efforts of the Four Masters to create a strict mode of interpretation, subsequent events in the Order overshadowed, at least in practical consequence, their achievement. Three years after the publication of the *Exposition,* Crescentius of Jesi became General. An elderly man, he might not have been held responsible for further decline in observance were it simply due to incapacity. However, he combined a lack of concern about maintaining the interpretation promulgated in 1241 with an active persecution of the friars known for their zeal for material poverty. He is regarded as having fostered "relaxation" and possibly even soliciting the two papal rescripts that would create major breaches of strict observance, *Ordinem vestrum* and *Quanto studiosus.* Lambert writes: "It was under these circumstances, with the Papacy under Innocent IV occupied by a man who cared little for Franciscan poverty, and the generalate held by a relaxing Conventual, that the order came to take a formal step down from the standard of observance prescribed by *Quo elongati.*"[47]

Promulgated by Innocent IV in 1245, *Ordinem vestrum* obliterated the distinction between the *nuntius* and the *amicus spiritualis.* Superiors received full authority to use agents to take monetary alms when ever they wished to do so. Innocent

[46] Lapsanski, 175-176.
[47] Lambert, *Poverty,* 96.

further declared that the dominion of all goods belonged to the papacy, an arrangement that was a legal fiction, since the papacy enjoyed no actual benefit from such dominion.[48] Two years later *Quanto studiosus* transferred property rights in the Order to a single agent, an apostolic syndic who was given wide legal powers. Because these syndics were at the disposition of the friars, both appointed by and completely answerable to them, the use of money was in effect unregulated by external limits. Lambert describes the results:

> With the issue of *Quanto studiosus* in August, 1247, the formal development of the observance of poverty by means of Papal privileges had reached its term, for the time being. It was still hardly more than twenty years after the death of Francis. In that short time, which could easily be included in a single life-span, the friars through the use of intermediaries had gone a long way towards obliterating the distinctive features of their observance of poverty.[49]

The combined effects of the temporizing of Crescentius and Innocent IV were, however, mitigated by the election of John of Parma as General in 1247. His term witnessed a return to a vigorous style of personal visitation, strict interpretation, and inspiration by example of personal poverty in dress and behavior. His identification with the views of the simple brothers who championed the primitive ideals of the Order earned him the adulation of the leaders of the Spiritual party. His greatest tactical victory was the decision of the Genoa Chapter in 1249 to refuse the permission contained in Innocent's bulls and

[48] Lambert finds precedent for this in the action of Cardinal Hugolino receiving the property of the Poor Clares in Tuscany in the name of the Holy See in 1217.

[49] Lambert, *Poverty,* 100-101.

return to the standards of *Quo elongati*. For nearly a decade
(1247-1257), John of Parma gave vigor to the highest ideals of
poverty. Both the dates of his generalship and the close affinity
that existed between him and yet another respected interpreter
of the *Later Rule*, Hugh of Digne, bear significant relevance to
Clare's *Rule*.

Hugh of Digne's Rule Commentary

Hugh of Digne was a learned and eloquent friar from Provence
who was singled out to provide yet another extensive commentary on the *Rule*. Again, the initial stimulus seems to have
originated within the Order itself. Hugh, according to Lapsanski,
"sought to explain and defend the *Rule* against those who found
it too strict and too difficult to observe."[50] David Flood also
disagrees with those who believe that Hugh wrote primarily to
counter external influences: "Hugh did not set out to correct the
Four Masters and *Ordinem vestrum* which he emended where
necessary, but new opinions which distorted the Franciscan
mind. Hugh sought to insert sound concepts of Franciscan life
into those areas of understanding which, he believed, suffered
from confusion and false teaching. With the support of authority, Hugh wrote to influence the reality definitions by which the
Order lived."[51]

Hugh's methodology involved personal investigation of living witnesses from the earliest days of the fraternity, as well as
investigation of documents. He gave first place to the *antiqui*
and *patres precedentes*, creating a powerful appeal to tradition
for new generations. He, too, favored strict standards of
interpretation for inculcation of poverty and humility. His
influence was to have far-reaching effects, becoming a source
for papal pronouncements, internal authorities of later genera-

---

[50] Lapsanski, 177.

[51] David Flood, *Hugh of Digne's Rule Commentary* (Grottaferrata, Romae:
Collegii S. Bonaventurae ad Claras Aquas, 1979).

tions (e.g., Bonaventure), and for notable Spiritual voices like Angelo Clareno and Ubertino of Casale. It will suffice here to summarize his position on Chapter Six of the *Later Rule*. In this part of his *Commentary*, Hugh defined the heart of material poverty as the abdication of possessions and expanded this definition in five points: 1) the friars have no possessions and no right to acquire them; 2) this standard applied to commercial contracts; 3) the "use" of things should be according to a poor standard; 4) he warned against the spirit of appropriation; 5) he praised mendicancy.[52]

The late Duane Lapsanski described many of the nuances that Hugh of Digne brings to his considerations of poverty. Hugh saw mutual love as essential to fostering this form of poverty. Likewise, minority prevented the friars from losing the inner qualities of poverty of spirit. In Hugh's thought poverty was defined as that which "makes them [the friars] conscious of their dependence on God and thus helps them to remain humble. Moreover, by encouraging them to be generous with others, poverty helps to maintain a sense of love and brotherhood among the Friars Minor."[53] Finally, it should be noted that David Flood holds that Hugh composed the *Commentary* no earlier than 1246 and most likely in 1252. Should the later date be the acceptable one, the possibility of a direct influence upon Clare's thought is somewhat removed, since by that time she had finished, for all practical purposes, the composition of her *Rule*. However, the situations and debates which engaged Hugh's reflective genius were in motion well before 1252. It may be a bold step to propose a link between the thought of Hugh and the thought of Clare, but the personal linkage—the proximity of the early companions to Hugh and to Clare—suggests some basis for doing so. Of no small importance is Celano's account that present during Clare's last hours (in the cloister!) were Juniper, Angelo and Leo. Further, Leo entrusted to the Poor

---

[52] Flood, 78-87.
[53] Lapsanski, 190.

Ladies for safekeeping some of his most precious items, including the scrolls of his own records and the breviary used by Francis. To the extent that Hugh so constantly appealed to the moral authority of these "elder statesmen," it can be assumed that in their continued communication with Clare and her sisters, the thoughts and fears they shared with Hugh became the subject of many conversations at San Damiano.

This brief summary of events spanning the years from 1230 to approximately 1253 shows us the complexity of the questions facing the Friars Minor in their observance of the *Rule*. Pressure to adapt their internal economic structures in order to respond to ecclesiastical expectations and regulations concerning the preaching ministry altered the original concept of the evangelical life. Factors affecting their own consensus regarding the observance of the *Rule* included internal changes in membership and attitude, the varying capabilities of the generals who succeeded Francis in the first century, the broad geographic distribution of membership, and works which complicated communication or formation of norms. As a result of these factors, the papacy came to weigh more and more as the court of last resort for the Friars Minor. Clare, on the other hand, administering a small and stable community of women could deal at close range with the various interpretations placed before her. When she finally proceeded to write her *Rule*, it included a profound awareness not only of the literal texts that preceded hers (the texts of Francis, Hugolino and Innocent); she drew from living fonts of experience as well. These living fonts included her own awareness of: 1) the changing economic circumstances of the women of central Italy; 2) the broad phenomenon of women seeking identification with groups committed to a poor evangelical life; and 3) the crises in which the Friars Minor had attempted to re-define the obligations of the *Rule* and to re-interpret the mind of Francis.

Clare's Definition of Evangelical Poverty

Clare sought a new way to define evangelical poverty for her sisters "present and to come" (TestCl 39). Examination of Clare's *Rule* provides an invaluable tool for determining how she accomplished this task. There are sections of the *Rule* which clearly intend to furnish precise, canonically tenable norms. Other sections of the *Rule* define the attitudes and describe the daily actions that constitute the incarnation of a commitment to evangelical poverty. At times it is helpful to refer to the documents she received from Francis and from Church officials as well as to her other writings. The spirituality invested in the *Rule* can be viewed with greater clarity as a result of such analysis.

Poverty as the Center of the Rule *(Chapters VI, VII,VIII)*

It has been noted that Clare inserted the three chapters (VI-VIII) which treat of poverty and its ramifications directly in the structural center of her text.[54] Placing her text alongside the *Rules* of Hugolino and Innocent produces no parallel passages to clarify the manner in which Clare wrote the almost autobiographical explanations of the life of poverty contained in these three chapters. Why do these chapters immediately follow the comparatively technical discussion of "Silence, the Parlor and the Grille" of Chapter V? And why, when she completes the description of the life of evangelical poverty that these three chapters contain, does Clare continue with two chapters on correction and admonition (IX, X) and then provide another lengthy chapter (XI) on the "Custody of the Enclosure"? In outlining the material of both Hugolino's and Innocent's *Rules,* one is confronted with lengthy descriptions, one after

---

[54] Notes on this point can be found in *Ecrits,* 141, Note 38; *FF,* 2256, note 15; Armstrong, *Works,* 218, note 19. Also, see TestCl 24-43 in which parallel passages are found.

another, of juridical cautions, prohibitions and permissions. Although pastoral concerns are not lacking, these texts are preoccupied with the exposition of weighty obligations. The very language employed embodies the steely quality of the physical facts described. While Clare is most careful to endow her text with the precision required for both approbation and good governance, personalism and delicacy break through time and again. How could it be otherwise? Hugolino and Innocent live *outside* the enclosure, regarding it from an impersonal and juridical distance. They understand and describe its objective physical components: silence, mortification, discipline, iron bolts, wooden beams, keys, locks, black curtains, metal grilles. Clare lives *inside* the enclosure. She knows and describes its physical dimensions as well. However, it does not exist as something outside of her. Rather, it exists as a space within which a precious treasure is guarded. Open on the one side the door of silence, fasting and enclosure; open on the other side the door of custodial protections (grille, visitation rights, chaplains). In the center—inside those doors—Poor Sisters live, rejoicing in "divine inspiration" (RegCl 6: 3) and in "the example and teaching of our most blessed Father Francis" (RegCl 6: 1). They are "serving and working" (RegCl 7: 1) but remain given over to "the Spirit of holy prayer" (RegCl 7: 2). They are "pilgrims and strangers" (RegCl 8: 2) on this earth who know themselves to be "heiresses and queens of the kingdom of heaven" (RegCl 8: 4). This is the astonishing difference that the reader discovers within these central chapters. Here Clare speaks confidently and authoritatively. Here Clare explains both in canonically precise forms the profession of poverty and the ordinary activities by which this profession is manifested as "day unto day imparts knowledge" (Ps 18).

The sources that Clare had before her as she composed her *Rule* dealt with poverty in various ways. In the *Rule of Hugolino* there is no specific mention of possessions. Earlier, as papal legate, Hugolino had dealt with the property questions of the monasteries in his legation by means of separate rescripts.

Innocent's *Rule,* in section eleven, provided for a procurator accountable to the abbess and her advisors, permitted possessions that could provide stable income, and allowed for small gifts of moveable goods. Present in this section are elements comparable to those that figure in the decisions of *Ordinem vestrum* and *Quanto studiosus.* Only in the *Later Rule* of Francis, then, can Clare trace the description of poverty that is the foundation for her own. From Francis she had already taken the first pivotal sentence: "The form of life of the Order of the Poor Sisters that Blessed Francis established is this: to observe the Holy Gospel of our Lord Jesus Christ, by living in obedience, without anything of one's own, and in chastity" (RegCl 1: 1-2).[55] However, in the first of these three central chapters, it is the primitive *Form of Life* (RegCl 6: 3-4) combined with the *Last Will* (RegCl 6: 7-9) that strikes the dominant note. There is also a citation (6:12) from Francis' *Later Rule* (RegB 4: 1). Once again, Clare did not use her sources in literal or automatic fashion.[56] She determined what she needed to define. Then she used the source text that most clearly supported or explained her stance.

Juridical Foundation of Poverty

Chapter VI: 10-15 of Clare's *Rule* uncovers the kernel, precise and legally clear, that grounds the form of poverty of the Poor Sisters:

> Just as I, together with my sisters, have ever been solicitous to safeguard the holy poverty which we have promised the Lord God and blessed Francis, so, too, the Abbesses who shall succeed me in office and all the sisters are bound to observe it inviolably to the end: that is to say, by not receiving or having possession or

[55] See *Ecrits,* 142-143, note 41.
[56] See *Ecrits,* 42-44.

> ownership either of themselves or through an
> intermediary, or even anything that might
> reasonably be called property, except as much
> land as necessity requires for the integrity and
> proper seclusion of the monastery, and this land
> may not be cultivated except as a garden for the
> needs of the sisters.

This description derives from the earliest legal document which Clare sought for confirmation of her intent to live *sine proprio*, the *Privilege of Poverty.*[57] Both forms of the *Privilege* (1216 and 1228) summarize the proposal in the words, "no one can compel you to receive possessions." In the intervening years, Clare learned through her experience of receiving existing foundations or beginning new ones, with the attendant questions of how much or how little land and accommodation would be required for the Poor Sisters living there. Her experiences enabled her to further nuance her definition. She also had the experience of having to refuse possessions from the very personage to whom she had recourse for this exemption, Gregory IX (LegCl IX: 14). Iriarte points out that it is unmistakable from Clare's wording that she wanted to avoid creating the juridic fiction which was becoming normative among the Friars.[58] She acknowledged that property which belonged to the monastery and set the norms for limiting its size. The "Mandate of 1238"[59] presents a good example of how she and the community adhered to this limitation. Additional comment on this will be made in Chapter Five.

[57] See Armstrong, *Clare,* 83-84. Also, Bolton, "Mulieres Sanctae," 149, as well as Optatus van Asseldonk, O.F.M. Cap., "Santa Chiara d'Assisi nei suoi Scritti e nelle Biografie." *La Lettera e lo Spirito, Vol. II* (Roma: Editrice Laurentianum, 1985) 222-224.

[58] Lazaro Iriarte, O.F.M. Cap., *La Regola di Santa Chiara: lettera e spirito* (Milano: Biblioteca Francescano Provinciale, 1976) 139-141.

[59] Armstrong, *Clare,* 107-108.

In further defining the actions by which the profession of the sisters of San Damiano would be guaranteed, Clare stated in Chapter II: 7 that the candidate must distribute her goods to the poor or, at least, have the intention to do so. The Abbess and sisters are not to become entangled in this procedure: "Let the Abbess and the sisters take care not to be concerned about her temporal affairs, so that she may freely dispose of her possessions as the Lord may inspire her. However, if some counsel is required, let them send her to some discerning and God-fearing men, according to whose advice her goods may be distributed to the poor" (Reg Cl 2: 9-10).

Furthermore, the profession made is specifically one of "promising to observe perpetually our life and form of poverty" (RegCl 2: 13). No one may continue to live in the monastery who lacks this formula of profession (RegCl 2: 23). To underscore this obligation, Clare repeated it again in giving the qualifications for election as abbess (RegCl 4: 4-5).

Incarnational Aspects of Poverty

Having provided for strictly legal and minimal norms, Clare then addressed in several sections of the *Rule* what may be considered her standard for the daily incarnation of a truly poor style of life. She placed upon the abbess and her vicar the important obligation of preserving common life (RegCl 4: 13-14). In all things in which there was a question of choice, of making provisional legislation, of settling conflicts, Clare urged an overall spirit of moderation, mutual consultation and discernment.[60] She indicated clearly the concrete aspects of daily life of the sisters in which the poverty of the Gospel becomes incarnate.

The sisters engage in manual work for the common good and for their support (RegCl 7: 1-3). This validation of manual labor finds precedents in the *Rule of St. Benedict* and that of Francis.[61]

[60] *Ecrits,* 44-46.
[61] RegB 5:1-2; 8:4.

Even though the value does not originate with Clare, it appears to have been a prominent feature of the sisters' witness. Jacques de Vitry characterized them in the following terms: "The women live near the cities in various hospices.[62] They accept nothing, but live from the work of their hands" (JdV 5-6). To read this description is to want to know precisely what "the work of their hands" was. Several source citations tell of the spinning and weaving done by Clare (Proc I: 11; VI: 14; LegCl 28).[63] One instance even indicates that silk coverings were made for the corporals which the bishop blessed and then had sent to the churches of Assisi (Proc VI: 14). In addition to seeing this work as a form of cooperation in the Eucharistic reforms of the Lateran Council, it can well be imagined that the parishes which received these gifts repaid in some sort of alms. Also, there was a garden to tend, and nursing service was often a wearying occupation (CantExh 6). Add to these bits of evidence the ordinary functions of a monastery of thirty to fifty members, and one can understand why there was no lack of "the grace of working "(RegCl 7: 1).[64]

The reception and use of alms is matter for the weekly chapter (RegCl 7: 44-45). It is most noteworthy that Clare permits the reception of money.[65]

---

[62] Armstrong, *Clare,* 246, note 5 refers to a definition provided by Margaret Wade Labarge, *Women in Medieval Life: A Small Sound of the Trumpet* (London: Hamish Hamilton, 1986) 182. "Medieval charters and wills tend to describe as a hospital any building specially designed to harbour those who needed temporary hospitality. These might include pilgrims, both sick and well, the wandering poor, the impoverished aged or the ill. The first two categories usually took refuge in what is more accurately called a hospice, designed for the temporary lodging of a wayfarer rather than the more specific care of the sick."

[63] Shahar describes the role of women in the medieval cloth-making industry. Many women did spinning and weaving in their own homes and had their work supervised and reimbursed according to guild regulations. See Shahar, 189-91.

[64] cf. *Later Rule* V: 1-2 and Armstrong, *Clare,* 70, note 37.

[65] Armstrong, *Clare,* 71, note 42. Also, *Ecrits,* 149, note 52.

> Let no sister be permitted to send letters or to
> receive or give away anything outside the
> monastery without the permission of the Abbess.
> Let it not be permitted to have anything that the
> Abbess has not given or allowed. Should any-
> thing be sent to a sister by her relatives or others,
> let the Abbess give it to the sister. If she needs it,
> the sister may use it; otherwise, let her in all
> charity give it to a sister who does need it. If,
> however, money is sent to her, the Abbess, with
> the advice of the discreets, may provide for the
> needs of the sister. (RegCl 8: 7-11)

This reveals a development indicating Clare's realization of
her own authority for the interpretation of Francis' charism.
Whereas numerous texts could have been cited in which
Francis expressly forbade the use of money as a medium of
exchange (e.g., RegB 4), Clare, fully cognizant of the developments described previously, and equally aware of the type of
internal economy required by a group of totally enclosed
women, allowed the reception of money to provide for needs.
Moreover, in the routine functioning of the community, (the
weekly chapter), there was an adequate safeguard against
abuse of this accommodation. In making such clear provision,
Clare did not attempt to do violence to this inevitable form of
benefaction. She made it an occasion in which each sister must
exercise personal discretion. The permission for the sister to
receive a gift, or for the monastery to benefit from a family's
generosity, did not nullify the responsibility of all to candidly
determine the use of such alms in a spirit of true poverty.[66]
Finally, Clare made provision for the needs of the sick in much
the same way as did Francis, although adding some specific
items of clothing and furnishing (RegCl 8: 12-18).

---

[66] Iriarte, *Regola*, 152-153.

Perhaps the most revealing section in the *Rule* on material poverty is Clare's heartfelt plea to the sisters regarding clothing. In the text of Hugolino's *Rule* there is evidence that agreement about the types of clothing was not easy to obtain (RegHug 9). In giving specifics, Hugolino's *Rule* is full of phrases such as: "may," "if they wish," "should," "if it seems fitting." In Clare's effort to give sufficient room for local and personal contingencies (RegCl 2: 16) she found that there was still room for confusion, and distortion. This occasions a particular urgency and personal zeal in this text : "I admonish, beg and exhort my sisters to always wear cheap garments out of love of the most holy and beloved Child Who was wrapped in such poor little swaddling clothes..."(RegCl 2:24).[67] For the sake of this Child and "of His most holy Mother" she begs for fidelity to this norm. The tone indicates that she fears relaxation on this point.[68]

Sources of Clare's Vision of Poverty

Having summarized the legal parameters of Clare's *Rule*, it is appropriate to ask what formed the spiritual basis for her legislation. The *Rule* itself contains valuable indications: the poverty of Christ; the inspiration derived from the teachings of Francis; and the relationship with him and his brothers.

---

[67] Compare her language here with Francis' expression of his plan for the *praesepio* at Greccio, 1 Cel 84.

[68] See LegCl 17, Armstrong, *Clare,* 207, note 86. Armstrong indicates in his notes on the description of her clothing in the Legend that the interpretation of her poverty in dress as a form of mortification signals a shift in the spiritual theology of the period. We also know that clothing functioned as a sign of social status and solidarity of groups such as guilds of workers and religious fraternities. This leads us to wonder if clothing that initially aligned the Poor Sisters with other poor women of the working class, did not gradually come to be a privatized, ascetic sign and thus open to accommodation in internal religious legislation. See also, Gabriele Andreozzi. *San Nicolo "De Pede Plateae" dove nacque il movimento francescano* (Roma: Editrice Franciscanum, 1986) 22-23.

Divine inspiration had led Clare to choose the way of "the most high poverty." With an enlightened heart Clare saw the goodness of God expressed ineffably in the Christ (TestCl 1-4). She could not let the thought of Him leave her for an instant (LEr 11). The image of Him that resonated most completely in her spirit was the image of one who is poor: poor as a needy infant, poor as a dying outcast.

When, however, she contemplates the Mirror that is Christ Crucified, she is by her own inner "coincidence of opposites" drawn deeply into the mystery of the exalted King of Kings who draws her and adorns her with riches beyond imagining.[69] The outer poverty and hardship to which she is pledged and for which she fights is swallowed up in an inner relationship with a Royal Bridegroom who transforms her identity. So comforted and emboldened with hope is she, that she can walk as a pilgrim and stranger and exhort her sisters to do likewise (RegCl 8: 2).[70] She knows here on earth no lasting city (RegCl 8: 6). Like Francis, she constantly discovers that this trust in the goodness of God is rewarded by providential wonders. Empty oil jars and shrinking stores of bread are mysteriously replenished (LegCl 15, 16; Proc VI: 16 ; I: 15; II: 14). Defenseless women find their

---

[69] Ewert Cousins, "Introduction" in *Bonaventure* (New York: Paulist Press, 1978) 33. Bonaventure proposes in metaphysical language the "coincidence of opposites" in Christ: "the eternal is joined with temporal man...the most actual with the one who suffered supremely and died...." In comparable fashion Clare's letters often draw upon such comparisons of poverty with riches. Christ is always the mediator of this exchange. See, for example, 1LAg 15-17; 19-20; 30; 2LAg 18-23; 3LAg 7; 24-27; 4LAg 15-25. ˙

[70] Clare's use of this image may seem somewhat ironic in view of the cloistered life of the Poor Sisters. However, the rich spirituality of the pilgrimage in the Middle Ages could have its counterpart even in this situation. For further exploration of the spiritual significance of the concept see: Brown, *The Cult of the Saints* 86-87; Raffaele Pazzelli. *St. Francis and the Third Order* (Chicago: Franciscan Herald Press, 1989) 24-26; Régine Pernoud, *I Santi nel Medioevo* (Milano: Rizzoli Editore, 1986) 9-27; Iriarte, *Regola*, 129-141.

enemies repulsed by unseen force (Proc IX: 2-3) and various illnesses yield to restorative prayers and signs (LegCl XXII).[71]

The Bond with the Friars

Clare is forever mindful of the particular grace of God that drew her to Francis and allowed her to become a companion of his, a co-worker, a disciple (TestCl 5; 3LAg 4). The moment of conversion that the encounter with him represents is never far from her consciousness (TestCl 6-17). Having sought the Lord and the way of his commandments from her youth, she can clearly remember the point of transformation of her hopes into certainty (TestCl 27-29). The confidence of this grace is so complete that she is able to profess obedience to Francis (TestCl 24-26). The bond created with him and with his brothers by this profession was not simply a legal necessity, it was an expression of conviction that together they were recipients of an inspiration whose validity they could never be persuaded to doubt (TestCl 17, 29). To profess her belief in this way of poverty, minority and fraternity, Clare summoned the primordial and graced energies of her entire human existence and focused them into a laser point of light and fortitude. The relationship with Francis and his companions always remained an essential element of her vocation; to suffer separation or diminishment of this bond was to permit a corroding rust to threaten the treasure of her soul.

One must know this, and meditate on it to fully grasp the meaning of Clare's continued struggle to maintain her relationship with the friars. She is clear in the *Rule* that the brothers accompany the sisters "in support of our poverty" (RegCl 12: 5-6). Practically, they are the questors for the sisters. They are also the chaplains and preachers for the sisters. Clare is adamant that both services enjoy equal esteem (LegCl XXIV: 37). If papal

---

[71] Note a similar juxtaposition of poverty and providential miracles in *Legenda maior* VII: "On his love of poverty and the miraculous fulfillment of his needs."

scruples would bar the friars from entering the monastery to preach, Clare's tenacity would bar the questors from carrying food to them. She would not allow the friars and the papacy to redefine what she and Francis had so clearly determined without making a vehement protest.[72]

This arrangement by which San Damiano and affiliated monasteries enjoyed the spiritual and temporal services of the friars was neither a unique nor a new concept. "Double monasteries" had been present in the Church for some time. Jane Tibbets Schulenberg writes that many of these "were initiated primarily for female religious"[73] and "then supported a supplementary community of monks or priests and male servants who provided the necessary sacerdotal functions and performed manual labor."[74] Recent research on the nature of the relationship between the nuns of Fontevrault and the monks who shared the Order with them indicates a precedent for a group of women being served by brothers who clearly accepted such a position of service. While it is obvious that neither Francis nor Clare intended to create a Franciscan equivalent for this famous house, it is also possible that new roles and relationships in the evangelical movements of the twelfth and thirteenth centuries created a favorable climate for testing new ground.[75] Significant

[72] The decision referred to was contained in *Quo elongati* issued in 1230 (*BF* I, 68) or *Etsi omnium* issued in 1236 (*BF* I, 206).

[73] Jane Tibbets Schulenberg, "Women's Monastic Communities, 500-1100: Patterns of Expansion and Decline," *Sisters and Workers in the Middle Ages,* eds. Judith M. Bennett, Elizabeth A. Clark, Jean F. O'Barr, B. Anne Vilen, and Sarah Westphal-Wilh (Chicago: Chicago UP, 1989) 219.

[74] Schulenberg, "Patterns," 219.

[75] Penny Schine Gold, "Male/Female Cooperation: The Example of Fontevrault," *Distant Echoes* 151-162. Gold suggests that among many groups attempting a kind of symbiotic monastery, Fontevrault succeeded due to careful legislation and Robert of Arbrissel's clearly expressed intent that the monks were to value their call to be of service to the nuns. She writes: "The structured inclusion of men was also very important to Fontevrault's success. In most other cases, arrangements were made with men on a more casual basis, using whatever resources were available locally. There were several

as well is the fact that contemporary heretical movements gave places to women, which accorded them power and status, thereby attracting large numbers of female adherents. Francis wanted the Poor Sisters treated with the same care as that given to the friars. To the extent that the new Franciscan movement was promoted as an orthodox alternative to the orders created by the heretical groups, the effort to maintain a bond of equality among men and women might have served as a proselytizing function.[76]

It has already been indicated that when Clare lay dying the Friars who were present at her death-bed were Francis' companions Juniper, Angelo and Leo (LegCl XXIX: 45). Source material reveals that Angelo was in tears and Leo could not refrain from kissing Clare's bed (LegCl XXIX: 45). The grief which the *Legend's* author ascribes to them—and the fact that

variables in the arrangements: would the fulfillment of the material and spiritual needs of the nuns be cast as service or supervision, would they be fulfilled by an individual man or a community of men, and would that individual or community reside with the nuns or at a distance? The particular arrangement could make a great difference in the reliability of services for the nuns. Those nuns dependent on priests from a neighboring community, for example, had a less convenient and secure arrangement than nuns who could call on a resident chaplain or group of chaplains. Whether this male participation was structured as service or supervision also made a difference" (162). We might even hypothesize that lack of clear legislation within the Order of Friars Minor eventually created problems about relationships with the Poor Sisters that led to later conflicts on this point.

[76] Giovanni Gonnet, "La donna presso i movimenti pauperistico-evangelici," *MRFF,* 103-129. For example, Gonnet states: "Given the consistency of a feminine presence, it is not surprising to discover in their line women of superior quality worthy to recover the roles, until now reserved for the men, of "the perfect ones," or "teachers." If in the north of France, in Belguim, in Holland and in the Rhine region, the women's question finds an opening between orthodoxy and heresy in the beguine movement, in the south of France and in Italy, it is channeled into the dualistic ambience of the Cathari, or in the evangelical ambience of the Waldensians and those currents affiliated with them, such as the Humiliati, to say nothing of contemporary or later monasticism."

they are clearly within the enclosure as was Jacoba at the death of Francis—is evidence of a powerful bond with Clare and her community.[77] These bits of information confirm that these early companions continued to communicate with one another.[78] As has been stated in the discussion of Hugh of Digne's work, they also continued to serve as a source of oral tradition for younger generations; one may suppose that the friendship linking the early companions was a friendship which included Clare and the sisters. It was a friendship that endured. Duncan Nimmo, in his major work on the history of the Order, cites Leo's gift of Francis' breviary to Clare and the sisters at San Damiano as reason for acknowledging the continuing communciation between the sisters and friars. He also says that Leo collaborated with Celano on the *Legend of Clare*.[79] Knowing the crucial role that these friar-companions played in preserving loyalty to Francis, it can safely be assumed that Clare was part of that continuing effort. What she wrote and taught was part of the patrimony intended to preserve the charism of Francis just as surely as the wealth found in Celano's *Second Life*, in the *Assisi Compilation*, or in the *Commentary* of Hugh of Digne.

[77] The material in their Greccio letter also relates that they at that time (1246) had communication with Brother Philip, "Visitor of the Poor Ladies," and with Brother Bernard "of holy memory" who had accompanied Clare to Sant' Angelo di Panzo.

[78] See Lazaro Iriarte, O.F.M. Cap., "Clare of Assisi: Her Place in Female Hagiography," *Greyfriars Review* 3 (August 1989) 173-206. Pages 190-194 especially focus on the relationship of Clare and the early companions. Iriarte says Clare played a significant role in preserving the primitive ideals of Francis.

[79] Duncan Nimmo, *Reform and Division in the Franciscan Order (1226-1538)*. (Rome: Capuchin Historical Institute, 1987) 85-86. Nimmo cites Joergensen's *Life of Francis* (note 183) as the source of this information.

Summary Observations

1. Clare lived during a time of widespread rejection by the Christian laity of the inequities and violence which accompanied the rise of new economic systems. Through their marriages, women of Clare's social standing were tools of social and economic aggrandizement. By rejecting the marriage plans her family had entertained in her regard, Clare—in her determination to "do penance"—did not choose a path of simply personal renunciation/consecration. She chose a path that had powerful social consequences whose effects were reflected in the violent reaction of her family and in the initial social opprobrium she and her companions endured.

2. The Friars Minor, for their part, struggled with the problem of how to observe their *Rule* and how to deal with questions of property, money and resources during the decades in which Clare was leading her sisters in facing the same issues. The friars were, at times, blessed with internal experts and leaders who promoted a high standard of observance and loyalty to the traditions of Francis and the early fraternity. At the same time, they were often forced to turn to the papacy for solutions to their internal "disputed questions." Papal interpretations and permissions served, at times, to allow more latitude to those within the order who favored more lenient prescriptions and accommodations to new situations. Between 1230-1250, commentaries upon the *Rule*, papal declarations that interpreted the *Rule*, and new legislation produced a body of literature that had observance of the *Rule* as its theme, even if the purposes and viewpoints of the various texts differed greatly.

3. Clare's determination to write a *Rule* of her own resulted in one of the most important Franciscan sources handed down to modern times. The *Rule* has only recently been subjected to careful analysis from linguistic, structural and historical viewpoints. (It has always, of course, been the subject of assiduous

study and meditation as a source for life among the thousands of Poor Clares for whom it is foundational.) The sources Clare used for her text created a document that successfully achieved papal approbation and served as a clear instrument of governance. Clare employed what was useful and necessary from the *Rules* of St. Benedict, Hugolino and Innocent IV. She also uses extensively the *Later Rule* of Francis as the source from which she took her primary thrust and spiritual authority. This spiritual authority derives from the inspiration which gave it its breadth of vision: the determination to live the poverty of Christ and his Mother with complete confidence in 1) the goodness of God, 2) the validity of the teaching of Francis, 3) the enduring bond with the Friars Minor, and 4) the charity which bonds the Poor Sisters to one another.

4. The manner in which Clare developed the teaching of Francis in her *Rule* and the understanding of his intentions that she demonstrated in her relationship with pontifical authority and with the Order of Friars Minor suffices to demonstrate that she was, for the span of her lifetime, one of the true authorities guiding the Order and providing it with written source material. It is equally clear that Clare's jurisdictional authority was limited to the exercise of governance of her own monastery and a very small number of affiliated convents. Her moral authority continued to exercise some influence in the small circle of Francis' intimate companions whose representatives were present at her death-bed. This same moral/spiritual authority was accorded public respect by prelates who visited her and, in particular, by Raynaldus and Innocent IV, who granted formal recognition to the *Rule*. The question that remains is the question of why her wisdom and knowledge were not more actively sought by those friars who were the key agents in the on-going crises concerning the interpretation of the obligations of poverty as delineated in the *Later Rule*. Why is it that when the history of juridic and spiritual interpretation of Francis' wishes is recounted, Clare's text with its superb blend of fidelity to inspi-

ration and prudent adaptation to new situations, becomes a footnote and not, as it deserves to be, an important chapter?

Chapter Four

CLARE'S INCARNATION OF MUTUAL CHARITY

The Medieval Woman's World of Relationships

The rescript which introduces the *Rule of Clare* contains the praises of Innocent IV regarding the intentions of the Abbess and her sisters. He affirms that "the form of life which Blessed Francis gave you" consists especially in "unity of mind and heart" as well as in "the profession of highest poverty."[1] The Brady-Armstrong edition of the writings points to this characteristic of the life at San Damiano: "Clare...describes a life integrally tied to a monastery and caught up in the struggle to preserve 'unity of mutual love, which is the bond of perfection.' The life of the Poor Ladies developed through an essential preoccupation with the interior life, that is, the spiritual life of each sister, and its external manifestation in the community of love that was formed by the sisters."[2] And again: "More than a community of support, the sisters are seen as a means of salvation in manifesting the profound relationships that exist in the Inner Life of God....The genius of Clare's perception of the spiritual life can

---

[1] Armstrong, *Clare*, 61.
[2] Armstrong-Brady, *Works*, 174-175.

be seen in this aspect of her *Rule*, for she penetrated, as Francis did, the marvelous mystery of the Revelation of God Who reveals Himself as a Community of Love. There can be little doubt that the enclosed life of San Damiano struggled on a daily basis to express that Unity of God."[3] This fascination with the incarnation of love within the confines of San Damiano is also the focus of Optatus van Asseldonk:

> The form of life consisted particularly of two parts, i.e., in a life of holy unity and in a life of highest poverty. The words used by Pope and by Cardinals almost suggest that Clare had used the same or similar words in the request. Besides, it seems that this form of life may have been received in words and in writing, from Francis himself, at least substantially. This is a thought which corresponds precisely to that of Clare and it has been repeated often in her writings.[4]

No matter how inclined one may be to find beauty in these words, it is still possible to ask in what way such concern for mutual charity was unique to Clare. Is not such a pursuit of divine charity of the essence of all Christian life and particularly that of religious persons in the Christian community? In consequence, another attempt to paint the "triptych" places charity in focus. In order to appreciate the primacy and the particular urgency for Clare of this call, one must ascertain what kinds of relationships comprised the ordinary experience of medieval women. How did they know or experience human affection, loyalty, solidarity, intimacy? What boundaries existed between one individual person and another, or between the individual and the community? Further, how did the Friars Minor confront

---

[3] Armstrong-Brady, *Works*, 185.

[4] Optatus van Asseldonk, O.F.M. Cap., *La Lettere e lo Spirito*, 2 vols. (Roma: Editrice Laurentianum, 1985) 2: 154.

the same requirement? How were they able to carry out the injunction to "witness that they are members of one family" (RegB 6: 7)?

Affectivity in Medieval Life

Medieval historians have had difficulty in determining what the emotional experiences of medieval persons were. David Herlihy affirms that practically the only sources from which such information can be gleaned are the lives of the saints. He credits the *Acta Sanctorum* with being a valuable repository of information about the domestic life of this period.[5] However, some caution is advised, since the hagiographic devices employed often depict family relationships with reserve, even with contempt. Saints are depicted as struggling to overcome claims of family in order to be faithful to divine callings. Their counsel to their followers often includes encouragement to flee excessive attachment to relatives. On the other hand, family relationships appear as a source of metaphors in describing mystical experiences and measuring the impact of saints upon their contemporaries. Herlihy believes that the constant use of this frame of reference belies the hostility towards family obligations implied in the more didactic aspects of these *vitae:*

> My point is that the evocation of motherhood, childhood, and fatherhood contained in the lives must bear some correspondence with the ways in which mothers, children, and fathers were viewed in the real world. These images were designed to evoke an emotional response on the part of readers or listeners; the sentiments expressed in a devotional context must have had parallels in feelings that prevailed in the natural family, for which we have no

[5] Herlihy, 113.

records....Family imagery, family models, in
religious devotion and in daily experience: each
echoed and reinforced the other.[6]

Before proceeding to a consideration of family relationships
as models of affective life, however, consideration must be
given to some important distinctions offered by Caroline Bynum
as warnings to the twentieth century reader who is in danger of
interpreting certain terms in equivocal ways. She begins by
reminding us that there is a school of thought among medievalists that locates the "discovery of the individual" in the twelfth
century. In examining this theory, Bynum offers some important refinements of the proposition. She states: "For twelfth-
century religion did not emphasize the individual personality at
the expense of corporate awareness. Nor did it develop a new
sense of spiritual and psychological change, of intention, and of
personal responsibility by escaping from an earlier concern
with types, patterns, and examples."[7]

She goes on to define the "discovery of the self" as evidenced
by an increase in interiority after 1050 and by an increase in
literary exploration of this topic in this period.[8] Unlike their
twentieth century counterparts, however, twelfth-century men
and women did not discover individual identity by rejecting
imposed patterns of behavior, but precisely by adopting appropriate behavior in order to arrive at conformity with a chosen
model. The saints became models because of their power of
personal attraction, even as they tried to model themselves
upon Christ. Interestingly, this concern also gave rise to fierce
competition among groups as new models replaced old ones in
the Christian economy.[9] Bynum asserts that the late medieval

[6] Herlihy, 115.

[7] Bynum, 85.

[8] Bynum, 87-88.

[9] Bynum, 92-94. The author also notes in this regard that while such
competition revealed a preoccupation with personal prerogatives of vocation, it also ultimately fostered an acceptance of variety of callings within the
body of believers.

"self" that was capable of reflection and choice, was—for all that—a "self" oriented towards choice of a group that could enable conformity to a model, a saint or sage, who would facilitate identification with the ultimate Model, Christ, as discovered in the Scriptures. She finds that the twelfth century equilibrium between self and group culminated in Lateran IV and that the prohibition of new religious life forms led to a certain rupture between individual religious experience and that of the group.[10]

Familial Relationships

The pattern of medieval marriage described in Chapter Three with its age gap between husband and wife gave rise to a high incidence of young widows or to women living a good part of their lives with their husbands at some distance due to war, crusades, or trading expeditions.[11] While records demonstrate that medieval marriage partners did, in some instances, enjoy a deep emotional rapport, there is substantial evidence that personal bonds were not always achieved. A powerful factor in shaping societal attitudes towards women and marriage was what Herlihy terms the "profound ambivalence" of the Church in its treatment of women. Following the Fathers of the church, Jerome in particular, medieval teaching presented woman as the very embodiment of carnality and of uncontrollable appetite. This misogynist tendency was related to the reform goals of imposing clerical celibacy. One of the strategies of the campaign was to render woman suspect and repugnant to clerics who might otherwise be tempted to either light dalliance or serious involvement.[12] At the same time, the monastic clergy

[10] Bynum, 108-109.

[11] For some descriptions of the rapport between husband and wife see: Meg Bogin, *The Women Troubadours* (New York: W.W. Norton and Co., 1980) 20-36; LaChance, 53-54; Herlihy, 103-104, 110-111 and 157-158.

[12] For additional treatment of this topic: Vern L. Bullough, *The Subordinate Sex: A History of Attitudes toward Women* (Chicago: University of Illinois Press, 1973) 169-179; R. Manselli, "La Donna nella vita della chiesa," *MRFU,*

developed the cult of the Virgin Mary in ways that supported both a popular piety and a body of theological and devotional literature that exalted woman in the person of Mary. This reverence for the Virgin Mary stood side by side with the didactic literature and its antagonistic treatment of women.[13]

In this context the rise of the troubadour poetry and the the courtly love *genre* of literature must be examined.[14] The existence of this body of song and poetry has been interpreted as a sign that women of this period enjoyed improved status and treatment. The characteristic exaltation of the lady and the fervent promises to live as her vassal imply a dramatic reversal of the masculine social domination usually associated with feudal life. In point of fact, however, the courtly love literature, while rooted in an actual phenomenon, reflects a social luxury of the elite without in any way proving that women in general enjoyed better treatment in law or in social and moral respect. In fact, at least one commentator on the courtly love tradition believes that these poems really had as their goal the ad-

243-255; Frederic Raurell, *Lineamenti di Antropologia Biblica* (Casale Monferrato: Edizione Piemme, 1986) 159-168; A. Valerio, "La donna nella 'societas christiana' dei secoli X-XII," *Rassegna di teologia* 3 (1983) 435-446.

[13] Jean Leclercq, Francois Vandenbroucke, Louis Bouyer, *A History of Christian Spirituality, Vol. II: The Middle Ages* (Turnbridge Wells: Burns & Oates, 1968) 250-254.

[14] Bogin, 37-61; Leclercq, Vandenbroucke and Bouyer 277-282; Andreas Capellanus, *The Art of Courtly Love*, trans. John Jay Parry (New York: W.W. Norton and Co., Inc, 1969) 3-24; Norman F. Cantor, *Medieval History*, 2nd ed. (London: Collier-Macmillan Limited, 1969) 377-386. Of special interest is Cantor's comment on page 385: "The romantic literature also instructed the aristocracy that the sensibility which had hitherto been regarded as a mark of feminine inferiority was now made into a virtue practiced by heroes such as Lancelot, Parsifal, and Tristan. By making feminine qualities heroic, the romantic poets enhanced the dignity of woman and made her a being with distinctive and valuable qualities. The teaching of the fourth-century church fathers on sex and marriage was the first stage in the emancipation of women in western civilization. The romantic ethos of the twelfth century marked the second stage."

vancement of the troubadour's own career by the device of public flattery of the patron's wife.[15] In reality, the lot of the married woman was full of contradictions. She might enjoy the happiness of companionship and respect. She might just as well find herself alone for lengthy periods or widowed at a young age. A new poetic fashion led to improved manners and a definite refinement of emotional life. But this did not eradicate the misogynist tendencies which characterized much ecclesiastical literature and affected in deepest consequence both her self-image and the image that men carried regarding her.[16]

Then, there is the role of woman as mother. Parent-child relationships have been the subject of some controversy in the medievalists' camp.[17] Herlihy sees the marriage patterns as promoting a family system in which the mother was the primary socializing influence and the mediator between children and father. Mothers spent more consistent time with their children and probably had the greatest influence upon their formation. In making her critique of assumptions about Italian historiography, Diane Owen Hughes points out that it was precisely in the "private, generational time of the family" that Italian women were accorded their greatest historical significance.[18] While this resulted from a diminution of woman's role in the public sector, it cannot be denied that the role of the family as a social institution in the culture was vastly important. So this 'private' sphere of women was in reality a source of enormous power. This primacy of the mother's role is reflected in much of the imagery found in the saints' lives, in which mothers often are seen as gathering spiritual "families," or guiding spiritual "children."[19] Clare's own mother, Ortulana, is without doubt an excellent personification of this reality. If one recalls the life of

[15] Bogin, 51-56.

[16] For a contemporary response to the historical impact of this point of view see Raurell, 167-183.

[17] Herlihy, 207, note 1 Chapter 5. See also Shahar, 98-106.

[18] Hughes, 34.

[19] Herlihy, 122-124.

Clare as a young girl at home and its penitential practices, there
is no question of the reality of her mother's influence; there is
also the testimony that Ortulana had gone "beyond the sea for
reasons of prayer and devotion" (Proc I: 4). It is likewise
significant tht Ortulana herself and two of Clare's blood sisters
entered San Damiano.

Horizontal Relationships of Medieval Women

The family patterns of medieval life were often replicated in
the monastic world, especially when monasteries functioned as
a method of providing for women in the extended family who
were widowed or for whom marriage was not a possibility.[20] It
was in the monastic world of the Middle Ages that women
achieved the greatest measure of administrative power and
spiritual authority. Eleanor McLaughlin asserts that even though
women in the heretical sects were given the right to preach,
their brief egalitarian experience did not endure. It was only in
the "special vocation of holiness" to which monastic life was
oriented that "women found the most enduring and powerful
roles."[21]

In secular life the extended household presented the space in
which women might forge relationships to one another.[22] The
ideal mistress of such a household is portrayed as a good
administrator and a wise provider for her serving men and
women. Her care manifested a personal quality in that she not
only organized and directed the tasks of the house, but also

[20] Leclercq, *MRFF,* 65-66 and 79-83; Herlihy, 89 and 101-103.

[21] Reuther and McLaughlin, 124. It should be noted, however, that within
these monasteries the social stratification of secular society continued.

[22] Many studies of medieval households and daily life exist. We cite a few:
Eileen Power,*Medieval Women,* ed. M.M. Postan (London: Cambridge, 1975);
Labarge, ...*A Small Sound of the Trumpet,* see especially Chapter Eight:
"Medieval Women as Healers and Nurses"; Shahar, 149-154, 204-210, 239-250;
Christine Klapisch-Zuber, "Women and the Family" in *Medieval Callings,* ed.
Lydia G. Cochran (Chicago: U Chicago Press, 1990) 285-311.

personally provided for ample food and drink, medication and care in time of sickness, and so forth. In the thirteenth and fourteenth centuries, the church promoted the servant girl as a model of humility and holiness. This promotion was aimed at enforcing a moral standard for poor girls who came from rural areas into the cities as servants. The ideal was, in a sense, an echo of the servant motif in the lives of many sainted noble women, in which the reversal of roles expected by "worldy values" took place. Adoption of humble behavior towards one's social inferiors became one of the hallmarks of sanctity seen in the *vitae* of many women saints. While social barriers still existed between these classes, the ideals presented in the lives of the saints bridged the gap by inculcating attitudes of humility and charity that were blind to social distinction.[23]

The women of the merchant and artisan classes of the communes enjoyed the greatest measure of liberty in the later Middle Ages.[24] They participated in the creation of a new economic and social order which was antithetical to the older feudal way. Even though limited in political rights and roles, in view of their work, these women did enjoy some public *persona*. Ironically, it was the women of the middle class, those who exercised a trade in their own right or in cooperation with their husbands, who were more influential in the new social order than their social betters, the women of the nobility. Hughes demonstrates that the communes deliberately sought to restrict the power of these women:

> As cities of the twelfth and thirteenth centuries forced into political submission the noble feudatories that challenged their new and still fragile authority, they confronted women who

[23] Michael Goodich, "Ancilla Dei: The Servant as Saint in the Late Middle Ages," Julius Kirshner and Suzanne F. Wemple eds., *Women of the Medieval World: Essays in Honor of John H. Mundy* (London: Basil Blackwell, 1985) 119-136.

[24] Shahar, 189-203.

> through inheritance or marriage exercised con-
> trol over lands and men in the Italian country-
> side and even in the city itself....Women's
> centrality in that private world of family and
> patronage which the communes strove to
> weaken by insisting on the public institutions of
> law and contract, made them seem dangerous.
> Rooted in that older private world, they could
> not respond to the individual and civilizing
> impulses that drew men out of a blood-based
> network of corporate obligation. Women could
> not rise to the cultural demands of the city,
> which required its citizens—much as Gregorian
> reforms had required priests—to abandon those
> obligations and to create new ties and loyalties
> based on common belief and shared enterprise.[25]

Hughes believes that from this point forward, women were denied a share in the "changing encounters of an age of contract," but that they were expected to celebrate "the end-lessly repetitive rite of an age of blood."[26]

Based upon the preceding material, a few conclusions can be drawn. In spite of warnings by historians that a true estimate of emotional life in the Middle Ages does not come easily to the modern investigator, some patterns indicate how relationships were created and sustained. The notion of marriage is vastly different from our own post-Romantic, post-Freudian era in which the personal intimacy of the married (or unmarried) couple is promoted as an essential experience of personal development. While medieval marriages may have provided such personal affection, such was neither a prerequisite nor an indispensable goal. The beginnings of a cult of romantic love emerge at this period, witnessed in the troubadour literature.

[25] Hughes, 30-31.
[26] Hughes, 34.

The literature, however, was more cause than effect, and such respectful sentiment towards women as normative was a later development.

Women of the nobility lived long portions of their lives in the company of other women and children. Affective bonds with children were often more intense and efficacious than those with husbands. As time passed, this maternal role gained increasing importance; there is also plentiful evidence that it was experienced as a powerful and assuring relationship. In addition, women formed multiple relationships in the large households of the upper classes. Other family members, servants and other workers were often in the care of the mistress of the household for significant portions of time and relied on her for the maintenance of basic needs. Such interaction, when influenced by Christian ideals, fostered an ideal of humble service and mutual love that stamped the lives of saints of both noble and servant classes.

Because women in monastic roles enjoyed both the network of relationships that an extended family could provide (sometimes the monastic and natural family coincided), and the administrative powers that secular roles denied them, female monasteries became an important source for the development of talent and power among women.

Women in the communes who were members of the mercantile class were able, at least initially, to escape the gradual erosion of rights and roles that noble women endured after the feudal era. They were able to respond to the new relationships and contractual obligations that made the commune successful. Women of noble birth, on the other hand, found themselves increasingly isolated, caught between the determinisms of the male oligarchs of their families and the freedom of the new women who worked side by side with men in creating a social order based on personal industry rather than on family lineage.

The Friars and the Experience of Fraternity

How can the way in which the friars of the early decades experienced their fraternal life be ascertained? In what ways did their daily existence bear the stamp of brotherly relations? What difficulties did they encounter in giving actuality to this fraternal spirit advocated so insistently by Francis? In dealing with this question regarding medieval women, a general portrait of the ordinary relationships that constituted the woman's world at the time of Clare was presented in order to describe general patterns and the affective bonds that analysts of medieval life associate with these relationships. A general understanding of how women of Clare's time might encounter the demands of relationships leads to better understanding of her teaching and practice regarding the nature of communal relationships in the monastery. Now, in turning attention to the friars, it is possible to glean some insights drawn from more immediate sources regarding their particular social experience. First, however, it is necessary to develop a context for evaluating the uniqueness inherent in Francis' vision of organized religious life as it touched the interdependence of individual men in the fraternity.

Théophile Desbonnets, in his contribution to the 1982 "Corso di Formazione Francescana" of the Pontifical Athenaeum Antonianum, discussed the process by which the early Franciscan *fraternitas* evolved into an *ordo*.[27] In pursuing his topic he offered a valuable synthesis of the meanings of *fraternitas* Francis encountered in the lived reality of his society. Having its roots in the social conventions of Roman antiquity, the medieval notion of fraternity covered a large assortment of groups having social, religious and economic purposes. Various terms (*fraternitas, congregatio, gilda, conventus*) were used to depict those associations not clearly entitled in either canon or civil law, whose descriptions are found in local civil and ecclesias-

[27] Théophile Desbonnets, O.F.M., "Dalla fraternità all'ordine." *Temi di vita francescana: la fraternita...* eds. G. Cardaropoli e C. Stanzione (Roma: Ed. Antonianum, 1983).

tical archives.[28] Pointing out the guarded and even hostile reactions of established religious orders to this proliferation of new forms, Desbonnets contends that they appeared "as the black beast" of the older groups. Quoting Michaud-Quantin he describes this fear:

> In a vertical organization of society, in which each one is bound to both superiors and to inferiors, without taking into account the relationships which exist between individuals situated in the same level, the mutual oath replaces an horizontal organization where relationships on the same level, take the primary place....The feudal society was connected to physical persons as such: the lord to whom fidelity was owed, the vassals to whom protection was due; but the member of a collective society is bound to the moral person of the society itself.[29]

Desbonnets holds that the early horizontal structure of the Franciscan fraternity gradually evolved into a more "regular" structure as a result of the initiatives of the Roman curia, the friars' own desire for recognition and the speedy growth of the order. He points out, however, that one must beware of approaching Francis as a "mythic hero" whose work can be interpreted in black and white absolutes. Desbonnets does not see the evolution as a falling away from the ideals of fraternal relationship. Rather, he maintains that even in his lifetime Francis guaranteed that the structures indicated in the *Rule* would support this kind of evangelical bond of brother with brother. He concludes: "In this structure, relationships (we would say vertical relationships) between superiors and inferi-

---

[28] Desbonnets, 72.

[29] Desbonnets, 88, quoting P. Michaud-Quantin, *Universitas, Expressions du mouvement communitaire dans le moyen age latin*, (Paris, 1970).

ors had sense only if they are at the service of horizontal relationships among equals; therefore, in the *Earlier Rule* it is written: 'No one is to be called prior...'."[30]

Another force that supported this renewal of relationships is cited by Michael Hart in his study of Franciscan fraternity. Basing his observations on those of M. D. Chenu, Hart reminds us that "a new hermeneutic, or way of applying Scripture texts in real life, emerges in a society when there are new social and cultural conditions."[31] Chenu sees fraternity as an important value in this medieval development. For Francis and his brothers the shift from a hierarchical view of the universe led to a re-reading of the gospel and an understanding of Jesus as "one who is Brother." Thus the friars were both giving expression to profoundly felt aspirations of their times and shaping the perceptions of subsequent generations in the Christian community by their ability to incarnate this intuition.[32]

What concrete evidence supports these assertions? What are the dangers of trusting memoirs of the ideals and pedagogy of the friars without investigating their real experience? Would Clare and her companions have been able to turn to the brothers for living examples of Francis' teaching on this point? Chapter Three surveyed documentation such as expositions and papal decrees to describe the manner in which the friars sought to understand their obligations regarding poverty. At this point, information should be sought from a different *genre,* the chronicles which portray the ordinary round of activities of the brothers. However, the cautions explained by Cajetan Esser in discussing his own use of sources for *The Origins of the Franciscan Order* still apply. Esser pointed out the danger of

[30] Desbonnets, 95.

[31] Michael Hart, "Dynamics of Franciscan Fraternity: A Study of Spirit, Word, Obedience and Poverty in the Writings of St. Francis of Assisi," Diss. Pontificium Athenaeum Antonianum, 1988, 81-84.

[32] For a contemporary reading of this subsequent incarnation, see Dominic Monti, O.F.M., "Franciscan Ministry—Changing Contexts and Historical Developments, *The Cord* 41 (March 1991) 66-79.

trying to understand the Order's early years solely through materials such as the biographies in which the point of view often was determined by the author's position on the various poverty controversies. He turned to "writings which go back to eyewitnesses of the primitive Franciscan movement or to contemporaries not belonging to the Order."[33] In describing the fraternal reality of the primitive Order, Esser writes:

> That love which prompts a man to serve his neighbor, to care for him and provide for him with the necessities of life, is aroused by this radical poverty. It is precisely this immediate and practical brotherly love that sets its special seal on the new Order. It is one of the outstanding traits of the Christian example given by the community which grew around Francis—a fact that has been overlooked too frequently up to this. Contemporary sources do not give very much information on this subject. They tend rather to present the external picture of the new Order.[34]

Esser continued, however, with additional materials that demonstrated the effect that the life of *minoritas* and *fraternitas* had upon various observers. These observations are included in the letters of Jacques de Vitry, the *Chronicles* of Jordan of Giano and Thomas of Eccleston, and the *Sacrum Commercium*.[35] Esser stated that these works, overlooked by Sabatier and those who entered the fray to do battle with or for him, "report simply and directly on the life of the friars as it was **actually** lived in the first decades of the thirteenth century; that is to say, on the

[33] Cajetan Esser, O.F.M., *The Origins of the Franciscan Order* (Chicago: Franciscan Herald Press, 1970) 4.

[34] Esser, *Origins,* 240.

[35] Esser, *Origins,* 241-251.

questio facti."[36] They demonstrated that the *Rule* served neither as a rigid nor infallible guide and that daily life gave rise to many practices that became normative with time.

The Chronicles of Jordan of Giano and Thomas of Eccleston

The *Chronicle of Jordan of Giano* stands as one of the most precious documents of early Franciscan history.[37] It is, in its very essence, a "fraternal" document in so far as it was written at the request of a provincial chapter. This chapter decision reflected the friars' desire to preserve histories of the early days of the Order, and especially of the German province. Clearly these recollections both reflected and fostered a sense of "the ideal-ism and the courage of the brothers as they lived and spread their message."[38] Another facet of the chronicle that adds to its importance is the service it provides in helping modern readers to see members of the Order living out their vocation at some geographical and psychological distance from Francis himself. Jordan admits to the fact that while he had known Francis he had not held him in sufficient reverence until the experience he had when he carried some of his relics back to the province after a stay in Italy.[39] This small indication gives insight into something of the experience of men who entered the Order not with an expectation of being actual companions of Francis, but of the other brothers encountered during preaching expeditions. Jordan, in other words, provides a glimpse of the fraternal dynamics of those brothers who accepted the rule and life of the

[36] Esser, *Origins,* 7.

[37] H. Boehmer, *Chronica Fratris Jordani (Edidit, notis et commentario illustravit)* (Paris: Librairie Fischbacher, 1908). English translation: Placid Hermann, O.F.M. *XIIIth Century Chronicles; Jordan of Giano, Thomas of Eccleston, Salimbene degli Adami* (Chicago: Franciscan Herald Press, 1961). Cited hereafter as *Jordan* with section number.

[38] Lapsanski, 191-192.

[39] *Jordan,* 41.

Friars Minor and lived out its demands far from the events that constitute the gravitational center of many of the biographies and other sources.

Some indications of the day to day features of fraternal life are quite clear. Jordan recalls the brothers travelling to visit Caesar of Speyer. They were hungry and their begging was fruitless because they could not speak German. One of the brothers devised a way of feigning ignorance in order to cajole people into contributing bread, eggs and milk to the larder of the mendicants. Having discovered this stratagem, he used it repeatedly to get food for the brothers who were not so lucky.[40] Jordan also describes the humility of Nicholas, who could not bear being made a superior, but who, while in office, endeared himself to all by sharing in the menial duties of the house and by doing with his brothers the penances he imposed on them.[41] Another of the superiors, Brother John, embodied perfectly the injunction of the *Rule*: "He cherished and ruled over all his brothers as a mother her sons and a hen her chicks in peace and charity and in all consolation."[42] In a negative form, reaction to the damage done by Elias demonstrates the anger of the brothers at having their unity disturbed by his excesses.[43]

Jordan always perceived the grace of God strongly at work in bringing the Order through difficult beginnings in Germany and bringing abundance upon the province. What is striking about these reflections upon such growth is the vertical dimension of his acknowledgment of Providence and the horizontal dimension of his joy and satisfaction in recounting the goodness of the brothers and their willingness to suffer for and with one another. This extends the experience he describes of being present at the Chapter of 1221: "Who can explain how great was the charity among the brothers at this time, and the patience, humility,

---

[40] *Jordan*, 27.
[41] *Jordan*, 47-49.
[42] *Jordan*, 55.
[43] *Jordan*, 61.

obedience and brotherly cheerfulness?"[44] Such witness is what Jordan sees and remembers, beginning at the early chapters and extending through the four decades that followed until his writing in 1262.

Thomas of Eccleston presents the earliest information concerning the friars who were first to live beyond continental Europe. In *The Coming of the Friars Minor to England,* he preserved recollections and factual information spanning the years 1224 to 1258.[45] In spite of his biases, identified by Lapsanski as a prejudice against the other Orders and an intense patriotism, Thomas's work is invaluable as a source for a thirty year interval in the primitive history of the Friars Minor.[46] It should be noted as well, that Eccleston clearly showed the development of patterns of conventual life. The information he supplied shows a stability in terms of dwelling places, horarium, community discipline and other expectations. Given such parameters for the actual practice of fraternal life, it is easy to see how Eccleston succeeded in capturing these vignettes of daily experience with such clarity.

He described the brothers at collation as they "drank with joy" even the dregs of the brew available.[47] He shared the marvelous story of Brother Solomon who was suffering intensely from the cold. "But since the brothers did not have anything wherewith they could warm him, holy charity showed them a kindly remedy. All the brothers gathered closely around him and warmed him by huddling up against him as pigs are wont to warm each other."[48] This same brother, afflicted with spiritual

[44] *Jordan,* 16.

[45] A.G. Little. *Fratris Thomae vulgo dicti de Eccleston: Tractatus de Adventu Fratrum Minorum in Angliam* (Manchester: Manchester University Press, 1951). English translation: Hermann, cited hereafter as *Thomas* with section number.

[46] Lapsanski, 99. See also Lapsanski's views concerning the monastic elements of life that attract Thomas' praise, 200-201.

[47] *Thomas,* 1.

[48] *Thomas,* 3.

distress at death, asks the brothers who were his close friends to pray with him. Thomas lauded these early brothers who served God "not by means of constitutions" but in fervor and "the free affections of their devotion."[49] This fervor, however, was joined to fraternal joy. He recorded that they "could hardly keep from laughing when they saw one another"[50] and recounted their efforts to keep such levity from interfering with the decorum required in choir. He reported that when Brother Stephen ruled over Salisbury "mutual charity flourished in a special way," and that Stephen "would permit no one, to the best of his ability, to be sad."[51] Then there was Brother John, whose skill at comforting the brothers was so highly regarded that "many from other provinces who were desolate came to him and seemed to prosper under him."[52] The charity to be exercised toward the sick, exhorted in the *Rule,* was present, apparently to an heroic degree, in the case of Brother William who remained with a plague-stricken brother when others fled and died himself as a result.[53] The brothers could hardly bear the separation resulting from new assignments and often accompanied each other to the new mission and then parted with tears.[54]

Thomas also provided a glimpse of some of the problems of these friars, whose merits he generally upheld. He recalled John of Parma's warnings that the brothers have failed to build up the humility and meekness of their lives to the same level as their zeal for study.[55] Another brother had a vision in which the devils revealed how busy they were "when the brothers sit gossiping over their drinks at the hour of compline."[56] And the visitator sent by Elias managed, with "very strict and subtle" instructions,

[49] *Thomas,* 5.
[50] *Thomas,* 5.
[51] *Thomas,* 7.
[52] *Thomas,* 9.
[53] *Thomas,* 13.
[54] *Thomas,* 5.
[55] *Thomas,* 13.
[56] *Thomas,* 11.

to stir "mutual accusations within the Order"[57] so that another cleric likened the situation to a diabolical snare. A "certain lector" (who was charitably left nameless) was criticized for being "too intimate with seculars"[58] and, as a result, lacking in sufficient familiarity with the brethren. Thomas of Eccleston depicted honestly the daily experiences, the usual dispositions and the harmful lapses of the early English friars. His general regard for them was, however, full of praises for "the humility and meekness, the simplicity and zeal, the charity and patience of the brothers of England."[59]

Both the efforts of modern scholars to analyze the beginnings of the Order, and the chronicles and documents that report the experiences of the first few decades, show a substantial degree of admiration at the mutual love exhibited in the far-flung fraternities of the first decades. Descriptions of actual events taking place in friaries, during journeys, or between individuals show the friars true to the admonitions on mutual charity that Francis often gave. In addition, observations from sources external to the Order, such as Jacques de Vitry, confirm the sense of admiration evoked by this new spirit of equality and love.[60] In his summary of the presentation "Istituzioni comunali di Assisi," Daniel Waley offers the interesting observation that Francis' optimistic view of the possibilities of peace, liberty and the capacity of people to work together in communal structures was undoubtedly influenced by his own experience of the rapid developments by which Assisi achieved the status of commune.[61] Francis was seventeen years of age when this civil event took place. In his formative years he had witnessed the process by which Assisians rapidly developed institutions through which

[57] *Thomas*, 7.

[58] *Thomas*, 11.

[59] *Thomas*, 14.

[60] See Esser's summary of de Vitry's observations in *Origins*, 241-243.

[61] Daniel Waley, "Istituzioni comunali di Assisi." *Assisi nel tempo di San Francesco* (Assisi: Società Internazionale di Studi Francescani, 1978) 55-70.

various social levels hoped to achieve peaceful means of resolving disputes. It seems that, in addition to the information gleaned from sources already cited, this final observation is well worth recording in order to understand how Francis tried to express and to create fraternal relations. The friars, fired by the words of the Gospel and the power of the Holy Spirit, would be messengers of this peace which they would first demonstrate among themselves, and by which they would hope to make of all men and women brothers and sisters.

Clare's Definition of Mutual Charity

The search for the pattern Clare used to present mutual charity in her *Rule* demonstrates that her entire text is thoroughly infused with this spirit. It is not simply a matter of offering a certain few prescriptions or ideals.

In fact, the *Rule* in its structure does not have a positive instruction on mutual love, although it does contain a chapter on the "Admonition and Correction of the Sisters" which deals with violations of charity.[62] Consequently, it is impossible to locate her thoughts in a single chapter or sequence of articles. Instead one must examine the text as a whole and try to assess the entire range of Clare's thought. This approach reveals three major aspects of the value of mutual charity: 1) individual sisters in their activity contribute to a loving environment; 2) the abbess and other officials of the community have specific responsibilities to foster charity; 3) the structures and norms of the community contribute to a basic justice that make charity possible. Supporting all of these elements, and the prevailing point of view of Clare is a spiritual foundation drawn from the Gospel and celebrated liturgically.

---

[62] Use of the word *caritas* occurs in the following verses: 8:5, 8:7, 9:3, 10:1; *amor* in 4:7, 4:8; *diligere* in 8:9, 10:7.

The Individual Sisters and Mutual Charity

The image of the individual Poor Sister in her life of love for her co-sisters emerges from certain specific details of the *Rule*. Perhaps the first and most fundamental expression of this mutuality is the simple directive that "they can communicate always and everywhere, briefly and in a low tone of voice, whatever is necessary" (RegCl 5: 4). This may hardly seem much of a teaching on charity until it is measured against the severity of Hugolino's *Rule* with its instruction: "Let a continuous silence be kept by all at all times, so that it is not allowed either for one to talk to another or for another to talk to her [the abbess] without permission, except for those on whom some teaching office or duty has been enjoined, which cannot be fittingly discharged in silence. Permission may be given to these to speak about those things which pertain to their office or duty, where, when, and how the Abbess sees fit" (RegHug 6). Clare, in her major amendment of this practice, indicates the need for basic human communication to proceed untrammeled by the scrupulosity that invariably results from universal prohibitions. She affirms the necessity and value of ordinary human speech as a form of facilitating work, the service of others and the general life of the monastery. She further permits conversation in the infirmary, not only for the service, but for the "recreation" of the sick (RegCl 5: 3). The sick, in turn, are to respond with "good words" to those who enter the monastery to help them (RegCl 8: 19). Here, again, she shows an appreciation of ordinary conversation as a means of exercising love. Care of the sick is cited as a particular index of the charity of the community (RegCl 8: 14).[63] In the same section of the *Rule* (8: 15-16), Clare echoes Francis in calling for a mutual manifestation of need

---

[63] Further, the *Process* and the *Legend* abound in descriptions of her personal care of the sick; for example : Proc I 12, 16, 19; II 3, 13, 16; III 10, 11, 17; LegCl 12, 35, 38. Francis, too, in writing the CantExh urges patience in care of the sick.

rooted in the trust that each sister loves the others with an
affection that rivals that of a mother for a daughter. This deep
affection is demonstrated in specific ways. Each sister works for
the common good (RegCl 7: 1). When a sister receives something
as a gift she gives it "in all charity" to another sister should that
sister have greater need (RegCl 8: 10).

In dealing with the topic of reconciliation, Clare specifies
actions that must be performed to repair damage done to
mutual love. In the weekly chapters the sisters acknowledge
their shortcomings to one another (RegCl 4: 15). Clare is quite
specific regarding the form of reparation when an individual
seriously offends one of her sisters:

> If it should happen—may it never be so—that
> an occasion of trouble or scandal should arise
> between sister and sister through a word or
> gesture, let she who was the cause of the trouble,
> before offering her gift of prayer to the Lord, not
> only prostrate herself humbly at once at the feet
> of the other and ask pardon, but also beg her
> simply to intercede for her to the Lord that He
> might forgive her. Let the other sister, mindful of
> that word of the Lord: "If you do not forgive
> from the heart, neither will your heavenly Father
> forgive you," generously pardon her sister ev-
> ery wrong she has done her (RegCl 9: 6-10).

Clare teaches a process of reconciliation in this text. First, the
offending sister must acknowledge her guilt, and she must carry
out the Gospel injunction of begging pardon (as Francis also
demanded). She must add a step (asking for prayer), one that
proceeds from a clear realization of the nature of sin and of the
teaching of the Gospel. The offended sister must also allow the
Gospel to be her guide and must pardon "generously." By
requiring that the injured party promise to pray for the other,

Clare includes in the process a further guarantee that the forgiveness will not be superficial.[64]

Special instructions for the serving sisters set clear standards of conduct designed to protect the monastery from the effects of gossip and social entanglements. These sisters were to be outside the monastery only because of necessity, were to say little, were to do nothing to promote gossip about the Poor Sisters, and were not to repeat the gossip of the world inside the monastery (RegCl 9: 11-16). It is evident that Clare was determined to deal forcefully with anything that would seriously harm the reputation of the sisters.[65] While allowing for human weakness, she reserves her most severe language for such infractions: "But if a sister does this *through vicious habit* let the Abbess with the advice of her discreets, impose a penance upon her according to the nature of the fault [emphasis added]" (RegCl 9: 18). Perhaps it is in seeing Clare exercise this faculty of judgment that one gains a precise notion of the charity she wanted to inculcate: "In fact, I admonish and exhort the sisters in the Lord Jesus Christ to beware of all pride, vainglory, envy, avarice, care and anxiety about this world, detraction and murmuring, dissension and division. Let them be always eager to preserve among themselves the unity of mutual love which is the bond of perfection" (RegCl 10: 6-7). This list of what the sisters must avoid suggests a reverse image of the community she sought to form with its members committed to humility, generosity, trust, charity, forgiveness, reconciliation.[66] A further depth is touched in the subsequent lines in which the sisters are

[64] Garrido, 147-148.

[65] See Adm 25, RegNB 5: 13-14.

[66] Iriarte, *Regola,* 202-203. Iriarte points out that Clare adds the words "discord and division" to the text from Francis which is her base (RegB 10: 7). While agreeing that Clare and her sisters most likely experienced in an intense way the dangers of discord in their enclosed monastic community, it is difficult to agree that "suscettibilità femminile" [feminine sensitivity] is completely responsible for this danger when one examines the parallel divisions that were operative among the friars at this period.

counselled: "...to have humility, patience in difficulty and infirmity, and to love those who persecute, blame, and accuse us, for the Lord says: 'Blessed are those who suffer persecution for the sake of justice, for theirs is the kingdom of heaven' (Mt 5: 10). But 'whoever perseveres to the end will be saved'" (RegCl 10: 10-13). It is difficult to know exactly how to evaluate this admonition. Is Clare reflecting the experience of internal trials that exist when charity is not present? Are persecutions fomented by agents outside the monastery? Or is she pointing to the sufferings created within the community by slander, detraction and calumny? Since this same biblical citation is found in the chapter on mission in the friars' *Earlier Rule* (16: 12), the different use and placement here must be noted. It is possible that Clare might be implying that the persecution which Francis identified with vulnerability to "enemies" ("Saracens and other nonbelievers") may be present to the Poor Sisters in forms more subtle but no less efficacious for meriting salvation.[67]

Responsibility of the Abbess for Mutual Charity

Clare unequivocally stated that "all who hold offices in the monastery" are chosen "by common consent" and that the primary characteristic of their service is "to preserve the unity of mutual love and peace" (RegCl 4: 22). She even presents incompetence in this charge as the reason for the community to "elect another as abbess and mother" and she further admon-

---

[67] Iriarte, *Regola,* 207. There must have been some troubles of external origin which occasioned this item of encouragement in the *Rule.* Is this perhaps an oblique reference to Clare's struggle to maintain the *Privilege of Poverty?* Would, for example, Crescentius of Jesi have been affirming or antagonistic in his attitude toward the monastery? Or, what sort of difficulties were encountered by a sister sent from San Damiano to another house for the purpose of leading a reform there? Such an interpretation does not contradict the basic premise that Clare is speaking of the hardships of daily life in community, but simply adds a second level of possible meaning.

ishes that this is to be done "as quickly as possible" once the situation is evident (RegCl 4: 7). The maternal solicitude that Clare expects of the abbess is manifested in such actions as providing suitable clothing "with discernment...as it shall seem expedient to her by necessity" (RegCl 2: 16) and dispensing from the fast the young, the sick, or those working outside the monastery (RegCl 3: 10). She makes work assignments "in the presence of all" RegCl 7: 3-5) and announces and distributes alms in the same way. In her preservation of common life, she creates a principle by which the resources of the house will be fairly distributed (RegCl 4: 13). Further, she must consult every sister, including young members whose wisdom may serve all (RegCl 4: 17-18). The abbess herself must not only be ready to help those who are troubled in spirit (RegCl 4: 11-12), she must carefully avoid particular friendships that fragment the group (RegCl 4: 10). By such selfless presence to every one of her sisters, she will be able to prevent the "sickness of despair" from attaching itself to an individual's spirit, since even the weakest members will be able to approach her.

When exercising her function as the corrector of the sisters, the abbess is warned "not to become angry or disturbed" so that her example will set the tone for the community's response to the erring member.[68] She here repeats the marvelous warning of Francis that even such apparently justified anger will "prevent charity in oneself and in others" (RegCl 9: 5).[69] Furthermore, her corrections are to be given "humbly and charitably" (RegCl 10: 1) for she is to be a servant (RegCl 10: 5).

Undoubtedly, Clare sees the abbess as one who must behave in certain ways so as to inspire and teach mutual charity (RegCl 4: 9). It is also obvious that she legislates many details that contribute to this environment without being specifically identified with charity. A moment's reflection upon the actuality of

---

[68] RegNB 5: 7 and RegB 7: 3.

[69] The *Admonitions* contain an entire "program" of spirituality on this point: Adm 9, 11, 13, 14, 17. 2, 18.

monastic life enables one to see this more clearly. The long history of conventual monasticism is full of documents of practical wisdom expressed in regulations governing daily life and of descriptions of the recurring patterns that comprise it.[70] The many details that develop in such legislation, while potentially open to misinterpretation, also function as a source of protection for individuals and for the group. Behavior is inculcated that enables persons of varying temperaments to agree to common standards. Routines are devised that free individual energy for more important contemplative and organizational work. Expectations of members, norms for belonging to the group, and sanctions for failures are specified. While this aspect of tradition can give rise to a certain tedium or formalism, it can also serve as the guarantee of a basic justice.[71] It allows each member to know clearly what is required and what the individual in turn may expect in return for compliance with the group's standards. A group in which such clear norms do not exist becomes victimized by either social anarchy or by the despotism of forceful personalities. Therefore, the care with which Clare and her sisters evolved the practices found in many sections of the *Rule* reflects an understanding of that very ordinary justice essential for growth in more evangelical charity. Some of these norms deserve additional attention.

The consent of all is required before permission to admit a new member can be asked of the Cardinal Protector (RegCl 2: 1). The new candidate's decisions about distribution of goods must be left to her freedom (RegCl 2: 9). Any involvement in decisions which may have subsequent negative repercussions in internal relationships is forbidden. The reasons given for going out of the enclosure—"for any useful, reasonable, evi-

[70] JoAnn McNamara treats of early stages of the evolution of this wisdom in difficult circumstances in "The Ordeal of Community: Hagiography and Discipline in Merovingian Convents," *Vox Benedictina* 3 (1986) 293-326.

[71] For some interesting examples of how St. Bernard, for one, directed monastic women tempted by these dangers, see Leclercq, "Does St. Bernard Have a Specific Message for Nuns?" *Distant Echoes,* 269-278.

dent and approved purpose" (RegCl 2: 12)—indicate a great
reliance upon the individual good will and prudence of the
sisters. Clare's *Rule* provides "inner space" for judgement and
discernment rather than subjecting the members, as Hugolino
and Innocent did in their *Rules,* to the destruction of mutual trust
by giving the abbess no latitude for such permission.[72] The
education of the young girls who come to the monastery
combines "a holy way of life" with "proper behavior" (RegCl 2:
19). This proper behavior socialized the aspirants into the group
so as to allow them to contribute to the concord of the monastery.[73]

Clare stipulates that the office is to be read "without singing"
(RegCl 3: 2). One possible interpretation of this directive is that
the monastic cult of the Benedictine and Cluniac traditions
required elaborate preparation for liturgical service.[74] Such
preparation was possible in a monastery in which lay sisters
carried out domestic duties, freeing choir sisters for the education
and rehearsals needed to competently complete the sung office.
In San Damiano, with its equality of members (RegCl 2: 21), the
sung office might become a source of division that would

---

[72] The comparable passages of the two previous *Rules* are: (RegHug 4) "After
they have entered the enclosure of this Order and have assumed the religious
habit, they should never be granted any permission or faculty to leave [this
enclosure], unless perhaps some are transferred to another place to plant or
build up this same Order"; (RegInn 1) "After they have entered the enclosure
of this Order and have been professed, promising to observe this rule, let them
never be granted any permission or faculty to leave this enclosure unless
perhaps some are transferred to another place by the permission of the
general minister of the Order of Friars Minor or the provincial of the province
of that Order in which the monastery is situated....They can at times be
transferred for some even pious and reasonable cause beyond those mentioned above, at least, as a general rule, with the permission of the General."

[73] Herlihy's comments on the social function of youngsters being raised in
households other than their own during this period may be of interest in this
regard. See Herlihy, 155-156.

[74] See Leclercq, Vandenbroucke and Bouyer, "Cluny and Unceasing Prayer,"
106-110.

destroy a fraternal spirit.[75] The liturgy also functions to reinforce and express this mutuality when the chaplain is permitted to celebrate inside the enclosure on the special feasts on which Holy Communion is to be received (RegCl 3: 15). Thus both sick and healthy were joined together more closely for these festive celebrations of Mass. The sermon to be offered by the Minister of the Friars Minor prior to elections also had charity as its goal: "Let him dispose them, through the Word of God, to perfect harmony and the common good in the election that is to be held" (RegCl 4: 3). Even the request for prayers for a deceased sister employs a curious word, but one that may indicate the relationship that for Clare and the sisters did not end with death. She writes: "When a sister of our monastery shall have departed this life, *[migraverit]* however, they should say fifty 'Our Fathers'" (RegCl 3: 7). The use of *migraverit* conveys an image of the sister as one who has "emigrated" to another country or monastery or place. It is almost an echo of the Preface of the Requiem that assures the faithful that "life is changed, not ended." The English translation "shall have departed this life" has unfortunately become a colloquial expression that loses some of the apparent freshness of this Latin verb.

While a more thorough study of the governmental structure of the monastery will be taken up in Chapter Five, suffice it to say at this point that several items indicate a concern for mutual trust as a pre-requisite for charity. Among these would be the stipulation that all be consulted in the matter of contracting debts (RegCl 4: 19), and the use of the weekly chapter to correct problems, organize work and discuss major decisions (RegCl 4: 15-18).

[75] The equality of members that Clare establishes by such prescriptions will be treated in greater detail in the following chapter.

The Language of Love

One of the most basic means by which Clare inspired a sense of mutuality through the *Rule* is the language she employs. Matura has pointed out that Clare herself does not use the term *Rule* and that it occurs neither in the body of the text nor in the Bull of approval. Rather, Clare uses the term *forma* seventeen times in the *Rule* (four in the *Testament)* in the following combinations: *forma professionis* (five times), *forma vitae* (four times), *forma paupertatis* (three times). What is just as worthy of comment is the manner in which Clare uses the possessive form to qualify this term. Often one finds such expressions as *nostrae professionis formam* (the form of *our* profession), *paupertatis nostrae* (*our* poverty), *vitae nostrae* (*our* life). In one of the most poignant departures from the curial *Rules*, she uses this last expression in a manner that signals a world of meaning concealed within the tiny form of the possessive adjective *(noster)*. Hugolino had written: "The hard and austere realities, through which according to the Religion one is led to God and which must necessarily be observed, must be explained to all who wish to enter this Religion and are received, before they actually enter and change their garb, lest ignorance be their excuse later on" (RegHug 4). In describing the same procedure of entrance, Clare loses nothing of the required canonical precision, but ends her opening statement with the words: "Let the tenor of *our life* be thoroughly explained to her" (RegCl 2: 6).[76] The simple addition of "our" to "life" betrays a world of meaning, a love for the form of life so faithfully treasured and advanced. With one small stroke of the quill it separates Clare's

---

[76] See Manselli, "La donna nella vita della chiesa tra duecento e trecento." *MRFU*, 243-255. Of particular interest in regard to Clare's use of the first person in her *Rule* is his observation: "The first consideration, and it deserves to be kept in mind, is the decision of the woman to get out of an economic, juridical, and social situation, which tends to reduce her to the condition of being an object, refusing her every or nearly every possibility of expressing herself as a subject [one who acts, not one who is passive]."

perceptions from Hugolino's far more dramatically than the enclosure walls could ever separate outer perceptions from inner realities.

Finally, Clare, at times, breaks with the sober and restrained language befitting a "legal" document and allows herself the privilege of addressing the sisters directly and in highly personal, emotive terms. In Chapter Eight the opening paragraph of six lines is divided in tone. In the first three sentences she maintains an objective voice by using the subjunctive. "Let the sisters not appropriate anything, neither a house nor a place nor anything at all; instead, as pilgrims and strangers in this world who serve the Lord in poverty and humility, let them confidently send for alms. Nor should they be ashamed, since the Lord made Himself poor in this world for us." (RegCl 8:1-3) Then a sudden break occurs and she changes into a direct appeal using the terms "my dearest sisters," and "my most beloved sisters." This tone resonates with the first-person recollection of the beginnings of life at San Damiano that figures so importantly in Chapter Six. Even there, though, when Clare recalls the foundational experiences of her vocation, she clearly sees herself not as an isolated individual but united to the others in a personal way: "... I, together with my sisters, willingly promised him obedience."

The last word belongs to her choice of designation for the members of her community: *Sorores Pauperes.* Godet discusses the significance of the use of the title "sister":

> "Lesser Brothers" and "Poor Sisters" expresses therefore a program of life which is qualified not only by the following of Christ but also by a certain type of interpersonal relationship. Francis did not call his "companions" "friends," "comrades," "monks," "religious"; he called them "brothers." Clare, choosing from among different possibilities of the same type, called her companions "sisters." This means that for Clare

> as for Francis, the relationship of fraternity is
> fundamental and primary.[77]

While it is true that in one instance Clare uses the preferred canonical term of the time *(monache),* she is consistent in all other cases in employing a term that simultaneously expresses and reinforces the fundamentally relational nature of the form of life that she and her sisters have embraced.[78] In the name by which each is called—"sister"—and in the commonality of "our" enterprise, as well as in the admonitions, policies and Gospel teachings, Clare teaches the theory and the practice of a life of love. This horizontal, mutually caring relationship parallels, if it does not surpass, the concept of fraternity in the chronicles discussed in Chapter Three.

Summary Observations

1. The founding of the Poor Sisters coincides with a period in which women of the nobility were experiencing major dislocations of social power and prestige. The rising power of the merchant class and the reduction of the prerogatives of feudal leaders had notable impact upon the standing of women. It has been posited that this period marks a point at which women became less visible on the stage of historical action and more valued for their domestic, private lives and honor. Women who belonged to the merchant class enjoyed greater social and economic liberty than their counterparts among rural peasants or noble houses. They were, nonetheless, still banished from any role of entitlement in governmental affairs in the communes.

2. Monastic life provided one of the enduring forms of feminine culture from late antiquity into the High Middle Ages.

---

[77] Godet, *Progetto,* 240.
[78] *Soror* appears sixty-eight times in the *Rule.*

Within the monastic enclosure women had access to education, administrative and economic power, and held a respected position in church and society. However, in spite of occasional reform efforts, a class structure dominated female monasteries, allowing for different levels of membership and rights within these communities.

3. Early chronicles and other sources attest to the fact that among the Friars Minor the early decades of the Order's development witnessed a healthy expansion of a fraternal social structure. In spite of the obvious reversals involved in legislative and governmental structures, a basic commitment to an open system which recruited from all levels of society was much in evidence. These same sources offer evidence that this fraternal *milieu* had strong roots in Gospel values, new social institutions, and the personal sanctity of many of the brothers.

4. Clare made mutual charity a focus of her *Rule*. She did this in a way that evokes in feminine terms the twin realities of minority/fraternity and poverty in the thought of Francis. The courage to accept the constraint of material poverty is, in part, born of confidence in this mutual love and service. Individuals and community officials shared the responsibility for this call. Clare made explicit provision for the tensions and inevitable failures that would occur. The *Process* demonstrates that her actions, more than the text of the *Rule* document, carried the force of this teaching into the lives of the sisters.

5. A sisterhood which guaranteed equality combined with sensitive and affectionate regard provided a new possibility of social relationships for the women who comprised it. Freed from the social constraints and traditions of the secular and monastic forms of their day, these Poor Sisters identified in a dramatic and unsettling way with groups of women seeking their own place in a nascent social-ecclesial urban reality.

Chapter Five

CLARE'S DEFINITION OF GOVERNANCE

Medieval Women and the Search for Religious Identity

Introduction

The *Rule of Clare* and her *Testament* speak always of a *"forma vitae,"* a form of life given to the Poor Sisters by Francis. When describing this "form" Clare usually stresses both the essential element of evangelical poverty and the mutual solicitude of the brothers and sisters. Because of the constant return to these themes in her writings (and those of Francis for the Poor Sisters), it would be tempting to conclude that less attractive concerns such as government, correction of members, or rules of enclosure, are somehow "beyond the pale" of concern for those who try to understand the *"forma"* of early Franciscan women. This is far from the truth, however. A religious form of life, no matter how idealistic and spiritual its aspirations, must ultimately find structural expressions for those ideals. As a result, concrete structures of authority and decision-making emerge from the fabric of human communication and commitment to mutual rights and responsibilities. A religious community is not exempt from creating its own "polis" in which its "citizenry" forges the governmental realities that makes its sustenance feasible.[1]

For the religious foundation in the ecclesial tradition, there is not only the inevitable tension between individual aspiration and common good that its internal structures must mediate, but also the tension between the foundation itself and demands of higher ecclesiastical authorities for compliance with general norms. If approval for its way of life is sought from the Holy See, or from the ordinaries of dioceses, a religious institute must take into account, at some stage in its development, the necessity of adherence to canonical norms.[2] In view of these two levels of need, how did Clare develop the structures of her community? What evangelical principles are evident in the choices she proposed and which she and her sisters obviously endorsed? The answers can once again be viewed as a third "triptych," this time with the images of governance as the theme. What historical influences were at work in shaping the authority structures which Clare included in her *Rule*? What specifics of Church legislation was she required to incorporate? How were these

---

[1] Lozano, *Discipleship,* 221-223.

[2] It is interesting to examine the line of argumentation used by Hugolino in providing the Benedictine Rule for the Poor Sisters: "Every true Religion and approved institute of life endures by certain rules and requirements, and by certain disciplinary laws. Unless each sister has diligently striven to observe a certain correct rule and discipline for living, she will deviate from righteousness to the degree that she does not observe the guidelines of righteousness" (2). And again: "So that the order of your life, firmly built and established on Christ after the manner of and in imitation of those who have served the Lord without complaint and have crowned the beginning of their blessed and holy way of life with the most blessed conclusion of perseverance, may be able to grow into a holy temple in the Lord and by following the footsteps of the saints may be able to reach the reward of such a high vocation directly and happily, we give you the *Rule of Saint Benedict* to be observed in all things which are in no way contrary to that same *Form of Life* that was given to you by us and by which you have especially chosen to live. This *Rule of Saint Benedict* is known to embody the perfection of virtue and the greatest discretion. It has been devoutly accepted from the very beginning by the holy Fathers and venerably approved by the Roman Church"(3). Armstrong, *Clare,* 88-89.

same concerns understood by the Friars Minor? In this chapter, however, the approach to this second "panel" of the triptych will differ somewhat. In previous chapters it has been asked how the Friars in their own experience responded to the crises affecting poverty and the continuing need to witness to divine love among themselves. In this chapter the question addressed is how the Friars were drawn into the controversies concerning the governance and supervision of the Poor Sisters. This shift in perspective is dictated by the Friars' perception of their **legal** bond with the Poor Sisters and a more intimate connection perceived in the norms articulated by Clare.

Monastic Developments before the Thirteenth Century

In his article entitled "Incarcerate e recluse in Umbria," Mario Sensi writes: "The vocation of Clare of Assisi occurred between two antithetical moments: the monasticism of the Benedictine Order and the urban reclusion of the penitential movement already in motion. And the movement of the Poor Lardies, guided by Clare, represented an overcoming and a synthesis of these moments: the traditional monasticism and the new style of semi-religious life that was the *bizzocaggio*."[3] In order to understand this assessment of Clare's achievement, it is necessary to trace, however briefly, the monastic developments passed on to her when she set out upon the path that led from the Portiuncula to San Damiano.[4]

[3] Sensi, *MRFU*, 93-94.

[4] The material that follows is indebted to Jacques Leclercq, "Il monachesimo femminile nei secoli XII e XIII." *MRFF*, 61-99; Edith Pásztor, "I papi del Duecento e Trecento di fronte all vita religiosa femminile," *MRFF*, 29-65; Raoul Manselli, "La chiesa e il francescanesimo femminile," *MRFF*, 239-261; Jane Tibbets Schulenberg, "Strict Active Enclosure and its Effects on the Female Monastic Experience (500-1100)." *Distant Echoes*, 51-86; Mary Skinner. "Benedictine Life for Women in Central France, 850-1100: A Feminist Revival." *Distant Echoes*, 87-113; Sally Thompson, "The Problem of the Cistercian nuns in the twelfth and early thirteenth centuries," *Medieval Women*, 227-251; Brenda

From the beginnings of the Church's emergence in the West, monastic life for both men and women had been part of its presence in the world. Early female monastics could base their lives upon rules emanating from such luminaries as Jerome, Augustine, Cassian, Columba, Caesar of Arles.[5] The *Rule of Benedict* was not the sole option, even though it is often treated as if it were synonymous with the monastic vocation. It did, however, become the preferred form in the seventh and eighth centuries. Places of asceticism and contemplative flight from the world, these monasteries often served also as centers for education of the young and made a considerable contribution to evangelization.

The growth and spread of monasteries in the Merovingian and Carolingian dynasties resulted in three basic forms of monastic structures: 1) independent monasteries, 2) "double" monasteries in which bicameral houses were under a single authority, and 3) twin monasteries situated in geographic proximity, but lacking any legal dependence of one upon the other. Many of these monasteries were created and supported by noble families as extensions of family social responsibility for women who for some reason would not or could not marry. In an era of frequent, violent invasions, a protected environment for women who were unmarried or widowed was highly desirable. Additionally, the family, having decided the number and nature of marriages possible without prejudice to its property, found in these monastic households an honorable means of settling the women thus relegated to celibacy. The forms for religious life of this era were not monolithic. There were nuns, in the strict sense of the term, who lived as the monks did, with a religious rule. There were canonesses who lived a common life but retained

Bolton, "Mulieres Sanctae," 141-158; Adriana Valerio, "La donna nella 'societas christiana' dei secoli X-XII," *Rassegna di teologia* 3 (1983) 435-446; David Flood, "Cardinal Hugolino on Legation," *Haversack* 11 (December, 1987) 3-9, 24, and "Sisters Minor" 10-16.
    [5] The basic features of the historical outline that follows can be traced in Leclercq's article cited in the preceeding note.

ownership of their own patrimony. There were also recluses who lived alone in a cloistered cell or hermitage near an existing chapel or monastery.[6] The monasteries that did exist were relatively few in number and were comprised of twenty to thirty members.

The astonishing proliferation of monastic foundations for women that marks the twelfth century has been the subject of numerous studies.[7] Leclercq credits three factors with providing the environment for this growth: the stabilization of monastic observance, the liberalization of monastic recruitment and the diversification of institutional types. The stabilization of observance that preceded the foundation of these new orders might be best symbolized in the foundation of the monastery of Marcigny in 1061 with the authority of the abbot and customs of Cluny as its base. This provided a model of the "new" monastery in which free choice of the religious vocation was sought (rather than an imposed "family choice") and strict claustration imposed.

Perhaps the most famous "new" form of monastic life is the foundation of Fontevrault by Robert of Arbrissel in 1100. The women recruited for this foundation were those who had joined themselves to Arbrissel in response to his preaching. Their number included virgins, widows, and converted prostitutes. The male monastery connected to the female monastery was clearly ordered to the service of the women but the structures were designed to protect both the chastity and poverty of the nuns.[8] No less worthy of comment are the adaptations of the

[6] Leclercq, 65-66.

[7] This phenomenon must also be seen in light of the general awakening of a more scriptural and historicized spirituality. See, for example, M.-D. Chenu, O.P. *Nature, Man and Society in the Twelfth Century,* ed., trans. Jerome Taylor and Lester K. Little (Chicago: The University of Chicago Press, 1968). See, in particular, chapters 5 and 7.

[8] See Gold, *Distant Echoes,* 162: "These institutional arrangements enabled Fontevrault to survive the period of monastic retrenchment that occurred at the end of the twelfth and the beginning of the thirteenth century, and to escape the knife of necessity or convenience that severed women from many monastic communities. The woman-centeredness of Fontevrault was not

Benedictine usages introduced by Abelard in his rule for Heloise
and her nuns. The superior of the Monastery of the Paraclete
was known as a "deaconess." A program of study, much
indebted to Jerome, was laid down. Affiliated with the monastery
were "conversi"[9] to perform heavy manual labor, and chaplains
were available from a neighboring monastery. The general
supervision of the abbot was not intended as a dominative
power over the nuns. In England, the Gilbertines combined a
monastery of canons regular under the Augustinian rule with
the nuns who followed the Benedictine rule.[10] Another
foundation that numbered over one thousand members by the
middle of the century was the Premonstratensian Order, founded
by Norbert of Xanten. Founded at first as double monasteries,
practical difficulties forced a separation in 1137. By 1198 the
general chapter of the Order had ruled against further acceptance of groups of women, but such foundations did not cease
to develop. The growth of houses of women associated with the
Cistercian reform was also a feature of twelfth century monasticism. The first instance is that of the monastery of Jully which
housed the wives of the first companions of Bernard of
Clairveaux, and for which statutes developed between 1115
and 1132.[11] However, the Cistercians were most reluctant to
acknowledge the presence, let alone the claim for spiritual care,
of many of these foundations. It was not until the thirteenth

unique, but its firm institutional expression was, and this made it impossible
to view the nuns at Fontevrault as burdensome, unimportant, or peripheral."
Also, Jacqueline Smith, "Robert of Arbrissel: *Procurator Mulierum*," *Medieval
Women*, 175-184.

[9] See Pazzelli, 37-40; the sense meant here is that of "oblates" who served
God by "placing themselves at the disposal of" the monastery and its members
(38).

[10] Sharon K. Elkins, "All Ages, Every Condition and Both Sexes: The
Emergence of a Gilbertine Identity." *Distant Echoes*, 169-182.

[11] Leclercq, 67-73.

century that their general legislation indicates some attempt to cope with the phenomenon on the part of the monks.[12]

The Rise of Urban Religious Forms

While modern readers can experience some wonderment at the variety and apparent vitality of these foundations, it is clear that they did not succeed in creating a permanent response to the religious aspirations of women. This is not a consequence of a lack of zeal and pastoral initiative on the part of the great itinerant preachers of this century; rather, it is due to the changing sociological contours of society and of masculine forms of religious life. With the rise of the communes, of urban life with its forms of association for trade and government, and with the coming of the friars, "new wineskins" were sought by religious women as well, but the thirteenth century provided insufficient official opportunities to channel this evangelical energy. Brenda Bolton describes the situation:

> Women who had thus been catered for errati-
> cally in the twelfth century moved by 1200 into
> a different situation. They began to demand
> recognition of their real and separate identity.
> The question of their status in religion could no
> longer be answered solely by placing them in
> houses attached to the male orders, often as
> unwanted appendages. As enthusiastic women

[12] Thompson, *Medieval Women:* 242: "The gradual acceptance of nuns as members of the Cistercian order in the course of the thirteenth century, is reflected in the development in the codifications of the statutes of the general assembly. It was probably only during the years 1221-40 that the decrees concerning nuns were collected under a separate heading. Before this, edicts concerning religious ladies were placed under the title of *de capitulis quae non habet propriam distinctiones*—a heading which in itself suggests their relative lack of significance."

[13] Bolton, "Mulieres Sanctae," 143-144.

began to share the aspirations of the Friars and
like-minded religious groups, the logical out-
come ought to have been the creation of a
separate female order. Instead in 1215, the Fourth
Lateran Council issued a decree which epito-
mized the contest between those who would
have allowed new forms of religious life within
the church and those who supported the forces
of tradition and reaction.[13]

Mario Sensi, concentrating his attention on the Italian
manifestations of this phenomenon, characterizes the new
wave of feminine piety as flowing from the penitential movement and, using principally Franciscan sources, finds three
expressions of life-style emerging in the early thirteenth century:
cenobitic life with moderate cloister; urban or suburban
eremetical life; the *"bizzoche"*[14] who lived "in their own homes."[15]

There is no common agreement as yet on the origins of this
beguine/*bizzoche* movement and much study remains to sort
out the variety of models and titles used in various sources and
archives which testify to its existence. Dennis Devlin offers a
concise summary of four stages of development of the beguine
movement which extended over two centuries and which had
its best known manifestations in Belgium, Germany, southern
France and—with variations in form—Italy. Early beguines,
women inspired by new popular religious fervor of the twelfth
and thirteenth centuries, were regulated by neither vows nor

[14] The terminology used to designate these women who were the Italian
counterparts of the beguines is diverse. Sensi observes: (*MRFU*, note 85, 114-
115) "...on the feminine side: *beghine, bizzoche, incluse, recluse, incarcerate,
encarcerate, cellane, murate, evangeliche* are a few of the names which
served in the same penitential movement to indicate a multiplicity of experiences of secular eremetism, i.e., not stemming from a monastic background,
and without any official link with the "Order of Penitents" or with the
mendicant orders or in general with the monastic orders."
[15] Sensi, *MRFU*, 89. Origninal phrase is "in domibus propriis."

rule. They did not renounce marriage permanently. They usually lived in their own homes or in the houses of friends or relatives and supported themselves by manual labor, often in the cloth industry. By early in the thirteenth century, these women had coalesced into informal associations, usually finding spiritual guidance from monks or clerics sympathetic to their aspirations. Since beguines lived without formal rules, and allowed great freedom for each house to regulate its own devotional life, patrons such as the Cistercians and Jacques de Vitry protected them from civil and/or ecclesial interference. In 1233, Gregory IX granted an indirect recognition to these women in the bull *Gloriam virginalem,* which "was interpreted as sympathetic to the notion of beguine 'convents' or communal houses, and acted to spur their development."[16] Increasingly, as time passed, the women came under clerical control and supervision. Finally, beguine houses were officially grouped into parishes and given legal and civil recognition. They were also subjected to clear authority structures, most often under the Dominicans, losing most of their autonomy.[17]

As mentioned in Chapter Three, Sensi observes that various bishops were taken by surprise by the beguine phenomenon as it made its appearance on the Italian peninsula, and that the mendicants might be seen as the first group in a position to provide some form of pastoral response to them. At first (indeed at the last as well) the friars of both Dominic and Francis were most reluctant to accept any but the most limited association with such communities. Ultimately, in the *Later Rule* Francis forbade the reception of any women by the friars and made clear in the words preserved in Clare's *Rule* that it was for Clare and her monastery only that he pledged both material and spiritual support.[18] While there is no need to interpret the desire

---

[16] Fiona Bowie, ed., *Beguine Spirituality* (New York: Crossroads, 1990), 18.

[17] Dennis Devlin. "Feminine Lay Piety in the High Middle Ages: The Beguines." *Distant Echoes,* 183-196.

[18] RegNB 12, 13 and RegB 11. Comparable warnings were contained in the rules of other evangelical fraternities. See, for example, the citations from the *propositum* of Bernard Primus quoted in Lapsanski, 44-46.

to limit legal dependency as a declaration of disinterest or disregard (in fact, the sources assure us of Francis' contrary intentions[19]), it appears that Francis did not involve himself to a large degree with the governmental questions of San Damiano. A marked contrast can be seen in the efforts by which Jacques de Vitry publicized the life of Marie d'Oignies, for example, and sought some form of papal recognition of the beguines of Flanders.[20] That de Vitry saw parallels between the beguines of Flanders and the "sisters minor" whose lives he observed with such consolation in Umbria is evident from his correspondence. Yet, de Vitry and others who shared his enthusiasm for these *mulieres sanctae* did not succeed in creating a stable form of life with the kind of ecclesiastical support and cooperation that would have made the beguines a recognized order in the Church. In light of this, how did Clare and her sisters, living in the same period and faced with comparable difficulties, become an Order with its own *Rule*?[21]

First, there was Canon 13 of Lateran IV with its prohibition of new orders, which created an immense obstacle to dealing liberally with these small communities. Evidence that both Clare and Francis recognized the canonical precariousness of her position is found in the sequence of events that seem to have taken place as the council concluded. First of all, Clare obtained from Innocent himself the *Privilege of Poverty*.[22] This unusual permission appears to parallel his action in 1209 or 1210 in granting oral approval of Francis' establishment of the friars and giving them the right to preach. Clare also accepted the title of

---

[19] 2 Cel 205.

[20] Brenda Bolton. "*Vitae matrum*: a further aspect of the Frauenfrage." *Medieval Women*, 253-273. See also Jacques de Vitry. *De Maria Oigniacensi in Namurcensi Belgii Diocesi*, ed. D. P[apebroec] in *Acta Sanctorum*, Junii 5 (Paris, 1867)[June 23], 542-572. An English draft translation of this important work has recently been published by Peregrina Publishing Co., Saskatchewan, Canada, 1986. Trans. Margot King.

[21] Bolton, "Mulieres Sanctae," 49-150.

[22] Armstrong , *Clare*, 83-84.

abbess at this time, because of Francis' request (LegCl 12; Proc I: 6). Was this an action designed to forestall criticism that her community lacked the proper characteristics of one of the approved orders? It is one possible interpretation. In any event, Bolton asserts the uniqueness of Innocent's cooperation with Clare:

> It seemed that Innocent has, therefore, helped her to create an entirely new form of convent community, which maintained itself on alms and the profits of manual labor in the same way as the Franciscans....Is it possible that Innocent III's intervention on behalf of the Poor Clares might have led to the creation of a separate female order? A separate order for women would have horrified most medieval ecclesiastics. For this reason Clare represented a potential revolution within the church.[23]

Two years later Cardinal Hugolino dei Conti di Segni became the papal legate to Lombardy, Tuscany and Umbria.[24] When he rode into the territory of his charge he entered as well into the existing vacuum in episcopal policy and clerical pastoral care for the numerous groups of women wishing to participate in the evangelical poverty and penitential movements. The letter he received from Honorius III instructing him to proceed with his proposal for dealing with these groups is most instructive. Its central points include a description of the groups Hugolino encountered: "Very many virgins and other women desire to flee the pomp and wealth of this world and make some homes for themselves in which they may live not possessing anything under heaven except these homes and the oratories to be

---

[23] Bolton, "Mulieres Sanctae," 149.
[24] Armstrong, *Clare*, 85.

constructed for them."[25] Honorius continued with a description of the response of the faithful who wish to donate property to such groups of women, but who wish such property to be exempt from local episcopal control. He then confirmed the plan to provide houses under the control of the Holy See: "We command you through the authority of this letter to receive, legally as property, the foundations of this kind in the name of the Church of Rome and to ordain that the churches built in these places be solely under the jurisdiction of the Apostolic See."[26]

Sensi believes that this letter shows that Hugolino was trying to find a way to both honor the aspirations of noble families for the institution and preservation of these new monasteries and observe the regulations of the Lateran Council. Armed with this permission he proceeded to institute his program.[27] These monasteries were asked to accept an existing rule, in which case they remained under local episcopal jurisdiction. The other option was to accept special constitutions, or a "rule," written by him, that transformed the flight from the world into strict and perpetual cloister, but which permitted exemption from local bishops in favor of submission to the Holy See.[28] Hugolino in

[25] Armstrong, *Clare*, 85-86, "The Letter of Pope Honorius III to Cardinal Hugolino (1217)."

[26] Armstrong, *Clare*, 86.

[27] Sensi, *MRFU*, 93-100.

[28] In analyzing the intent and effect of this measure, Flood writes: "Honorius placed the properties of the holy women in the center of attention. He explained how land had been offered with the reservation that the benefactors retain a say about the communities. Therein lay a hindrance to the women's laudable desire. It forecast entanglements detrimental to the church's liberty. Having stated the case, Honorius proceeded to its resolution. He authorized his legate to take the lands as property of the roman church....As a result no authority, ecclesiastical or secular, would be able to exercise any right over them. But the women remained without possessions and without those revenues—tithes or burial taxes — which accrue to the prelates of local churches....Hugolino did not open a discussion on new forms of religious life while carrying out his duties as legate....Hugolino did his best to secure the

this way proposed to create a stable climate in which these communities could grow and prosper. Later, as pope, he would add the insistence upon fixed income. This change required Clare to ask again for a confirmation of the *Privilege of Poverty* which she obtained in 1228.[29] Sensi observes:

> The policy pursued by Cardinal Hugolino to-
> gether with whole Roman curia, and then per-
> sonally guided by Hugolino as Pope resulted in
> a remarkable fact: in the space of a few years the
> women's penitential movement of central Italy
> was placed completely under control. The
> majority of the new foundations, the result of
> the movement then in progress, were institu-
> tionalized with the Hugoline form of life. This
> explains the attraction of so many foundations
> linked to Clare during those years; and this
> places a new perspective on the problem of
> how many monasteries were formed by the
> community of San Damiano and as is said,
> therefore received their formation directly from
> St. Clare or her first companions.[30]

This, then, was the environment in which Clare acted, re-acted, lived out her promise of obedience to Francis. The possibility of maintaining allegiance to the goal of strict poverty

church liberties and advantages against the emerging institutions of the commune. He drew the church back out of the influence of forces organizing a new communal order into the feudal structure of the church. He drew the women out of the sphere where new liberties had been achievable into the feudal sphere of monasticism."

[29] Armstrong, *Clare,* 103-104.

[30] Sensi, *MRFU,* 98. He also claims that Gregory IX was "inflexible" about a religious house in Spoleto, what he calls a "*bizzocale*community wrongly held to be Benedictine" which was suppressed in 1235 when it apparently refused some form of episcopal control Gregory favored. *MRFU,* 100.

was achieved by overcoming almost insuperable difficulties. The general form of life insisted upon by Hugolino required acceptance of a strict claustration, a form that while it had a history in monastic practice, was not the only measure of enclosure documented prior to the thirteenth century.[31] In addition, by accepting Benedictine usage as a base, Clare was able to draw upon that tradition in the development of the internal structures of her monastery even as she struggled to maintain the essential features of the Franciscan project.[32]

Since Clare, unlike Francis, was legislating for a stable monastic community, she could draw upon a tradition of law and custom that brought certain strengths to her *propositum* even though it also had the potential to submerge it in the problems that Leclercq regards as "constant" in monastic history,[33] some of which have already been cited. The appeal the community

[31] Schulenberg, SAE, offers the following conclusions to her study of restrictive enclosure as a reform measure (78-79): The autonomy of nuns' communities suffered since "the ideology of enclosure was a basic assumption of the inability of the abbess and her community to order their lives." Loss in public influence and visibility, especially for abbesses, followed with new emphasis on her private role within the enclosure. Female monastic education suffered. Finally, Schulenberg notes the shifting rationale in the ecclesiastical legislation on this point. In its earliest expressions, enclosure was a protective measure for external defense. In the era of carolingian reforms, however, it became a means to remedy abuses and was advanced by mysoginist views "which one finds especially during periods of reform." Finally, it resulted that "nuns no longer had a choice between a strict, cloistered life and a more flexible cloister; whether they followed the Benedictine Rule or canonical regulations, all female religious were placed under strict enclosure."

[32] Thus writes Godet: "It is obvious that from the moment she accepted a determined *Rule* (notably that of St. Benedict) that was closest to her ideal but not completely satisfactory, Clare was constrained to accept the inevitable consequences, for example, the title of Abbess, and even more importantly, the example of not having community property. While Clare accepted the *Rule of St. Benedict* forced by circumstances, she asked the Pope without any delay for a special exemption from the common law to go alongside the Benedictine Rule."

[33] Leclercq, 79-83.

held for women of the nobility would invite problems not unlike those created by the practice of recruitment limited to upper classes in previous eras. The familial monasteries had fulfilled a social and political function for the aristocracy. They also had made the Gospel ideal difficult to attain since members of lower social classes in secular life remained in lower classes of membership within the monastery as well. In spite of attempts by reformers to correct such conditions, the natural tendency for the monastery to reflect prevailing social mores seemed pervasive. In terms of governance, the imposition of a superior chosen for administrative ability or sympathy to the family's political or military aims often created abuses and weakened religious spirit. The use of the monastery as a refuge for handicapped and unwanted family members also led to excesses of the kind that invariably resulted in advocating more severe forms of enclosure for women. Leclercq, however, maintains that a lack of genuine vocations in these institutions cannot necessarily be presumed, and that there is much evidence that good programs of religious life were faithfully followed.

Nevertheless, the lack of personal choice that was fundamental in the lives of many medieval nuns did lead to abuses and laxity.[34] These scandals generated reforms that evolved over the centuries into a program of more or less severe claustration. While the forms of enclosure advocated in earlier centuries differed from region to region and synod to synod, the development of a standard of strict enclosure at Marcigny signalled a new uniformity in approach. Particular material forms of claustration involving walls, grates for confession and parlor visits, distribution of keys for doors, and so on, evolved. At the same time documentation defended this practice with appeals to the fragility of the female nature.[35] These arguments often

[34] Leclercq, 83-87.
[35] Of particular interest on this point are E. Pasztor's comments in *MRFU*, 55-65, in which she describes the contrast between papal letters describing this "fragility" and the many women if this period living without the cloister but giving evidence of heroic forms of self-denial and service.

cloaked a fear of contact with consecrated women engendered as a subtle part of the Gregorian Reform's insistence upon clerical celibacy. Attempts to maintain a strict and uniform code of enclosure met with more or less success during the thirteenth century and culminated in the famous bull *Periculoso* issued in 1298 by Boniface VIII.[36]

The requirements of strict enclosure brought other consequences, unforeseen, perhaps, but important in their impact upon the practice of poverty. The strict regulations that made egress from the monastery impossible required the creation of extern sisters; even monasteries that otherwise would have promoted true equality of members were forced to admit members having two distinct roles that gradually involved distinct formation and life-style.[37] The same conditions required some dependence upon male communities for chaplains or procurators, with the usual result that autonomy and the ability to conduct the business of one's institution were often sacrificed by women to male counterparts out of necessity. Finally, repetitious warnings, sermons, and treatises dealing with women's ontological insufficiency and psychological instability left upon Christian theology and ecclesial praxis a mark that has overshadowed many of the achievements of the Catholic tradition regarding the dignity of woman. The deleterious effects of this are with us still.[38]

---

[36] *Sextus liber Decretalium*, 1. II, tit. XI, cap. un., ed. A Friedberg, *Corpus Iuris Canonici*, II, Leipzig 1922, 1053-1054.

[37] Iriarte, *Regola*, 183-187.

[38] Leclercq gives ample consideration to this last problem, demonstrating through the writings of Idung of Prufening, for example, the path by which views drawn in part from Greco-Roman philosophy, in part from the Fathers—particularly Jerome—found their way into the mainstream of theological consciousness in the Middle Ages (95-99). It is this pervasive and deeply rooted bias that is at issue in much of the literature on the current tensions over women's role in the Church and its ministries.

The Friars and Government

As illustrated in the preceding material, Clare was surrounded by various models of religious life that were simultaneously creating and expressing the evangelical ferment of her era. The thought, often expressed in the past, that she would naturally turn to a traditional monastic form because it was the only accepted form is not quite accurate. There were, in fact, in her immediate vicinity and in neighboring countries as well, several new attempts to create alternative religious life-styles for women. However, following the Lateran Council, papal policy increasingly advocated a return to a traditional monastic "form" with the additional requirement of strict material enclosure. The authority exercised in such monasteries would be of a hierarchical mode. At the same time, it would be authority always subject to some form of external control, whether that of the diocesan bishop or of a neighboring abbot or a visitator. In the case of the mendicant orders, for example, Innocent IV diligently attempted to create such dependency of the female houses upon the superiors of the masculine Order.[39]

Clare faced a considerable challenge in her desire to create a form of authority that would express the evangelical values Francis had insisted upon in his *Rule and Life*. When Clare looked to the Friars Minor for examples which would help to incarnate Francis' teaching on authority and obedience, what would she have been likely to see? She would have seen friars engaged in a parallel, yet very different, struggle to acquire adequate internal mechanisms by which to govern themselves and to deal with external offices in the church. She would have witnessed a series of initiatives which came from within the Order itself, from the ministers who succeeded Francis in office, from the cardinal protectors and the popes.

[39] Grundmann, 229-253.

The Friars' Search for Governmental Forms[40]

In trying to trace the first generations' response to the need for adequate internal machinery for the governance of the Order, it is important to consider that vast differences existed between the friars and the Poor Sisters in this regard. The friars were, after all, a single entity numbering thousands of members whose preaching missions were taking them far from their Umbrian cradle. They were uniquely constituted in having a single minister general with a direct authority over the members and the provinces. The very mobility of their situation meant that dealing with conflicts and policy matters would be diffused over a range of diverse structures and personal relationships. On the other hand, the Poor Sisters lived in individual monasteries in which a stable membership and an enclosed *modus vivendi* rendered clear forms of policy-making and governing relationships imperative. The very nature of the small, autonomous and practically unchanging membership group would have created internal pressures to face concerns which might not have had such urgency for the friars. A second aspect of this difference is that the very stability of the group in a monastic setting allows the service of authority to be refined in a comprehensive and consistent way, provided that officials and members desire such continuing conversion of forms and practices for the sake of authentic living. Such appears to have been the case for Clare and her sisters.

[40] Studies that deal with the internal development in the early decades of the Order include: Rosalind B. Brooke. *Early Franciscan Government: Elias to Bonaventure* (Cambridge: University Press, 1959); Justin Der, O.F.M. Cap. *The Capuchin Lay Brother: A Juridical-Historical Study,* diss. (Roma: Pontificia Studiorum Universitas a S. Thoma Aq. in Urbe, 1983); Lazaro Iriarte, O.F.M. Cap. *Franciscan History. The Three Orders of St. Francis of Assisi,* trans. Patricia Ross (Chicago: Franciscan Herald Press, 1983); John Moorman. *A History of the Franciscan Order from its Origins to the Year 1517* (Oxford: Clarendon Press, 1968) (See especially Part II, 83-122); Duncan Nimmo, *Reform and Division in the Medieval Franciscan Order* (Rome: Capuchin Historical Institute, 1986).

If the Friars were faced with significant organizational problems due to size and mobility, they had yet another set of difficulties to contend with in virtue of some of the problems created by Francis' characteristic ways of facing—or not facing—internal organizational demands. Duncan Nimmo speaks of his "blindness to organization."[41] Rosalind Brooke, in an even more sober estimate, asserts: "St. Francis had never really answered the problem of running an Order. His way was to put someone else, first Peter Catanii and then Elias, in charge of such things and rebuke him if he worried about it."[42] Given the fact that Francis did not leave a defined organizational structure as part of his legacy to the Order, those who had to supply such structures were faced with certain polarizing issues. Nimmo holds that the ensuing struggle resulted from three factors. First, the Order was divided by the problem of interpreting how best to preserve the true vocation of the friar. Was it in priestly service that required considerable education and ecclesiastical preferments or in humble evangelization by the example of a poor Gospel life? Secondly, there was the constant tension of reforming impulses calling for a return to the primitive experience of the Order. But how could that be done with so large a membership? Thirdly, there was the reality that the Order was, as is any institution, a political entity that had to define a way to reconcile ideological conflict—both internal and external.[43] In consequence, hermeneutical, theological and sociological factors combined in the early struggle.

It is imperative, however, to examine these difficulties, and their results, in concrete aspects. It seems the most direct route would be that already traced by Brooke in her study, *Early*

---

[41] Nimmo, 38.
[42] Brooke, *Government,* 283.
[43] Nimmo, 9-11.

Franciscan Government.[44] As she examines the manner in which the early ministers of the Order formed and reformed its physiognomy she offers many valuable indications of the governing style, Franciscan qualities, and institutional contributions or errors of the men who were Clare's contemporaries in the office of "minister and servant." Briefly recalling her synthesis, augmented at times by insights of other scholars, one can capture something of the environment in which Clare was developing her own form of service as an abbess who habitually called herself "the servant of the Poor Sisters."

Following the term Elias served after the death of Francis, John Parenti became the first elected minister general, serving from 1227 until 1232. It is Brooke's contention that his was an aristocratic rather than a democratic style. Parenti's agreement in seeking papal interpretation of troublesome points in the *Rule* led to the promulgation of *Quo elongati.* This was followed in 1231 by *Nimis iniqua,* which further exempted the friars from episcopal regulations regarding "the form of service they adopted, in administering the sacrament and in deciding how best to use donations from the faithful."[45] This began the process of a shared authority and power base in which internal governors gave up some prerogatives to the Roman curia.

The list of charges traditionally placed at Elias' door do not need lengthy elaboration. The most common allegations are his highly centralized and autocratic modes of exercising power, his use of lay brothers to conduct visitation, his failure to convoke a Chapter, and—most especially—his taxation of the provinces for construction of St. Francis' basilica, which gained him bitter enmity during his tenure from 1232 to 1239. Brooke holds that while Elias' personal weakness and procedural errors

[44] Brooke's study emphasizes the contributions of Haymo of Faversham. She demonstrates that much of the credit usually given to Bonaventure for stabilizing the Order should more justly be shared with Haymo. Iriarte is also of this opinion in *Franciscan History* (35, 41). The following analysis is drawn principally from Brooke's work.

[45] Iriarte, *History,* 33.

were considerable, the reaction against him was rooted in more subtle problems. Both by his refusal to follow the desires of the "enlightened ministers" and to give more power to the clerics within the Order, Elias maintained a middle course which avoided those progressive tendencies that resulted in the search for papal privileges and dispensations. When Elias fell from grace in the Order, the reaction to his independent style and authoritarian ways gave rise to a constitutional process that culminated in 1260 in the Constitutions of Narbonne.

Albert of Pisa, in his brief term (1239-1240), initiated this process. His lengthy experience in positions of leadership served him well; he confirmed the supremacy of the general chapter and replaced Elias' system of appointed officials with one of elected offices. It fell to his successor, Haymo of Faversham (1240-1244) to continue this development. Haymo began using a constitutional method to supplement the *Rule*; it was in his administration that the call for commentaries on doubtful points resulted in the *Exposition of the Four Masters*. He placed limitations upon the authority of provincials and custodians. His most drastic and far-reaching policy was the exclusion of lay brothers from office. This determination placed a new clerical and hierarchical stamp upon the exercise of authority within the Order. It is agreed that he was influenced by Dominican methods of organization.

With the election of Crescentius of Jesi in 1244, the trend towards seeking "relaxing" dispensations grew stronger. He appears to have sought the permission of *Ordinem vestrum*, and he persecuted the *zelanti* for their continued opposition to the perceived needs for progress. On the other hand, he called for the gathering of materials from the early companions of Francis; this resulted in the biographical materials upon which Franciscan historians and writers rely. This "gathering process" encouraged formation of a body of literature recalling Francis' insistence upon poverty and fraternity at the exact time when the government of the Order was allowing serious deviations from literal poverty to become legal options.

With Crescentius' deposition in 1247, John of Parma came to the office and remained for ten years. Iriarte characterizes his term as a happy "return to the past." John's style was, indeed, very evocative of Francis himself. He devoted himself to personal visitations, as well as to fidelity to poverty in both his personal life and in the policies he encouraged. He fostered a more united spirit by equalizing the number of chapters held in Italy and in Ultramontane provinces. He led the Order in seeking revocation of the privileges of *Ordinem vestrum* and *Quanto studiosus.* He relied more on these means than on continuing a constitutional approach. A man of very different character and vision, he, like Elias, fell because he incurred the displeasure of those in the "progressive party" who found in his avowed Joachimism[46] a way topple him and bring the Order back to the path in which the predominant tendencies toward relaxation would again be in the ascendancy. John's generalate ended with his exile in 1257, following his nomination of Bonaventure as successor.

Clare's Experience of these Events

Between 1226 and 1253, Clare must have viewed with some interest this succession of five Ministers General in the Order of Friars Minor. The opening chapter of her *Rule* presents with great clarity her interpretation of the original promise of obedience she had made to Francis in 1212:

> Clare, the unworthy servant of Christ and the little plant of the most blessed Francis, promises obedience and reverence to the Lord Pope Innocent and his canonically elected successors, and to the Roman Church. And, just as at the beginning of her conversion, together with

---

[46] See Iriarte, *History,* 51-52; Marjorie Reeves, *Joachim of Fiore and the Prophetic Future* (New York: Harper Torchbooks, 1977). "Joachimism" refers to the eschatological theories of Joachim of Fiore which were judged heretical.

> her sisters she promised obedience to the Blessed
> Francis, so now she promises his successors to
> observe the same obedience inviolably. And
> the other sisters shall always be obliged to obey
> the successors of Blessed Francis and Sister
> Clare and the other canonically elected Ab-
> besses who succeed her (RegCl 1:1-5).

In virtue of this promise, Clare had bound herself to the five ministers who had been the successors of Francis in her lifetime. It is worth noting that the sources preserve almost nothing of how this relationship was concretely experienced. Only the reference to Elias in her letter to Agnes of Prague and the letter of her sister Agnes to her[47] give any clues. On the other hand, there remain several other references to visits and correspondence with the hierarchy.[48] From some of the details of life at San Damiano, it is also possible to deduce some of the matters that required consultation with the leaders of the friars. There was the matter of assigning chaplains and lay brothers.[49] There was the service of carrying letters to distant monasteries. There was the necessity of harmonizing liturgical practices.[50] And, while there is no record of it, it is difficult to imagine that the promulgation of the *Rule of Innocent IV* did not occasion some serious discussions between Clare and the leaders of the Friars Minor.

She had witnessed, even from afar, the traumatic events of Elias' deposition. As mentioned above, she no doubt followed the various efforts of the generals regarding poverty with great concern. It is difficult to ascertain how she would have viewed the constitutional development that spanned the years from 1239 until her death. When the content of many of the directives

[47] 2LAg 15-16; LAgA 6.
[48] See, for example, LHug, LRay, Proc III: 14, LegCl 14, 27, 37, 47; Armstrong, *Clare*, 99-100.
[49] RegCl 5: 1-7.
[50] RegInn 2, 6, 12.

emanating from the ministers general during that period are examined, it is possible to identify parallel elements that recur in her *Rule*. Given what is known of Clare's personality and dispositions, it is not difficult to imagine that some of the dangers to her project of evangelical life which had arisen in the term of Crescentius made the appearance of a man of John of Parma's stature seem like a breath of new hopefulness. Surely, if he did not actively advise her to begin the composition of her own *Rule*, his example emboldened her to express again the conviction of how authority is called to protect and promote the charism. "By word and example" was a refrain both of Francis and of the reformers of the High Middle Ages. Clare had seen many examples of authority exercised for weal and for woe among the friars before she wrote her own words to define what evangelical governance must be among the Poor Sisters.

Clare's Definition of Governance

The Bull of Canonization summarized the gifts of Clare that pertain to her responsibility as abbess of the Poor Sisters of San Damiano.

> This woman, the first of the poor, the leader of the humble, the teacher of the continent, the abbess of the penitents, governed her monastery and the family entrusted to her within it with solicitude and prudence, in the fear and service of the Lord, with full observance of the Order: vigilant in care, eager in ministering, intent on exhortation, diligent in reminding, constant in compassion, discreet in silence, mature in speech, and skillful in all things concerning perfect government, wanting to serve rather than to command, to honor than to be extolled (BC 10).

An examination of the text of the *Rule* demonstrates that Clare, while at first resisting the title, nevertheless understood and articulated the role of the abbess with precision and pre-science.[51] It is possible to see her manifold prescriptions regarding the abbess under four headings. First, there are clearly disciplinary tasks, such as the daily and occasional duties that pertain to order in the community, correction of members, and so forth. Secondly, there are prescriptions that show the abbess in a formative role, either through her direct relationship with the sisters or by the services provided through others. Thirdly, there are concerns for observance of poverty. In Clare's thought these have a pre-eminent place and cannot be interpreted as merely routine observances, given her situation. Lastly, there are duties that fall upon the abbess relative to observance of enclosure.

It is helpful to begin with those items which are disciplinary in nature.[52] In the opening chapter, as already cited, the profession of obedience is assigned to the "canonically elected" successors of Clare. Norms for this canonical election are reviewed in the fourth chapter of the *Rule*. The somewhat terse prescriptions are seasoned, however, with Clare's particular stamp.[53] The responsibility of the Abbess is for the "service and common welfare" (RegCl 4:6) of the sisters. She is both "abbess and mother" (RegCl 4: 7). The personal qualities which she must

[51] It should be noted that Clare accepted the title of abbess, but does not use it in reference to herself except when absolutely necessary (e.g, RegCl 1: 5). Her habitual designation of herself is that of "handmaid," "little plant," "unworthy servant." See, for example, TestCl 37; salutations of the five letters to Agnes and Ermentrude.

[52] All reference to the *Rules* of Innocent, Hugolino and Clare will be made within the text.

[53] Referring to "Clare's particular stamp" does not imply that every thought or expression finds its origin in her. Rather, we indicate that she either makes an original contribution or uses pre-existing fonts with a particular personal insight or meaning. Clare's treatment of governance, for example, owes much to the *Rule of St. Benedict*.

bring to her duties are rooted in justice (in the preservation of common life), charity (in the refusal to take refuge in particular friendships) and compassion (in her concern for the troubled members). She is reminded of an account to be rendered at the judgment recalled in Mt 12: 36 (RegCl 4: 8-14).[54] This account-ability to the Divine Judge is complemented by an accountability to her own sisters exercised in the weekly chapter in which she and they confess their failings.[55] She can "mercifully" dispense the sisters from the fasts prescribed (RegCl 3: 10).[56] As she sees fit, she also provides for the clothing of the young girls who come to the monastery (RegCl 2: 17).

Beyond discipline, the formative role of the abbess is perva-sive in the life of the community. It begins with the discernment of the suitability of candidates. A list of impediments that the abbess must consider is provided (RegCl 2: 5).[57] This list is en-capsulated within the teaching function of the abbess who is to "carefully examine" the candidate herself or through another (RegCl 2: 3); she is also to "thoroughly" explain the "tenor of our life" (RegCl 2: 6).[58] The ultimate responsibility for the formation of the community falls to her: "The Abbess shall carefully provide a Mistress from among the more discerning sisters of the monastery both for these and the other novices. She shall form them diligently in a holy way of life and proper behavior according to the form of our profession" (RegCl 2: 19-20).

---

[54] *Rule of St. Benedict* 64: 7-8, 15 and 2 Cel 185. See also Armstrong, *Clare*, 66, n. 27.

[55] Iriarte, *Regola*, comments upon the importance of this requirement: "Every sister—the superior first of all—seeks, in humble and praiseworthy acknowledgement of her 'common and public negligence,' to make external reparation and also seeks the support of the sisters for the advancement of the common good and of feeling herself sheltered against her own instabiltiy."

[56] See above, p. 152.

[57] This list needs to be considered in light of the historical problems associated with the familial monasteries indicated earlier in this chapter.

[58] In the *Process* there is evidence of the personal involvement of Clare with testing and encouraging candidates (Proc VI: 15; III: 1; IV: 1; VI: 1; XI: 2).

In the on-going life of the sisters she continues in this pastoral capacity. She gives the permission for confession (RegCl 3: 12). She makes inquiry into the needs of the sick:

> Concerning the sick sisters, let the Abbess be strictly bound to inquire diligently, by herself and through other sisters, what their illness requires both by way of counsel as well as food and other necessities. Let her provide for them charitably and kindly according to the resources of the place. [Let this be done] because everyone is bound to serve and provide for their sisters who are ill just as they would wish to be served themselves if they were suffering from any illness (RegCl 8: 12-14).

In this instruction Clare gives concrete form to the admonition of Francis in the *Later Rule* regarding the maternal solicitude that must be mutually demonstrated:

> And wherever the brothers may be together or meet [other] brothers, let them give witness that they are members of one family. And let each one confidently make known his need to the other, for if a mother has such care and love for her son born according to the flesh (cf. 1 Thess. 2:7), should not someone love and care for his brother according to the Spirit even more diligently? (RegB 6: 7-8)

Clare's text synthesizes this in the following manner: "Let each one confidently manifest her needs to the other. For if a mother loves and nourishes her child according to the flesh, should not a sister love and nourish her sister according to the Spirit even more lovingly?" (RegCl 8: 15-26)[59] In addition, Clare outlines clearly the duties of the abbess in her general conduct towards all of the sisters. She is to admonish, visit and correct. Her commands are limited to the "form of our profession" and must respect the dictates of conscience. The sisters are likewise reminded of their serious obligation of obedience, framed within the same limits.[60] Having satisfied the requirements of canonical precision—as she always does—Clare goes on to imprint this obedience with the stamp of minority, giving an endearing feminine flavor to the parallel teaching of Francis: "Let the Abbess, on her part, be so familiar with them that they can speak and act with her as ladies do with their servant. For this is the way it should be: the Abbess should be the servant of all the sisters" (RegCl 10: 4-5).

The formative role of the abbess may sometimes be exercised through correction. This is treated clearly in Chapter Nine. The abbess has a responsibility to correct, although the other members are not exempt from this task (RegCl 9: 1). The severity of the penance is left to the discretion of the abbess (RegCl 9: 3). Both abbess and sisters, however, are cautioned—again using the insight of Francis—against anger towards the offending sisters (RegCl 9: 5).[61] Additional corrective measures regarding the serving sisters are "left to the prudence of the Abbess" (RegCl 9: 17-18) and she may, if need be, impose severe penances if the fault is grave. It is apparent that Clare's image of maternal solicitude does not eliminate authoritative response to harmful abuses.

---

[59] RegHug 8 and RegB 6. Sensitivity to and compassion for the sick was a characteristic of the confraternities and congregations of the period.

[60] Iriarte, *Regola,* 192-199. Clare follows the sequence of Francis but with some changes suited to a community of enclosed life. The same concept of loving obedience and authority exercised in a spirit of service is evident. The *Process* offers many instances of Clare exercising the role of correction: Proc VI: 2; VII: 3; XII: 6; XIV: 4.

[61] RegB 7: 3; Mt 5: 23; Mt 6: 15 and Mt 18: 35; *Rule of St. Benedict* 45: 1.

The third area of importance reveals that Clare's concern for the perfect observance of poverty induces her to require some specific actions on the part of the Abbess. She is not to become embroiled in the temporal affairs of candidates (RegCl 2: 9). She is to provide suitable clothing (RegCl 2: 16). This would seem a commonplace, except for her appeal at the end of Chapter Two (RegCl 2: 24) which leads us to speculate that this sensitivity provides a bulwark against possible abuses in this matter.[62] She incurs no debt without consultation with all the sisters, and she does not allow use of the monastery as a place of deposit for valuables (RegCl 4: 19-21). She must use the advice of her discreets "in those matters which our form of life requires" (RegCl 4: 23). In Chapter Six she specifically commands that the abbesses who will hold office after her are bound to observe inviolably "the holy poverty which we have promised" (RegCl 6: 11). By making assignments in the chapter, as well as announcements about alms received, she enhances the sisters' sense of material welfare and promotes the common obligation of ordinary labor. She is also responsible for the distribution of goods in a way that serves all (RegCl 7: 3-5). Chapter Eight opens with a beautiful exhortation in which Clare speaks directly to her sisters.[63] This is followed immediately with practical considerations. The permission of the Abbess functions as protection against an individual sister reaping private gain from relatives, but is linked with prudent communal acceptance of the charity families extend by their donations (RegCl 8: 7-11). She likewise is charged to provide for the sick material comforts that would otherwise be considered superfluous, such as feather pillows, woolen stocking and quilts (RegCl 8: 17).

Finally, many aspects covering observance of enclosure are assigned to the care of the abbess. All of Chapter Five is taken up with this material. It includes having the permission of the

[62] See above p. 111.

[63] Iriarte, *Regola*, 157-164. The pilgrimage theme introduced here is complemented by TestCl 15-16.

abbess to accept visitors and the obligation to assign members of her council of discreets as companions for such visits. Lest any form of elitism occur, the abbess and her vicaress are admonished to abide by the same restrictions (RegCl 5: 8). The abbess keeps one of the keys to the door of the grille. She has the right to permit visits, particularly for confession or similar urgent matters, during the two Lenten seasons (RegCl 5: 16-17). She assigns discreets as companions to the sick when they receive visits (RegCl 8: 20-21). In Chapter Eleven she is charged a second time to keep one of the keys to the main door, and to post someone at the door when workers are inside the monastery (RegCl 11: 4, 10). This chapter also contains an implicit right to allow someone to enter the monastery between sunset and sunrise where this is unavoidable (RegCl 11: 8). She also has the right to determine the number of persons admitted for funeral liturgies and for digging the sisters' graves (RegCl 12: 11).

Before passing from the office of abbess to the other persons and structures noted in the *Rule,* it would be beneficial to consider the manner in which both Hugolino and Innocent IV described the duties of the abbess in their respective rules. Hugolino gives many disciplinary obligations: granting permission to speak and to have visitors (RegHug 6); dispensing from wearing the scapular (RegHug 9); the obligation to answer the visitator honestly (RegHug 12); posting a guard at the door when workers are present (RegHug 13); permitting special bedding for the sick (RegHug 9). But she is given no right to admit anyone into the enclosure, except to arrange the chaplain's entrance for funerals (RegHug 10). On the formative level she appoints a mistress to teach reading to those who are capable (RegHug 5). She receives the profession of all (RegHug 4). In addition to discipline, there are many aspects of the *Rule of Hugolino* which imply a more pastoral responsibility for the abbess; for example, the care of the sick is one of the few aspects of this *Rule* which possesses some qualities of human sentiment that soften its hard canonical tone (RegHug 8). Hugolino uses words such as "kindly," "solicitously," "greatest care and diligence," and so forth in indicating the manner of service provided to the infirm.

Innocent's text adds little to that of his predecessor. What was added gave the distinct impression of being an effort to respond to experiential difficulties. For example, the abbess can give permission to the sick and those who serve them to speak (RegInn 3). She may dispense from fasting during blood-letting[64]—a practice which has other cautions noted (RegInn 4). In keeping with his provisions for business matters, he directed the externs and procurator to report to the abbess, a practice not accepted by Clare[65] (RegInn 10, 11). With the exception of granting the abbess "a place apart" from the common dormitory space of the others, Innocent offers no innovation regarding that role.

The first impression generated by reading the three documents sequentially is awareness of the broad combination of pastoral and juridical qualities that Clare managed to include in her document. Indeed, the abbess plays a much larger role in her *Rule*; the addition of her language creates a rounded portrait and conveys qualities such as mutuality, humility, and fairness not treated in the previous rules. The same impression is reinforced in examining the three texts in reference to other government structures and internal offices. Clare's *Rule* is the only text that clearly sets forth the information and the imagery needed to understand that her concept of authority is not monarchical and that the abbess, while clearly possessing central authority and responsibility is not an island. She governs within a collegial context.[66] She is always one among her sisters.

[64] See *Clare,* 112, note 10.

[65] Procurators for the sisters were not in keeping with Clare's concept of poverty.

[66] Garrido's comments on this point are instructive(315): "The Community is an **Order**, a religious Order. As such it has a structure according to the image of the eschatological Community of Jesus. It is **monarchical**, represented by the Abbess, and at the same time it is collegial, represented by the conventual chapter and the discretorium. It is a Community, and at the same time it is

The vicaress is mentioned by Clare in eight instances.[67] She is authorized to give the same permissions as would the abbess (RegCl 5: 5, 7, 17; 8: 20-21). She is obliged to provide an example of faithful observance (RegCl 4: 14; 5: 8). She is authorized to perform some of the functions of the abbess such as assigning work or distributing alms for the common good (RegCl 7: 3, 5). In addition to her vicar, the abbess has a council of eight discreets. From among these councillors she appoints companions who accompany sisters to the parlor or grille (RegCl 5: 7; 8: 20). She consults them regarding specific financial and material decisions (RegCl 7: 5; 8: 11) and regarding imposition of serious penances (RegCl 9: 18). The only other "officials" whose roles are indicated in the *Rule* are the sacristan and portress. Both are described as custodians of the keys of the enclosure (RegCl 5: 12; 11: 1).[68]

Another important internal structure clearly specified in the *Rule* is the weekly chapter: "The Abbess is bound to call her sisters together at least once a week in the Chapter, where both she and her sisters should humbly confess their common and public offenses and negligences. Let her consult with all her sisters there concerning whatever pertains to the welfare and good of the monastery, for the Lord frequently reveals what is best to the least [among us]" (RegCl 4: 15-18). This meeting was

personal. It must be added that, since there is question of a religious community, the structure does not rest in the government, but in a charismatic 'order' of life, which situates the entire Community in obedience to the Holy Spirit and in fidelity to the Gospel."

[67] Godet, *Progetto*, 268: "In regard to this matter, for Clare there is no intention at all of giving a "political reward" as if she sought to make the vicaress the psychological or political counterbalance to the abbess. The union of hearts, which is the fulcrum of communitarian life, must find its more influential expression in the harmony existing between the abbess and vicaress.")

[68] Godet, *Progetto*, 269-270. See *Fonti Francescane*, 2253-2254 for indications of the spirit in which abbess and vicar are charged to conserve common life. "The abbess has the duty of watching so that there does not arise in the community privileged situations for any of the sisters or in any house."

also the place where arrangements for community work and for distribution of common goods was handled. It can be presumed as well that the chapter sessions gave occasion for some of the teaching that is described in both the *Legend* and the *Process*.[69] There is a further indication in the *Rule* of the seriousness with which Clare regarded the collegial responsibility of the members of the community. Three instances of this are recorded in the fourth chapter: "If at any time it should appear to the entire body of sisters that she [the abbess] is not competent for their service and common welfare, the sisters are bound as quickly as possible to elect another as abbess and mother according to the form described above" (RegCl 4:7). And again: "Let all who hold offices in the monastery be chosen by the common consent of all the sisters....Moreover, the sisters can and should, if it seems useful and expedient, remove the officials and discreets and elect others in their place" (RegCl 4: 22, 24). The "Mandate of 1238" certainly provides a concrete proof of the actual application of this spirit. In the document it is clearly stated that Clare does not exercise the legal powers it contains unilaterally nor in her individual abbatial power. She does so "by the will the of the ladies or sisters listed below."[70] The forty-nine signatures affixed to this legal transaction are certainly testimony to how seriously Clare regarded this obligation of consultation and mutual responsibility. Finally, it should be noted once again, that neither these offices nor the weekly chapter are described in the *Rules* of Hugolino or Innocent.

A final observation regarding governmental structures concerns the offices of visitator and cardinal protector, the means by which the monastery was bound to ecclesial authority. Hugolino's *Rule* provided for this office with a description of the personal qualities expected of the Visitator and the edifying function he was to perform (RegHug 12).[71] Much of the material

---

[69] LegCl 36; Proc I: 9, 14; II, 10; III, 3; VI: 2; VIII: 3; XI: 2.

[70] Mandate, Armstrong, *Clare*, 107-108.

[71] Sensi, *MRFU*, 95. See, in particular, note 29.

in this section of Hugolino's text is directed at preventing any laxity in the observance of enclosure during the time of visitation and in warning the abbess and sisters of their duty to be honest with the visitor. The power of the visitator to correct is limited, but it extends to the chaplain as well as the nuns. Interestingly enough, the first official visitor was the Cistercian, Ambrose,[72] and not a Friar Minor. Innocent adds the obligation that the visitators should be accompanied by two companions and empowers him to remove the chaplain if he finds cause. One significant part of his legislation is the obligation given to the general chapter of the friars to assign the visitators (RegInn 8). Of far greater consequence, however, is the final section of this text, in which Innocent declares:

> So that it does not happen that, through the fault of some government, you fall back at a later date from the observance of the present *Formula* briefly described above, which we wish and decree is to be followed everywhere and by everyone in a uniform way; or, that you take up different ways of living under the teaching of various [persons], we fully entrust the care of you and all the monasteries of your Order— with the authority of the present [document]— to our beloved sons, the general and provincial ministers of the Order of Friars Minor. We decree that you remain under their—or others who might be ministers for a time—obedience, government, and teaching. You are firmly bound to obey them (RegInn 12).

---

[72] Rusconi, *MRFF,* 279-285. Rusconi deals with the apparently contradictory presentations of Philip's role with the Poor Sisters and discusses the necessity of a Cistercian visitor for the first years prior to the approval of Francis' *Rule.*

He then states that the election of the abbess is the prerogative of the community, but offsets this by giving the right of confirmation to the authorities of the friars. The right to establish new monasteries is likewise reserved to them. It is with keen interest then, that one ponders Clare's formulation on the delicate point of relationships to the friar-visitors and chaplains. She states simply: "Let our Visitator always be taken from the Order of the Friars Minor according to the will and command of our Cardinal" (RegCl 12: 1). She next summarizes in three brief sentences the multiple cautions of the previous *Rules* concerning his character and conduct during the visit. She then states: "We ask as a favor of the same Order a chaplain and a clerical companion of good reputation, of prudent discretion and two lay brothers, lovers of holy poverty and upright way of life, in support of our poverty, as we have always mercifully had from the aforesaid Order of Friars Minor in light of the love of God and our blessed Francis" (RegCl 12: 5-7). One could argue that this represents one of the consummate diplomatic expressions of relationship between a feminine religious superior and her male counterparts ever written. She leaves no doubt of the fact that the bond which unites the two is both recognized by the Church and stems from the express will of Francis. She also is clear that it is a bond of mercy and love, intended to support the commitment to absolute poverty, not to supplant the rightful government of the monastery. Thus she claims no right but asks this "as a favor (RegCl 12: 5)." And in her description of the election of the abbess she states that the Minister General must be invited—but to preach and dispose the sisters to their responsibility (RegCl 4: 2-3). At no point does she indicate the Minister General's right to confirm the election. However, she does acknowledge sharing the same Cardinal Protector appointed to the Friars Minor. She sees in that office what Francis himself first articulated: a relationship with the church is the guarantee of fidelity to the poverty and humility of Christ (she adds: "and of His most holy Mother") and the Gospel (RegCl 12: 12-13).[73]

A final aspect of Clare's understanding of government, obedience and ecclesiastical responsibility can be viewed through the prism of legislation regarding the enclosure.[74] As stated previously, the historic development of legislation and practice on this point was undergoing marked changes. Alexander III, in legislating for the Gilbertines in the late twelfth century, made the first papal intervention regarding material enclosure. The increased detail being legislated by the Roman curia reflected in the texts of Hugolino and Innocent is another effect of the codification of reforms proceeding from Lateran IV. As Leclercq and others have observed, in spite of the pluriform expressions of religious life that women in the twelfth and early thirteenth centuries supported, the curial program in the first half of the thirteenth century was in the direction of reinforcing an "old" model of strictly cloistered monastic life. A close examination of the details of the three *Rules* in this regard is instructive.

Hugolino's text is relatively limited in detail, but clear in the demand for strict adherence. He states:

---

[73]This is one of those points in which the reader wonders how detailed was Clare's grasp of the canonical and "political" ramifications of her legislation. She certainly acted with advisement and would not have received approval had the text neglected canonical form. Still, we have seen something of the complexity of Innocent's efforts to force a juridical bond between the two groups. It would be most helpful to know more of Clare's knowledge of these initiatives.

[74]It is important to note that the material of this segment is not intended as a discussion of enclosure from a theological viewpoint, nor is it the intention to answer questions regarding Clare's intentions (or those of Francis) in this regard. The point of view adopted is that Clare's inclusion of these points demonstrates her understanding of the responsibility of governing the monastery and her obedience to church authority. As a result of research done on this point, a manner for broadening the framework for discussion of the issue is proposed. The readers addressed are the many Franciscans of the First and Third Orders whose knowledge of the issue is limited or whose awareness of its post-councilliar development is from the "outside."

> Therefore, it is proper and it is a duty that all
> those women who, after condemning and
> abandoning the vanity of the world, have re-
> solved to embrace and hold to your Order,
> should observe this law of life and discipline,
> and remain enclosed the whole time of their life.
> After they have entered the enclosure of this
> Order and have assumed the religious habit,
> they should never be granted any permission or
> faculty to leave [this enclosure], unless perhaps
> some are transferred to another place to plant or
> build up this same Order. Moreover, it is fitting
> that, when they die, both ladies as well as
> servants who are professed, they should be
> buried within the enclosure (RegHug 4).

He reserves any right to admit outsiders into the cloister to the Holy See (RegHug 10) except in the cases of laborers and for the sacraments for the gravely ill (RegHug 11). Prelates who do enter are instructed with regard to the number of companions deemed proper (RegHug 10). He describes the grille and the times when it can be opened (for Communion, recitation of the office, for sermons) (RegHug 11). The greatest number of physical details are reserved to the description of the door and the regulations for guarding it and opening it to outsiders. He writes:

> Let the entrance be very well secured with door
> panels, strong beams, and iron bars. Let it never
> be left without a guard, except perhaps for a
> moment, unless it is firmly locked with a key.
> Nor should it be opened immediately at every
> knock, unless it is undoubtedly known be-
> forehand that it is such a person for whom the
> door should be opened without any hesitation
> according to the decree which is contained

> above in that *Form* about those who are about
> to enter religion (RegHug 13).

It is clear that by the time Innocent attempted to clarify problems arising from "the hard and austere realities," (a phrase used also by Hugolino), questions regarding the exact physical construction and maintenance of the enclosure had resulted in a multiplication of directives. The strict injunction that "they must remain enclosed the whole time of their life" (RegInn 1) is followed by an expanded version of the reasons for exemption:

> After they have entered the enclosure of this
> Order and have been professed, promising to
> observe this rule, let them never be granted any
> permission or faculty to leave this enclosure
> unless perhaps some are transferred to another
> place by the permission of the general minister
> of the Order of Friars Minor or the provincial of
> the province of that Order in which the mon-
> astery is situated to plant or to build up the
> Order, or to reform some monastery, or by
> reason of discipline or correction, or to avoid a
> great expense of some sort. They can at times be
> transferred for some even pious and reasonable
> cause beyond those mentioned above, at least,
> as a general rule, with the permission of the
> General (RegInn 1).

Again, no right is conceded to the abbess to allow entrance into the enclosure, but again a long list of situations that clearly have occasioned communications with the legislator is appended (RegInn 6).[75] Here are cited the doctor, the blood-letter, persons

[75] Schulenberg, SAE 64-65, offers some hints of the manner in which heroic observance of enclosure was recorded in medieval hagiography. Such inter-nalization of strict legislation no doubt led to many situations in which permissions were scrupulously sought and which Innocent is presumably trying to foresee. See also note 89 (83).

who come to protect from fire, danger, loss, destruction, and to perform work not able to be done outside the enclosure. Limitations on the entrance of prelates are repeated substantially unchanged from the Hugolino *Rule*. The chaplain's visits now include hints about the manner of being vested upon entrance and departure, rulings on his companions and the limitations upon situations that require his admission into the enclosure (RegInn 7). When it comes to the physical description of the enclosure, there is an explosion of detail. The grille with its drape, irons bars and key and the construction of the window for communion are prescribed (RegInn 7). Section nine requires that the door is to be placed in position so high that it can be reached only by a ladder. To this are added very specific instructions about times of the day when it is to be used. A turn (a small, revolving platform) is now included as a means by which goods are exchanged without contact with outsiders. The turn, like the other doors, has keys and locks. Avoidance of being seen by those on the outside is repeated in reference to sisters at the grille, the parlor, the door and the turn (RegInn 9).[76]

When Clare introduced the obligation of enclosure, she did so—as did Hugolino and Innocent—in the section dealing with reception of new members. This chapter in Clare's text is, however, more finely conceptualized and is definitely marked

---

[76] It is, perhaps, important to remember in reviewing this document that Innocent's efforts must be viewed within the context of the policy already in effect and within the context of his over-arching efforts to regulate multiple aspects of the mendicants' relationships to property and to convents of female adherents. As with his attempts to regulate the business affairs of the friars, so here. Once the practice of appealing for interpretation was in place, it was inevitable that legislation would tend to become more precisely detailed in an effort to avoid binding the consciences of those who found themselves in situations where recourse was out of the question. When Clare presented her text to Innocent for approval she would again face the delicate problem of presenting an alternative means of interpreting the obligations of enclosure to the pontiff who had attempted a "once and for all" solution and warned that it should not be opposed "with rash temerity."

by the spirit of Francis. She precedes this point about reception of members with important ideas about the divine inspiration that roots the vocation, the consent of the sisters to this new member, the testimony of orthodox faith, and instruction in the Gospel life, especially the requirement to sell one's temporal goods. Then, noting the fact of the new member's investiture she states: "Thereafter, she may not go outside the monastery except for a useful, reasonable, evident and approved purpose" (RegCl 2: 12). She continues immediately with other directives regarding the education of the sisters and girls. In Chapter Five she gives specific directives for permission to speak at the grille and for the physical construction of the grille. She repeats some of the previous restrictions regarding the locks and curtains and the times when the grille may be opened. Interestingly, she omits any reference to the sisters covering their faces when speaking at the grille. In the chapter on "The Custody of the Enclosure," she describes both the responsibilities of the portress and the physical structure of the door and the locks, that are part of it. In a very brief manner she comments upon the entrance of episcopal visitors and their companions, and describes the precautions to be taken with workers (RegCl 11: 7-12). She is content with one admonition that the sisters take care not to be seen at the door (RegCl 11: 12). She also regulates the entrance of the chaplain (RegCl 12: 8-10). It should be recalled[77] that she does make provision for "a manifest, reasonable, and un-avoidable cause" in which the sisters may allow someone to enter the monastery at night (RegCl 11: 8).

While it is obvious that Clare received and incorporated existing legislation governing monasteries of women, it appears equally clear that she gave that legislation a very personal and sisterly character. This is first observable in her choice of language and her enumeration of reasons for egress from the monastery. There is no reference to "hard and austere realities"

---

[77] See above, p. 190.

and instead of naming only the precise occasions for leaving the monastery (establishment of or reform of another convent) she gives a framework for discernment that allows maximum evangelical liberty to those making the decision. This seems to indicate that Clare has learned in her years as abbess that when a community uses a check-list approach to legislation, the list only tends to grow longer, scruples heavier and the time of superiors more encumbered with unnecessary adjudications. It should also be noted that Clare, while synthesizing the legislation required for approval of her *Rule*, does not attach to those prescriptions any personal or Scriptural commentary. These have a prominent, clear place in the *Rule* text in other areas. Yet, at no time does she make for the physical aspects of enclosure the kind of personal appeal that is found in reference to the observance of poverty nor does she cite any other sources in support of the prescriptions.

These observations are not intended as arguments regarding Clare's precise feelings or intentions regarding the enclosure legislation which she received and which she incorporated into her *Rule*. They are rather intended to point out how difficult it is to answer the questions frequently asked about Clare's intentions in this regard. It has been argued that the inclusion of these regulations should be seen as proof of her positive acceptance of this program. However, some of the material cited in the first part of this chapter should serve to indicate how the issue demands a more comprehensive approach. (And these few indications of enlightenment are gained when the *Rule of Clare* is read **after** a careful study of the *Rules of Hugolino* and *Innocent*). One must know the *Rule* text, and know its linguistic structure as well as its words. One must understand the historical juncture at which Clare wrote and try to measure how much intellectual or canonical freedom she actually had— or did not have—to consider another model of life. The role of Hugolino in shaping the early life of the monastery and his role in advancing contemporary attitudes toward the role of religious women in the post-Lateran IV church must be understood. One must take into account evidence of Clare's own preference for a "hidden" life as revealed in the canonization *Process*. Finally, a great deal more than is presently known must be discovered about the actual practices of similar monasteries and small communities of women who participated in the sweeping upsurge of urban evangelical piety in thirteenth century Umbria and Tuscany.

Summary Observations

1. The beginnings of the community of San Damiano coincides with the close of a period of great diversification of monastic life-styles for women. The monastic forms of the twelfth century made possible experiences of mutual service and spiritual development among groups of men and women in search of a new evangelical equilibrium. At the same time, a gradual centralization of policy-making power was affecting religious life for women. The activity of churchmen like Hugolino demonstrated a determination on the part of the Holy See to regulate what had previously been matter for regional authorities.

2. A second phenomenon, the emergence of the beguines or *bizzoche*, represented new possibilities for a form of Gospel life suited to current economic and social conditions. In spite of the impact made upon local church life, and the support these models gave to many individual servants of God, their general acceptance and integration into the stream of approved religious life never succeeded. Some observers do see in Clare's *Rule* and life a synthesis of elements that can be identified with the beguine movement. Among these elements are found identification with the economic activity of poor urban women, devotion to the Crucified Christ and the Infant Christ, and promotion of the Eucharistic cult.

3. The friars, faced with multiple problems of governance after the death of Francis, had to develop offices to meet their internal needs. Constant tensions between the groups that favored a life of simple evangelical witness, solitude and mendicancy, and the group Brooke refers to as "the enlightened ministers" characterized the early decades. Despite a series of major changes of leaders and philosophies of government, the Order did evolve means by which to protect itself against abuses of power. It also engaged in a continuous, and often contradictory, struggle to interpret the *Rule* by referral to papal authority and to internal experts.

4. Clare, in developing the role of the abbess and the government of the monastery, succeeded in creating a synthesis of legal and spiritual vision that might have served the entire Order in its early years. While Francis did not legislate for stable communities, but for an itinerant group, Clare was able to draft norms for a convent of some thirty to fifty members. These norms were cognizant of physical, psychological and spiritual needs without losing anything of the essential character of the Francis' dedication to poverty, contemplation and fraternity.

Chapter Six

THE CHARISM OF CLARE AND CONTEMPORARY RELIGIOUS LIFE

Post-Conciliar Developments in Understanding of Religious Life

The preceding chapters have surveyed in some detail material concerning the historical reality of Clare's experience of her Franciscan vocation. Throughout these attempts to recreate the social, economic, and ecclesiastical context of her lifetime, the question posed focused on how she received, shared, and developed the charism of Franciscan evangelical life in the Church. Now still another question must be added: has all of this been merely a kind of "archeological" expedition? Or an indulgence in antiquarian interests? Or, on the other hand, has this analysis cultivated knowledge of the past in such a way as to engender a sense of being stewards of the Franciscan charism in our own time? When Clare and Francis spoke of their followers who would come to the Order in the future, were they not speaking to us?[1] Clearly, they believed that responsibility for the vitality and integrity of the Gospel life did not die with them, but passed on to succeeding generations.[2]

Chapter Four alluded to Desbonnet's concern about creating mythic heroes of Francis and the early companions. The same fear might be extended to the case of Clare. When one studies the personality and experience of Francis, there are multiple early biographies and eye-witness testimonies to consult. One is not quite so fortunate in the case of Clare, though, indeed, there are invaluable sources for her life as well. Nevertheless, there is a danger that her life will be seen as lacking the active drama associated with Francis and the early friars. After all, one might be tempted to classify her among the "invisible madonnas" of history, even as one extols her in an "iconic" sense—to return momentarily to Diane Owen Hughes' assessment of how Italian historiography has treated the feminine presence. Falling into this way of thinking about Clare and her sisters, one runs the risk of failing to recognize the ways in which the experiences of Clare correspond to current experiences of religious vocation in the Franciscan family. To the extent that Clare is portrayed as an ideal "model" of feminine Franciscan virtue, there is also created a cultic distance between the real woman called Clare and ourselves. This distance may be dangerously comforting, however, insofar as it insulates us from the necessity of seeing ourselves as responsible for the continuation of the charism, as Clare knew herself to be in her lifetime.

---

[1] Clare speaks in her *Testament* (56-57): "In the Lord Jesus Christ, I admonish and exhort all my sisters, both those present and those to come, to strive always to imitate the way of holy simplicity, humility and poverty and [to preserve] the integrity of our holy way of living, as we were taught from the beginning of our conversion by Christ and our blessed father Francis." And Francis writes in the *Siena Testament*: "…Write that I bless all my brothers, [those] who are in the Order, and [those] who will come until the end of the world…."

[2] See Blessing: 5; Reg Cl 6: 6; TestCl 17, 39, 44, 50, 56, 79; "Mandate."

In many places this study has focused on the *charism* Clare shared with Francis. Before drawing any final conclusions one must ask precisely how to understand this term, which is so prevalent in discussions of contemporary religious life. What gave rise to the use of expressions like "rediscovery of the charism of the founder"? What theological content does such an expression contain? The more one probes the implications of a study such as the present one, the more one realizes that analysis of a spirituality, whether in its historic aspects or in its systematic theological exposition, requires attention to the larger field of the theology of grace. It appears that part of this task must be to place a rediscovery of the historic context of the founders and foundresses, and their proper spirituality, in dialogue with the developments taking place now in an articulation of the fundamental relationship between the divine and the human that is called grace. In fact, it is in the study of the history of spirituality that one finds some of the richest opportunities to behold grace at work in concrete persons and situations. Studies of this nature, then, should make a contribution to the immediate concern for the authentic expression of the spirituality of a given congregation or Order today. They should also serve as one intersection of theological reflection in which one escapes the danger of what Peter Fransen calls "an unhistorical conception of grace."[3]

John Lozano and Fabio Ciardi have traced how use of the term "charism" as defining the gift of religious life in the Church has developed since the close of the Second Vatican Council.[4] Lozano attributes the development to its use by Paul VI, princi-

[3] Peter Fransen, *The New Life of Grace,* trans. Georges Dupont, S.J. (New York: The Seabury Press, 1969) 146-147.

[4] John Lozano, C.M.F., *Founders, Foundresses and their Religious Families* (Chicago: Claretian Center for Resources in spirituality, 1983); Id. *Discipleship: Towards and Understanding of Religious Life* (Manila: Claretian Publications, 1986); Fabio Ciardi, *I Fondatori uomini dello spirito* (Roma: Città Nuova, 1982).

pally in *Evangelica Testificatio*(11)[5] and in other allocutions to groups of religious.[6] While John Paul II has continued to use the term in addressing the values of religious life, its development is most clearly seen in the 1978 document *Mutuae Relationes*.[7] Lozano points out that *Mutuae Relationes* is an important indication of the maturation of the concept of charism as related to religious life[8] because "charism" passed by means of this document from papal addresses into subsequent descriptions of the theology of religious life. It is somewhat meaningful that this document is the result of a joint effort of the Sacred Congregation for Religious and Secular Institutes (now the Congregation for Institutes of Consecrated Life) and the Sacred Congregation for Bishops. Lozano summarizes the document's contribution in the following way:

> Finally, this text further develops this thought by amplifying it with various aspects emerging from current theological reflection: 1) the founding charism is an experience of the Spirit granted to the founder or foundress; 2) this charism is a reality to be transmitted and safe-

[5] Paul VI, "Evangelica Testificatio. On the Renewal of the Religious Life: Apostolic Exhortation," *Acta Apostolicae Sedis* 63 (1971) 497-526. "Only in this way will you be able to arouse peoples' hearts to embrace the divine truth and love according to the charisms of your founders whom God has raised up in his Church." (English translation from Washington, D.C.: Publications Office, United States Catholic Conference, 1971.)

[6] Lozano, *Foundresses*, 27-28.

[7] *Directives for the Mutual Relations Between Bishops and Religious in the Church* (Vatican City: The Sacred Congregation for Religious and Secular Institutes and the Sacred Congregation for Bishops, 1978).

[8] T I,12 reads: "The specific charismatic note of any Institute demands both of the Founder and his disciples a continual examination regarding: fidelity to the Lord; docility to His Spirit; intelligent attention to circumstances and an outlook cautiously directed to the signs of the times; the will to be part of the Church; the awareness of subordination to the sacred hierarchy; boldness of initiatives; constancy in the giving of self; humility in bearing with adversities."

> guarded but also a dynamic reality to be con-
> stantly deepened and developed; 3) this charism
> encompasses a type of spirituality and apostolate
> which, in turn, gives rise to a special tradition.[9]

Even a casual survey of periodicals and publications on religious life in the past two decades will indicate how much this language, and its attendant concepts, has taken hold of our thinking about religious life.[10] This change in modes of thought and expression brings with it the danger that the language will take on a popular dimension separated from its deeper levels of meaning. Undoubtedly, few religious who use "charism" in daily speech realize, for instance, that it cannot be traced directly to the Council documents. It must therefore be asked how the Council prepared the way for the linguistic and attitudinal change in current understanding of this theological point.

It is to St. Paul that one must turn for the biblical basis of the term "charism." In his writing, he indicates the existence of these manifestations of the Holy Spirit seen as both transitory experiences and vocational (permanent) gifts. The three classic texts of the Pauline doctrine on charism (1 Cor 12: 28[11]; Eph 4: 11[12]; Rom 12: 7-8[13]) treat of ecclesiastical offices and manifold gifts directed to the works of mercy. In speaking of the charism of celibacy, Paul indicates that his directives come from the Lord

[9] Lozano, *Foundresses,* 29-30.

[10] Bibliographic information offered by Lozano in both of his publications bears this out. In *Foundresses,* see, especially, note 6, (93) and in *Discipleship* see 345-348.

[11] "Furthermore, God has set up in the church first apostles, second prophets, third teachers, then miracle workers, healers, assistants, administrators, and those who speak in tongues."

[12] "It is he who gave apostles, prophets, evangelists, pastors and teachers (12) in roles of service for the faithful to build up the body of Christ."

[13] "It may be the gift of ministry; it should be used for service. One who is a teacher should use his gift for teaching; one with the power of exhortation should exhort."

regarding this particular charism (1Cor 7:10-11). In making use of a rabbinical distinction between that which is commanded and that which is merely counseled (1Cor 7: 25),[14] Paul unknowingly created the foundation for a distinction that developed in Latin theology and flowered in the Scholastic period in the language of the "evangelical counsels." Lozano credits patristic writers with investing the concept of "counsel" with "profound intuitions" regarding the nature of consecrated life. To give but one example, the patristic writers, faced with a Hellenizing tendency to devalue marriage, argued that the charism of virginity or celibacy was offered to Christians by grace.

With Thomas Aquinas the concept of the "counsel" became equated with the term, "state of perfection." The problems raised in modern times by the use of such a description resulted in its being set aside in the Council's documents on the subject.[15] This option opened the way for a return to a more biblical conceptualization rooted in the Pauline teaching and a resulting change in terminology. The documents of the Council, however, continued to use the term *consilium* (counsel). Such a choice was inevitable in view of the fact that from the height of the scholastic period onward, this was the only technically accurate theological term used to describe the constitutive elements of religious life. In consequence, *Lumen Gentium* simply repeated what has been the commonly held doctrine of the last seven centuries in the Latin Church, namely, that the evangelical counsels of poverty, chastity and obedience, professed as the objects of vows, are essential components of the religious vocation.[16] However, in both *Perfectae Caritatis* and *Lumen Gentium*, the term *donum* is used as applying to the

---

[14] "With respect to virgins, I have not received any commandment from the Lord, but I give my opinion as one who is trustworthy, thanks to the Lord's mercy."

[15] Lozano, *Foundresses*, 30-35; *Discipleship*, 115-128;

[16] See Ciardi's exposition of *Lumen Gentium* on pages 33-35.

three counsels, and used in a way that the meaning is equivalent to that of *charisma*.[17] In this way the Council employed the traditional theological descriptions of the Gospel counsels but linked this formulation to citations from Paul, making possible a recovery of the original Scriptural understanding of the nature and role of the gifts within the Christian community.

Using the classic distinctions made between "sanctifying" and "actual" grace, it is possible to characterize this *donum* or this *charisma* of which Conciliar and post-Conciliar documents speak as a form of "actual grace." Speaking of these Pauline gifts, Donald Gelpi observes: "These gifts…were named 'gratuitous graces' by medieval theologians. As such they were distinguished from sanctifying grace *(gratia gratum faciens)*; for, it was argued, they are ordered, not to the sanctification of the one who possesses them, but to the edification of the Christian community."[18] Fransen explains "actual" as distinct from "sanctifying" grace as a constant influence of grace which empowers the free choice of will and which has been called in traditional theology by such titles as "assisting grace," "prevenient," "cooperating," and "efficacious." "All the different graces," he assures us, "can be reduced to light and certainty for the intellect, to strength and perseverance for the will, to consolation and comfort and joy for the mind."[19]

---

[17] The uses occur in the Prologue to *Perfectae Caritatis* with reference to Eph 4: 2; to PC #8 with reference to 1Cor 12 and Rom 12. Chapter VI of LG applies *donum* to the three evangelical counsels with reference to Mt 19: 11 and 1Cor 7: 7. LG #12 and #43 describe hierarchical authority vis-a-vis these gifts.

[18] Donald Gelpi, *Charism and Sacrament: A Theology of Christian Conversion* (New York: Paulist Press, 1976) 63.

[19] Fransen, 245. Fransen offers in this context a helpful observation: "We should be on our guard against the danger of taking our concepts and technical notions too seriously; otherwise the wealth of divine grace is analyzed and atomized to the verge of driving a normal man out of his wits. Unfortunately, we cannot be sure that such has never been the case in the history of theology; frequently, and under the influence of the reigning rationalistic tendencies, theology has devoted its attention more to abstract notions than to the one living reality which those notions and definitions tried to clarify and defend against heresy."

Many developmental approaches to the study of grace have followed the advance beyond scholastic and neo-scholastic modes of thought that was initiated in large part by the work of Karl Rahner.[20] Among these is an advancement of the pneumatological understanding of grace arising from both research in systematic theology and from a new experiential dimension present in the Church expressed in the literature associated with charismatic renewal. Heribert Mühlen is one contemporary theologian who addresses the need to define charism within this new perspective. He sees the Council as giving a new importance to the relationship of the Spirit and the Church, indeed defining the Church as "not so much a continuation of the Incarnation (as such), but rather a continuation of Jesus' anointing with the Spirit (Acts 10: 38[21]; Lk 3: 21[22], 4: 18[23])."[24] He further proposes: "By charism we mean an inward capacity insofar as it is freely given by the Spirit for the growth of Christ's body. All the charisms are a making-present of the Spirit (1Cor

---

[20] For a helpful summary of developments in the field following Rahner's work see: Francis Colborn, "The Theology of Grace: Present Trends and Future Directions," *Theological Studies* 31 (1970) 692-711; Leo J. O'Donovan, ed., *A World of Grace An Introduction to the Themes and Foundations of Karl Rahner's Theology* (New York: Seabury Press, 1980), especially Ann Carr, "Starting with the Human," (17-30) and Michael J. Buckley "Within the Holy Mystery," (31-49).

[21] "...God anointed him with the Holy spirit and power. He went about doing good works and healing all who were in the grip of the devil, and God was with him."

[22] "When all the people were baptized, and Jesus was at prayer after likewise being baptized, the skies opened (22) and the Holy Spirit descended on him in visible form like a dove."

[23] "The spirit of the Lord is upon me; therefore, he has anointed me. He has sent me to bring glad tidings to the poor, to proclaim liberty to captives."

[24] Heribert Mühlen, "Sacrament and Charism: the Spirit and the Church," *Theology Digest* 15 (1977) 46. Extracted from the original: "El Spiritu y la Iglesia: relacion entre sacramento y carisma," *Estudios Trinitarios* 3 (1975) 385-399.

12: 7[25]). The charisms are signs which contain God's salvific and missionary love for men."[26] In order to distinguish the grace resident in charisms from the grace of sacraments he points out that the sacraments also "contain" God's gift of grace, but only as an offer *(ex opere operato)*. The degree depends upon the dispositions of the recipient. He continues:

> These latter, [sacraments] involving some material object plus a vivifying word, come to us from outside ourselves and are anterior to the presence of the Spirit they bring. But charisms come from within and are a consequence of an already-present Spirit. Secondly, Baptism, Penance and the Anointing of the Sick relate primarily to individual salvation, while all charisms relate primarily to benefitting others.... Accordingly, "sacrament" and "charism," show the twofold meaning of God's grace: a) man's (individual) relationship to God—mediated by the Holy Spirit (sanctifying grace), and b) God's missionary relationship to men through a consecratory grace which must be handed on to others.[27]

Taking as our starting point this definition of Mühlen, one can come to deeper clarity about the experience of charismatic grace that is believed to be present in the great founders and foundresses of religious families in the Church. How does this "consecratory grace" manifest itself in concrete human action that both invites and enables others to participate in some

---

[25] "To each person the manifestation of the Spirit is given for the common good."

[26] Muhlen, 47.

[27] Muhlen, 47.

degree in the same experience of being led by the Spirit of the Lord?[28]

Founding Charism as the "Operation of the Holy Spirit"

In the second chapter of his book, *I Fondatori: uomini dello spirito,* Fabio Ciardi makes a thorough study of the process by which a charism is experienced and then results in certain human structures such as a congregation, spiritual writings, and rules.[29] He first offers a phenomenological presentation of the reception of the initial inspiration or awareness of the charism-gift. In some persons the inspiration comes as a direct intervention—an inner voice, dream or vision. There may also be a vision experienced in spirit (lacking corporeal form), or a great outpouring of light upon the intellect. At other times the charism is bestowed in the indirect form of human experiences. These may be experiences of life in the religious and social order. At first glance, such experiences may lack something of the intensity of the mystical phenomena, but the experience of the founders is of a clear and unique grace bestowing inner conviction and strength such as that described by Fransen above. Typical examples of such fruitful experiences might be a horror of evil witnessed in the workings of the Church or in society. Sometimes the grace is mediated in the suggestions of a third person. Examining sources for the lives of several founders, Ciardi also discerns stages in the gradual evolution of the

---

[28] Another way of articulating the experience of religious charism is offered by Bishop Joseph Galante, formerly Undersecretary of the Congregation for the Institutes of Consecrated Life: "A religious charism is an intensely personal reading of the Gospel resulting in an inner enlightenment that changes the way a person relates to God, to self and to others. This new way of relationship is so powerful that it has the potential to attract others who sense in themselves the same desire and capacity to read the Gospel in this "new key" ("Renewing Religious Life," unpublished lecture).

[29] Ciardi, 47-140.

charism.[30] At times this evolution is accomplished within an experience of "ignorance" in which the founder cannot see in advance the ultimate results of the graces received. Initial inspiration is followed by other divine interventions that confirm the inspiration received and move the person to the realization of its consequences.

One of the primary "consequences" of a charism is the formation of a new community of religious in the church. The foundress or founder is constituted as such when a group of "disciples" gathers with the intention of following the same call of the Spirit, of taking the new way inaugurated by this particular comprehension of the Gospel, of Christian life, and of accomplishing the work that flows from this new comprehension. The founding gift includes an extension to those who will maintain the original intuition with all of its spiritual vigor and potential and will foster its continued role of ecclesial service.[31]

The literature which records these experiences reveals images that often occur as descriptions of the relation between the founder and the disciples.[32] The first is the image of a plant with its associated activities of sowing, cultivating, harvesting. Another is the image of building, of making a foundation. Shepherding provides another analogy. Images of generation, of parenting spiritual sons and daughters, are likewise frequent. The new family which rises out of the founding charism is perceived as being a work of God. Sources that describe the birth of such foundations often record the founder's conviction of being simply an instrument. God is seen dynamically at work in the call and the response of the first generations of members. The work of this new group is not ordained to the good of the

---

[30] Among those he uses as "case studies" are Francis of Assisi, Ignatius of Loyola, Camillus de Lellis, Vincent de Paul, Paul of the Cross, Eugene de Mazenod, Don Alberione and Angela Merici.

[31] Ciardi, 313.

[32] Interestingly, the images reviewed by Ciardi are often found in the descriptions of Francis and Clare. He cites outstanding examples in his notes 334-343.

leader, but of the Church. The founding vocation is a prophetic one. The social and ecclesial dimensions of the charism's impact are significant aspects of its providential mission, so that the unfolding of the inspiration referred to as "institutionalization" is not a morally neutral event; nor can it be regarded as a merely sociological phenomenon. It is inevitable that an authentic founding charism will develop in this manner. It is **not** inevitable that the process of institutionalizing the founding intuition will result in its deformation, even though history attests to many such instances. In fact, it is possible to regard this process as another manifestation of the power of the charism incarnate in its corporate dimensions.[33] Ciardi sees the development of the community as an extension of a "living exegesis" in which a particular teaching of Christ is both interiorized and integrally lived, manifesting itself in an apostolic action, a ministry, or a style of life.[34]

Among these divine interventions is often found the impulse, experienced as a kind of revelation, to compose a rule of life for the community. Ciardi points out that the older *legenda* of the great founders tend to give this revelatory aspect of the rule a suspiciously triumphalistic tone. He maintains, nonetheless, that this insistence upon divine aid is rooted in an actual experience of personal inspiration on the part of the rule-giver. Further, the rule serves as a privileged witness to the charism of the foundress or founder. The conception of life, the fruits of experiences, the original inspiration, are here preserved "incorrupt" for future generations. Through the rule, Ciardi, states, the founder enters into dialogue with future followers, inviting and challenging them to embark upon the same way of the *sequela Christi* which inspired the text.

---

[33] For the origins of this insight I am indebted to a concept articulated several years ago by Thomas Clarke, S.J. in which he suggested that a full appreciation of Rom 5: 20 should lead the Christian to see the possibility that human institutions are as capable of mediating grace as of mediating its opposite (e.g., in the case of "unjust social structures").

[34] Ciardi, 220-221.

Another aspect of the refinement of this charismatic gift is the fact that its ultimate adjudication belongs to the Church.[35] This responsibility, recalled in *Lumen Gentium* (12), results in an encounter in which founder and church put each other to the test. A study of the founders' lives reveal a pattern of opposition and trial resulting from inevitable misunderstanding when new gifts erupt into the ecclesial community.[36] The nature of the trials endured often contributes directly to the growth in charity of the persons involved. These trials also provide a real test of the evangelical depth of the vision espoused and promoted. It is also important to realize that the charism is tested, not because of purely disciplinary aims, but because the overflow of the charism into the life of the church is part of its very nature. It is a gift for service to the Church, not service in terms of works performed, though these may be part of its efficacy, but the service of promoting "life and holiness."

Ciardi summarizes this experience of "evolution and continuity" discerned in various stages of institutional growth—establishment of the Order or institute, presentation of its spirituality in a rule—in the following words:

> Successive divine interventions centering around the first inspiration have shown the constant guidance of the Spirit either through an action of confirmation or through the completion of the work which the founders were called to accomplish. Now we are interested in seeing what connection can be found between the later interventions and the original inspiration. In this journey that leads the religious family to its definitive features, we discern

[35] 1Thes 5: 12; 19-21. See Ciardi, 268-297

[36] In this regard *Mutuae Relationes* I, 12 offers some candid observations regarding this "unvarying history of the connection between charism and cross."

a gradual evolution in its development and corrections of the understanding of the inspiring ideal, and in the forms which express that ideal. We also discern a basic continuity in comparison with the pristine inspiration itself. In the development of these two aspects of evolution and continuity stages of the process itself, the founders understand once more that they are led by the Spirit.[37]

Clare and Responsibility for the Charism

Having briefly examined the nature of that form of grace called a charism and having briefly considered the forms such charismatic experience takes in the formation of new religious ways of life, it is necessary to question a way of thinking about the charism that has resulted from an unwittingly one-sided approach in post-Counciliar renewal efforts. Paul VI articulated in *Evangelica Testificatio,* and also in *Ecclesiae Sanctae,*[38] the call to renew the constitutions and other aspects of religious institutes precisely by a return to the charism of the founder. He did this initially in *Ecclesiae Sanctae,* a document which specified activities of implementation after the Second Vatican Council. This was followed by his subsequent pastoral reflection on renewal of religious life, *Evangelica Testificato.* In many institutes an enormous effort to provide an understanding of the founding experience and of the written documents issuing from it resulted. The goal of these efforts was two-fold: a) to revitalize the institute by seeking to unleash the dynamic power of the charism in its corporate life, and b) to provide a new articulation of this gift in renewed constitutions. As a result, a good deal of historical study and recovery of lost or forgotten texts and

---

[37] Ciardi, 119.
[38] *Ecclesiae Sanctae, Acta Apostolicae Sedis* 57 (1966) 775-782.

traditions has engaged the energies of religious men and women for the last two decades. Few who have lived through the experience would dispute that, for all its difficulties, the effort has enriched contemporary religious life enormously. Part of this work has resulted in a greater mastery of historical sources. The other part has resulted in clear, and officially approved, written descriptions of the charism.[39] One hidden danger in the process remains to be faced. With these achievements comes the danger that success in describing one's present understanding of the charism may also tempt one into believing that the gift of grace the words define has been fully appropriated and internalized. Kilian McDonnell, in describing the experience of particular graces that accompany initiation into charismatic renewal, offers a warning that may be analogously applied to the experience of claiming rediscovery of the charisms for religious:

> There is a supposition abroad that at initiation one receives the Holy Spirit and the gifts of the Spirit. This supposition conceives of a gift of the Spirit as being an objectified spiritual reality, a pneumatic *res* which, once given, has its own independent existence. The gifts, however, are not spiritual realities having their own autonomous life. A gift of the Spirit is nothing else than the Spirit coming to visibility in the service of the community....A gift is a mode of the Spirit's life as it is turned toward the Church and the world.[40]

[39] In the case of the Franciscans of the Third Order Regular, it has even resulted in a completely revised Rule text that replaces the text promulgated in 1927.

[40] Kilian McDonnell, O.S.B. "Charismatic spirituality: one among many," *Theology Digest* 22 (1974) 213.

This warning invites a consideration of how Clare perceived and experienced the charism that, through Francis, had touched her and, in her own conversion, became hers in the fullest possible degree. In her *Testament* she eloquently recalled the experience: "After the most high heavenly Father saw fit in His mercy and grace to enlighten my heart, that I should do penance according to the example and teaching of our most blessed father Francis, a short while after his conversion, I, together with a few sisters whom the Lord had given me after my conversion, willingly promised him obedience, as the Lord gave us the light of His grace through his wonderful life and teaching" (TestCl 24-27). It is evident, in fact, that the entire *Testament* is a kind of homage to this experience. Clare described not an "objectified spiritual reality" but a relationship that embraced Christ as the Way, Francis as guide, and the sisters as fellow pilgrims. Had she experienced the charism as an object, rather than a living, relational entity of spirit, she might not have known the fear she shared in the same text:

> Therefore, I, Clare, a handmaid of Christ and of the Poor Sisters of the Monastery of San Damiano—although unworthy —and the little plant of the holy father, consider together with my sisters so lofty a profession and the command of such a father and also the frailty of some others that we feared in ourselves after the passing of our holy father Francis, who was our pillar [of strength] and, after God, our one consolation and support. Time and again we willingly bound ourselves to our Lady, most holy Poverty, that after my death, the sisters, those present and those to come, would never turn away from her (TestCl 37-39).

Not content with warning her sisters to remain steadfast, she appealed to the Cardinal Protector: "...[our Protector] may always see to it that his little flock, which the Lord Father has begotten in His holy Church by the word and example of our blessed father Francis by following the poverty and humility of His beloved Son and His glorious Virgin Mother, observe the holy poverty that we have promised to God and our most blessed father Saint Francis. May he always encourage and support them in these things" (TestCl 46-47). She then turned to the ministers of the Friars Minor with a similar plea: "I commend and leave my sisters, both those present and those to come, to the successor of our blessed Father Francis and to the entire Order, that they may always help us to progress in serving God more perfectly and, above all, to observe more perfectly most holy poverty" (TestCl 50-51). Finally, she charged all of the sisters with their share of this responsibility: "In the Lord Jesus Christ, I admonish and exhort all my sisters, both those present and those to come, to strive always to imitate the way of holy simplicity, humility and poverty and [to preserve] the integrity of our holy way of living, as we were taught from the beginning of our conversion by Christ and our blessed father Francis" (TestCl 56-57). Clare, keenly aware of the fact that the charism is neither received not sustained by personal acts of the will, finally reminded the sisters: "For this reason I *bend my knee to the Father of our Lord Jesus Christ* that, through the supporting merits of the glorious and holy Virgin Mary, His Mother, and of our most blessed father Francis and all the saints, the Lord Himself, Who has given a good beginning, will also give the increase and *final perseverance*. Amen" (TestCl 77-78).

All of the elements described earlier as components of the contemporary teaching concerning charism are present in the *Testament*. First, Clare speaks forcefully of the vocational grace as a gift. Further, it is a gift that is received "daily." The gift is not an abstract notion or ideological construct. It is a life. It is a Way. The Way is synonymous with the coming of Jesus into the world, a coming that demanded that he "empty himself" (Phil 2: 7). The person who first received this special under-standing of the Gospel of Jesus in the "key of poverty" was

Francis. Francis is therefore the Founder in Clare's vision. She and the Poor Sisters walk as itinerants along the "way" that he taught. In his own experience, Francis received this inspiration in a prophetic manner. Both Clare and Francis recognized the initiative for all of this as coming from "the joy and enlightenment of the Holy Spirit" (TestCl 11).[41] The very nature of the vocation was communal and the promotion of its vitality was fidelity to the call to be "a form" for others. This call does not remain an amorphous pledge of Gospel attitudes, but takes shape in a concrete proposal of life publicly professed in the church. The hierarchy approves and guards the essence of the proposal. (Yet here again, Clare reminds her readers/listeners that the proposal rests in a Person. It is Jesus in the crib and on the cross who gives it substance and meaning.) The responsibility to continue to live in this grace cannot be altered with geographical or governmental changes. Clare emphasized that the human structures of the community which are most clearly operative in the relationship of the abbess with her sisters guarantee the extension through time and space of the charism-vocation. Finally, she urged perseverance, warning that negligence and ignorance are capable of destroying the "integrity of our holy way of living"(TestCl 56). At the conclusion she returned one last time to the acknowledgement that "all is gift" and finished her *Testament* with Paul's prayer from Ephesians (3: 14).

The point of this reflection on the *Testament* is not simply to savor the beauty of its language, but ponder the document that describes Clare's clear and abiding—it might be said, urgent—sense of responsibility for the charism she shared with Francis. The intense language of Clare's *Testament* expresses with poetic and personal power what the achievement of approval of the *Rule* text represents canonically. The *Testament* allows all to

---

[41] For further reflection upon this prophetic moment in the story of Francis and Clare see Giovanna Mandelli, O.S.C., "Santa Chiara e profezia," Estratto della revista *Vita Minorum* 56 (1985) 1-24.

share her innermost reflections as she articulates this foundational experience of being called by the Lord to embrace the
same project of Gospel life that the Spirit of the Lord had poured
forth into the heart of Francis of Assisi.[42]

A potentially confusing question regarding Clare's relationship to Francis emerges at the end of these reflections. Clare
never spoke of herself as foundress, and in fact, was always
careful to ascribe to Francis the authority for the way of life she
and her sisters embraced. Others perceived her role as foundress
perhaps more clearly than she did.[43] Whereas it has become
customary to define the role of founding persons with ever
greater precision in recent years, it is disconcerting to find in her
discourse an absence of clear distinctions between her role and
that of Francis.[44] Her lack of precision, however, reveals something of major importance. It means that for Clare there were not
two projects of Franciscan Gospel life, but one.[45] It means that
for Clare there were not two founding charisms, but one. And
yet, in spite of the strength of her identification with Francis, she
did not regard herself as a passive recipient of a grace that came

[42] See Optatus van Asseldonk, O.F.M. Cap., "Lo Spirito Santo negli scritti e
nella vita di Santa Chiara," in *La lettera e lo spirito*, 137-151. See especially 141-
143 which treat of the *Testament*. In the same volume see also, "Lo spirito del
signore e la sua santa operazione negli scritti di Francesco (influsso di S.
Paolo)" 31-92; Armstrong, *Clare*, "Introduction," 17 ff.

[43] For example, there is the testimony of Ugolino in the *Process* (XVI: 2): "As
Saint Francis was the first in the Order of Friars Minor which, with the help of
God, he founded and governed, so this holy virgin Clare, as God willed, was
the first in the Order of the Enclosed Ladies. And she governed that Order in
all knowledge and goodness, as was seen and testified through public
knowledge." See also Edith Pasztor, "St. Francis, Cardinal Hugolino, and 'The
Franciscan Question'," *Greyfriars Review* 1 (September, 1987) 1-29.

[44] See Lozano's very helpful analysis of the founder's role in *Foundresses*,
Chapters I, II and III. The one drawback of this otherwise fine summary is
Lozano's lack of awareness of the actually vital relationship experienced by
many Franciscan congregations founded in the last two centuries with the
charism of Francis. See section 3, page 10.

[45] Jean-François Godet, unpublished lecture.

into her life as a "finished product." Clare's self-perception was that she received daily as a freely given gift the presence of the Holy Spirit in a special vocation. That vocation had been given to her at a new moment in the experience of the Christian people. In fact, a survey of her letters indicates that Clare always perceived a sense of endangerment regarding the fragility of this new form of life. Its sustenance required vigilance, discipline, prayer, counsel. All of these she enjoins in her letters to Agnes and Ermentrude. She and her companions bravely insisted against all odds their form of life was possible. So she advised Ermentrude: "Gladly endure whatever goes against you / and do not let your good fortunes lift you up: / for these things destroy faith and those demand it" (LEr7). And Agnes: "What you hold may you [always] hold, / What you do, may you [always] do and never abandon. / But with swift pace, light step...go forward...not believing anything, not agreeing with anything which would dissuade you from this resolution / or which would place a stumbling block for you on the way..." (2LAg 12-14).

Summary Observations

The Franciscan charism unfolds in the lives of actual men and women in each generation. It has been common to hear Clare described as a model of fidelity to the vision of Francis. It is less common to hear Clare described as sharing the responsibility and authority for the development of this grace.

1. In examining the relationship of Francis and Clare as described in the early sources, one discovers many instances which demonstrate Clare's autonomy and authority for her own life. She had clearly embarked upon some sort of program of religious dedication prior to her encounter with Francis. She attested always that his teaching represented for her the radical summons to "Look upon Him Who became contemptible for

you, and follow Him, making yourself contemptible in this world for Him" (2LAg 19). It is also clear, however, that she had already begun her journey along this path and was already part of the search for new religious forms. When she and Francis did succeed in accomplishing her incorporation into the Franciscan *fraternitas,* she assumed responsibility for the legal and canonical consequences of her choice. She confronted her family on the issue of her decision to embrace this form of life. She sold her patrimony. She supported her sister Agnes' intention to follow her in spite of violent reprisals. Her life in San Damiano revealed her as a woman of notable skill. She was not only the confidant of Francis and his closest friends, but also of Elias, of the prelates and pontiffs of her lifetime, and of leaders among religious women in distant countries. She exercised a healing role among the sisters, friars and townspeople. She governed her own monastery and was called upon to support reforms in others, and to establish new foundations. She was a woman whose gifts of contemplation and healing were sought by Francis as well as by others.

2. The second chapter presented a woman whose tenacious struggle to provide a secure base for the charism of her religious family lasted throughout her life. She is the one cited as requesting the *Privilege of Poverty.* She engaged in continual debate with cardinals and pontiffs over the advisability of absolute poverty. She continued to enter into discernment with the hierarchical officials regarding her life project. Finally, she wrote a *Rule* text and submitted it for pontifical approval. In an unprecedented act, approval was granted and she was able to pass on to her spiritual heirs a description of the essence of the vocational gift. The third chapter illustrated the context in which Clare's option for absolute poverty took flesh. She lived in a period of economic destabilization that affected her own social class most adversely. Instead of joining with the women of the noble class in a struggle to preserve their prerogatives in the private, domestic sphere, she joined with the women of the

"lesser nobility" and of the emerging mercantile class of the communes. By adopting a quest for a poor evangelical life in solidarity with these women, (expressed in its dress, its economic system, and its forms of religious devotion), she made a decision that was an even more dramatic break with her peers than the break created by the conversion of Francis.

3. Studying Clare in terms of social relationships and the Christian vocation to love revealed that Clare also confronted a society in which a woman's field of relationships derived from her role as wife and/or mother. For a woman, social position or marital status dominated the possibilities of knowing and working with others. In the creation of a small community in which there was neither the class division found in many monasteries, nor the class division of the commune (ameliorated though it was by this time) Clare allowed women a taste of proper human and Christian autonomy and authority. Moreover, she did not offer this equality as a "potential" achievement. She legislated in such a way as to guarantee the preservation of these rights of equality within the community. And, finally, the fifth chapter demonstrated that Clare, in devising the quality of government she did, made it possible for the Poor Sisters to taste some security and stability in this important component of monastic life. She created norms for governing all of the major functions within the monastery and she created policies to deal with serious structural issues. Yet there can be no doubt that the essential qualities of minority and mutuality Francis so insisted upon were equally protected by Clare's legislation. She was able to select stable, traditional elements required of monastic life without capitulating to prevailing hierarchical models. Considering that at the time she wrote this careful synthesis the friars' governing bodies were already undergoing major changes due to the clericalization process, it is quite extraordinary that she managed to preserve a form of life radically in harmony with the primitive communal experience promoted by Francis.

4. In all of this it is obvious that Clare was indeed faithful. In all of this, it is important to see that Clare understood herself as possessing a personal, unique responsibility before God. She had been taught by Francis. She was, in her own right, also led by the Spirit. She did not try to escape the consequence of this truth with its demand for continuing discernment and personal decision. She did not rest in a pattern of imitation. She faced situations for which Francis had provided no specific counsel. She faced situations in which his specific advice could not be applied. In all events she acted as a woman in whom the awareness of sharing the grace with another did not lead to a sense of false security. Rather, it led her to a vigilance and creativity which preserved and augmented the gift. Lozano, in describing the living tradition that flows from the experience of charism writes: "[The charism], because of its pneumatic origin and because of its destination for a Church which moves forward in history, produces different fruits in different times and places. It gives rise to various styles of life, through which it incarnates the Gospel in different tongues....Hence it is essential for religious communities to remain open and docile to the action of the Holy Spirit. Communion with the Spirit is the true source of renewal and adaptation of the religious life."[46] Clare of Assisi's response to the charism meant not only appropriating the *Rule* and life of Francis, but also exercising personal historic responsibility for the preservation of that gift throughout time in the Franciscan family and in the Church.

[46] Lozano, *Foundresses*, 92.

Conclusion

The relationship of Francis and Clare should be characterized as a communion of mutual charism and mission. Clare, a woman touched by the Spirit and committed to the path of holiness, found in Francis the perfect guide for the aspirations that had earlier moved her towards a form of evangelical witness. Francis, for his part, found in Clare a leader who could give shape to the hopes of women who sought to share the call to penance and poverty that the friars' preaching announced. Much of the mutual influence that these two leaders and mystics exerted upon one another is found in the writings they have left us. Using the biographical sources to attain an understanding of their life and work together requires careful attention to the findings of work done with form-critical methods in recent years. In addition, while using their own writings and analyzing materials contained in early *legendae,* other literary forms used to convey, however symbolically, their experience of friendship and love must continue to be studied.

Such study leads to a belief that the world of meanings Francis and Clare shared is not yet fully appreciated. The source of their own understanding of their relationship in an enterprise of grace at work in the world is still not fully understood. The inner and outer language with which they might have conveyed these meanings to one another and to their mutual friends and companions requires further analysis. Their relationship must be analyzed by minds free of unexamined stereotypes or preconceived images. A close examination of Francis' behavior, for example, shows that his commitment to a bond of loving care for Clare and her sisters never wavered, and that—in point of fact—included among his dying gestures were marks and expressions of the most tender affection for them. There is also a need to "de-privatize" one's images of this relationship and to consider the ways in which their friendship was just one relationship in a much larger network of relationships spawned by the dynamic quality of the Franciscan movement of the early days.

The *Rule of Clare* is one of the most important and least known documents of Franciscan spirituality. It is most important in that it provides an authoritative summary of the evangelical project of Francis written by one of his earliest companions. It admits the legitimacy of certain principles of adaptation yet simultaneously preserves almost everything essential in his original project, while adding measures that stabilize the life of those called to this *forma*. In saying that it is "least known," the point of reference is the many congregations of Franciscan women who follow the Third Order Regular *Rule* and the Franciscan friars who lack personal contact with the sisters of the Poor Clares. For these groups of Franciscans there is need to re-examine Clare's *Rule* as one of the most important Franciscan documents available, in that it offers a living commentary on the *Later Rule* of Francis. Clare's *Rule* also requires a more thorough analysis in view of what it gained from its two papal antecedents: the *Rules of Hugolino* and *Innocent IV*. Its presence in the historic period which combined the diminishment of the beguines with the stabilization of strict material enclosure should be further examined, if its role in the history of religious life is to be properly valued.

The point at which Clare began the composition of her *Rule* coincided with a period in which the first wave of relaxations sought by the friars from the papacy was in full vigor. This fact, which is almost never alluded to in descriptions of the text's history, needs to be considered if the formulation of the *Rule* is to be appreciated as an event in Franciscan history as well as a document. Clare is presented, often eloquently, as the most faithful disciple of Francis. This fidelity is usually described in terms of a personal affiliation. In this mode of thinking and speaking, Clare emerges as an heroic woman whose desire to embrace the way of Francis is an inspiration which resulted in a stable "Second Order" within the Franciscan family. Clare is rarely considered in her relationship to the friars themselves during the early years or later during the critical decades in which the structures and mindset of the Order were forged. It must be understood that Clare's initiative was of major significance not only in the internal world of the Poor Sisters, but also as a commentary upon the *Rule* written by Francis and its observance (or absence thereof) among the friars.

Clare, in founding her monastery upon the Gospel ideals she shared so completely with Francis, created a new possibility of relationships for the women of her *milieu*. By insisting upon an equality of formation and membership, she gave testimony to the aspirations of women of her era desiring new opportunities to participate in a world beyond the confines of the domestic sphere. In creating this form of life, she implicitly acknowledged the passing of the last remnants of the feudal order into which she had been born. Furthermore, in her willingness to accept her members from all social levels she dared to make common cause with the newly emerging mercantile class.

The form of governance that Clare evolved in her lengthy service as abbess of San Damiano is a synthesis of Franciscan spirituality concretely applied to an essential and traditional religious life structure. Its articulation owes much to the older monastic tradition, with its centuries of accumulated wisdom. It also results from the experience of living out in concrete and prosaic ways the charism of Francis. The elements of Clare's *Rule* regarding the material composition of the cloister must be evaluated within an historical framework in order to arrive at a

244

just estimate of their importance and their place in her thinking. A good deal of study has been devoted to the theological implications of Clare's option for a life of seclusion and contemplation. There is much more room for study of the particular stage of historical development in church legislation for religious women in which her work is located. Clare's option for an enclosed life is not in question. The actual physical form, canonical sanctions, and historical ecclesiastical motivations for such legislation, are open to scrutiny and discussion. It is necessary, however, to approach the history of legislation governing enclosure—and its motivations—with open-mindedness and experientially-based questions which are respectful of and attentive to the lived experience of enclosure.

The manner in which the charism that Clare shared with Francis was articulated in her *Rule* and thereby preserved for future generations presents opportunities for reflection on the very nature of religious charism as it is understood in a contemporary theology of religious life. Placing both Clare's text and modern studies about a "founding charism" within the larger context of the theology of grace highlights the importance of understanding the spiritual dynamic unleashed when a charism is received and transmitted by the mediation of human interaction. There is, in addition, greater appreciation of the charism not as a quantity that can be defined, but a gift that is received and, if possible, described, in order to witness to its power as it comes from the Holy Spirit.

It is fair to conclude that Clare shared authentically and originally in the charism of Francis. She gave the charism a new dimension by her own discernment of how best to make it operative in her ordinary life and the ordinary existence of her sisters. She did this by describing it and providing for its continual efficacy in the *Rule*. She did this long after the death of Francis, surrounded by situations that made it appear that the early dream of the Franciscan movement was seriously endangered. The feminine incarnation of the Franciscan evangelical life emerges in Clare not only as a model for the inspiration of

Franciscan women. The feminine incarnation of the Franciscan evangelical life emerges in Clare as a testimony to the fact that the charism of the Franciscan vocation is given by the Holy Spirit equally to women throughout the history of the Orders. It also emerges for subsequent generations of Franciscan women and men as a paradigm of the ineluctable responsibility that each Franciscan man and woman possesses for the continuation, the preservation and the radical appropriation of the Franciscan vocation in our time.

BIBLIOGRAPHY

1Cel = Thomas of Celano. *Vita Prima S. Francisci. AF* X, 1-117.

2Cel = Thomas of Celano. *Vita Secunda S. Francisci. AF* X, 129-260.

1LAg = Clare of Assisi. *First Letter to Agnes of Prague.*

2LAg = Clare of Assisi. *Second Letter to Agnes of Prague.*

3LAg = Clare of Assisi. *Third Letter to Agnes of Prague.*

4LAg = Clare of Assisi. *Fourth Letter to Agnes of Prague.*

Actus-Fioretti = Actus Beati Francisci et sociorum ejus. Ed. Paul Sabatier. Paris: Fischbacher, 1902.

Adm = Francis of Assisi. *Admonitions.*

AF = Analecta Franciscana. Quaracchi/Grottaferrata, 1885 ff.

AFH = Archivum Franciscanum Historicum. Quaracchi/Grottaferrata, 1908 ff.

Andreas Capellanus. *The Art of Courtly Love.* Trans. John Jay Parry. New York: W.W. Norton and Co., Inc., 1969.

Andreozzi, G. *San Nicolò "De Pede Plateae" dove nacque il movimento francescano.* Roma: Editrice Franciscanum, 1986.

AP = L. Di Fonzo, O.F.M. Conv. "L'Anonimo Perugino tra le fonti francescane del sec. XIII." *MF* 72 (1972) 117-483.

Armstrong, R. J., O.F.M. Cap. "The Spiritual Theology of the *Legenda Major* of Saint Bonaventure." Ph.D. Dissertation, Fordham University, 1978.

Armstrong, *Clare* = *Clare of Assisi : Writings and Early Sources.*
    Edited by R. J. Armstrong, O.F.M. Cap. New York:
    Paulist Press, 1988.
Armstrong-Brady, *Works* = R. J. Armstrong, O.F.M. Cap., and I.
    C. Brady, O.F.M. *Francis and Clare: The Complete Works.*
    New York: Paulist Press, 1982.
Baker, D. *Medieval Women.* Oxford: Basil Blackwell, 1978.
Bartoli, M. "Analisi storica e interpretazione psico-analitica di
    una visione di S. Chiara di Assisi." *AFH* 73 (1980) 449-
    472.
Bartoli, M. "Donna e Società nel Tardo Medioevo: Guida
    Bibliografica." *Cultura e Scuola* 73 (1980) 81-88.
BC = *Bull of Canonization of Saint Clare.*
BF = *Bullarium Franciscanum,* vols. I-IV ed. J. H. Sbaralea,
    1759-1768, vols. V-VII. Ed. C. Eubel, 1898-1904; new
    series vols. I-III, ed. U. Hüntemann — J. M. Pou y Marti,
    1929-1949.
Bogin = M. Bogin. *The Women Troubadours.* New York: W.W.
    Norton and Co., 1980.
Bolton, B. "Mulieres Sanctae." *Women in Medieval Society.* 141-
    158. (Originally published in *Studies in Church History*
    10. London: Basil Blackwell, 1973).
Bolton, B. "*Vitae matrum*: a further aspect of the Frauenfrage."
    Ed. Derek Baker. *Medieval Women,* 253-273.
Bowie, Fiona, ed. *Beguine Spirituality.* Trans. Oliver Davies.
    New York: Crossroads, 1990.
Brooke, *Government* = R. B. Brooke. *Early Franciscan Gov-
    ernment: Elias to Bonaventure.* Cambridge: Cambridge
    University Press, 1959.
Brooke, *Work* = R. B. Brooke. "Recent Work on St. Francis of
    Assisi." *Analecta Bollandiana* 10 (1982) 653-676.
Brown, P. *The Cult of the Saints.* London: SCM Press, Ltd., 1983.
Bullough, V. L. *The Subordinate Sex: A History of Attitudes
    toward Women.* Chicago: University of Illinois Press,
    1973.

Bynum = C. Walker Bynum. *Jesus As Mother: Studies in the Spirituality of the High Middle Ages*. Berkeley: University of California Press, 1982.

CantExh = Francis of Assisi. *The Canticle of Exhortation to Saint Clare and her Sisters.*

Cantor, N. F. *Medieval History*. 2nd ed. London: Collier-Macmillan Limited, 1969.

Chenu, M-D., O.P. *Nature, Man and Society in the Twelfth Century*. Ed. and trans. J. Taylor and L. K. Little. Chicago: The University of Chicago Press, 1968.

Cheriyapattaparambil, F. X., O.F.M. Cap. *Troubadour Influence in the Life and Writings of the Man-Saint of Assisi*. Rome: Antonianum, 1985.

Ciardi = Ciardi, F. *I Fondatori, uomini dello spirito*. Roma: Città Nuova, 1982.

Clare of Assisi. *Writings*. See Armstrong, *Clare;* Armstrong-Brady, *Works; Écrits;* Omaechevarría, *Escritos.*

Colborn, F. "The Theology of Grace: Present Trends and Future Directions." *Theological Studies* 31 (1970) 692-711.

Conciliorum Oecumenicorum Decreta. Bologna, 1973.

Conti, M., O.F.M. *Lettura biblica della Regola francescana*. Roma: Ed. Antonianum, 1977.

Cousins, E., trans. *Bonaventure*. New York: Paulist Press, 1978.

Cuthbert of Brighton, O.F.M. Cap. "A disputed story concerning St. Clare." *AFH* 6 (1913) 670.

Der, J., O.F.M. Cap. *The Capuchin Lay Brother: A Juridical-Historical Study*. Diss. Roma: Pontificia Studiorum Universitas a S. Thoma Aq. in Urbe, 1983.

De Robeck, N. *St. Clare of Assisi*. Milwaukee: The Bruce Publishing Co., 1951.

Desbonnets = T. Desbonnets, O.F.M. "Dalla fraternità all'ordine." *Temi di vita francescana: la fraternità*. Eds. G. Cardaropoli and C. Stanzione. Roma: Ed. Antonianum, 1983.

Desbonnets, T., O.F.M. "Legenda Trium Sociorum." *AFH* 67 (1974) 38-144.

Desbonnets, T. — Godet, J-F. — Matura, T. — Vorreux, D. Eds. and trans. *François d'Assise: Écrits.* Sources Chrétiennes 285. Paris: Les Éditions du Cerf & Les Éditions Franciscaines, 1981.

Devlin, D. "Feminine Lay Piety in the High Middle Ages: The Beguines." *Distant Echoes,* 183-196.

Directives for the Mutual Relations Between Bishops and Religious in the Church. Vatican City: Sacred Congregation for Religious and Secular Institutes and the Sacred Congregation for Bishops, 1978.

Distant Echoes = J. A. Nichols and L. Thomas Shank, eds. *Medieval Religious Women, Volume One: Distant Echoes.* Kalamazoo: Cistercian Publications, Inc., 1984.

The Documents of Vatican II. Eds. Walter M. Abbott, S.J. & Msgr. Joseph Gallagher. New York: Guild Press, 1966.

Dozzi, D., O.F.M. Cap. *Haec Est Vita Evangelii Jesu Christi: Il Vangelo come vita nella "regola non bollata" di Francesco d'Assisi.* Roma: Pontificio Istituto Biblico, 1987).

Dronke, P. *Women Writers of the Middle Ages: A Critical Study of Texts from Perpetua (d. 203) to Marguerite Porete (d. 1310).* Cambridge: Cambridge University Press, 1984.

Écrits = M-F. Becker, J-F. Godet, T. Matura. *Claire d'Assise: Écrits.* Sources Chrétiennes 325. Paris: Les Éditions du Cerf, 1985.

Eliade, M. *Myths, Dreams and Mysteries.* Trans. Philip Mariet. Glasgow: Harvill Press, 1960.

Elkins, S. K. "All Ages, Every Condition and Both Sexes: The Emergence of a Gilbertine Identity." *Distant Echoes,* 169-182.

EpCust = Francis of Assisi. *Letter to the Custodians.*

EpFid = Francis of Assisi. *Letter to the Faithful.*

EpLeo = Francis of Assisi. *Letter to Brother Leo.*

EpMin = Francis of Assisi. *Letter to a Minister.*

Erickson, C., and Casey, K. "Women in the Middle Ages: A Working Bibliography." *Medieval Studies* 37 (1975) 340-359.

Esser, K., O.F.M. "The Definitive Rule of the Friars Minor." *Round Table of Franciscan Research* 34 (1969) 4-67.

Esser, K., O.F.M. *The Rule and Testament of St. Francis.* Chicago: Franciscan Herald Press, 1978.

Esser, *Opuscula* = K. Esser, O.F.M., ed. *Opuscula Sancti Patris Francisci Assisiensis.* Bibliotheca Franciscana Ascetica Medii Aevi XII. Grottaferrata: Collegio S. Bonaventura, 1978.

Esser, *Origins* = K. Esser, O.F.M. *The Origins of the Franciscan Order.* Chicago: Franciscan Herald Press, 1970.

Esser, K., O.F.M., and Hardick, L., O.F.M. *The Marrow of the Gospel.* Trans. and ed. I. Brady, O.F.M. Chicago: Franciscan Herald Press, 1958.

FF = *Fonti Francescane.* Ed. Movimento Francescano Assisi. Padova: Edizioni Messaggero, 1980.

Figueira, R. C. "Legatus apostolicae sedis: the Pope's 'alter ego' according to Thirteenth Century Canon Law." *Studi Medievali* 27 (1986) 527-574.

Flood = D. Flood, O.F.M. *Hugh of Digne's Rule Commentary.* Grottaferrata, Romae: Collegii S. Bonaventurae ad Claras Aquas, 1979.

Flood, D., O.F.M. "Cardinal Hugolino on Legation." *Haversack* 11 (December, 1987) 3-9, 24; "Sisters Minor," 10-16.

FormViv = Francis of Assisi. *Form of Life given to Saint Clare and her Sisters.*

Fortini-Moak = A. Fortini. *Francis of Assisi.* Trans. Helen Moak. New York: Crossroad Publishing Co., 1981.

Francis of Assisi. *Writings.* See Armstrong-Brady, *Works;* Desbonnets—Godet— Matura—Vorreux; Esser, *Opuscula.*

Fransen = Fransen, P. *The New Life of Grace.* Trans. Georges Dupont, S.J. New York: The Seabury Press, 1969.

Garrido = J. Garrido. *La forma de vida de Santa Clara.* Aranzazu, 1979.

Gelpi, D. *Charism and Sacrament: A Theology of Christian Conversion.* New York: Paulist Press, 1976.

Gilliat-Smith, E. *St. Clare of Assisi: Her Life and Legislation.* London &Toronto: I.M. Dent & Sons, Limited, 1914.

Godet, *Progetto* = J-F. Godet. "Progetto evangelico di Chiara oggi." *Vita Minorum* 56 (1985) 198-301.

Godet, J-F., and Mailleux, G. *Opuscula sancti Francisci, Scripta sanctae Clarae.* Corpus des Sources Franciscaines, V. Louvain: Université Catholique, CETEDOC, 1976.

Gold, P. S. "Male/Female Cooperation: The Example of Fontevrault." *Distant Echoes,* 151-162.

Gonnet, G. "La donna presso i movimenti pauperistico-evangelici." *MRFF,* 103-129.

Goodich, M. "Ancilla Dei: The Servant as Saint in the Late Middle Ages." *Women of the Medieval World: Essays in Honor of John H. Mundy.* Eds. J. Kirshner and S. F. Wemple. London: Basil Blackwell, 1985. 119-136.

Grau = E. Grau, O.F.M. "Die Schriften der heiligen Klara und die Werke ihrer Biographen." *MRFF,* 195-238.

Grundmann = H. Grundmann. *Movimenti religiosi nel medioevo.* Trans. M. Ausserhofer and L. Nicolet Santini. Bologna: Il Mulino, 1974.

Hart, M., "Dynamics of Franciscan Fraternity: A Study of Spirit, Word, Obedience and Poverty in the Writings of St. Francis of Assisi." Diss. Pontificium Athenaeum Antonianum, 1988.

Herlihy = D. Herlihy. *Medieval Households.* Cambridge, Mass.: Harvard University Press, 1985.

Hughes = D. Owen Hughes. "Invisible Madonnas? The Italian Historiographical Tradition and the Women of Medieval Italy." *Women in Medieval History and Historiography,* 25-57.

Iriarte, *History* = Iriarte, L., O.F.M. Cap. *Franciscan History. The Three Orders of St. Francis of Assisi.* Trans. Patricia Ross. Chicago: Franciscan Herald Press, 1983.

Iriarte, *Regola* = Iriarte, L., O.F.M. Cap. *La Regola di Santa Chiara: lettera e spirito* . Milano: Biblioteca Francescano Provinciale, 1976.

JdV = Jacques de Vitry. *De Maria Oigniacensi in Namurcensi Belgii Diocesi,* ed. D. P[apebroec] in *Acta Sanctorum,* Junii 5 (Paris, 1867) [June 23], 542-572. An English draft translation of this important work has recently been published by Peregrina Publishing Co., Saskatchewan, Canada, 1986. Trans. Margot King.

Johnson, T., O.F.M. Conv. "Liminality and the Religious Experience of Saint Francis of Assisi." *The Cord.* January 1985. 19-27.

Jordan = H. Boehmer. *Chronica Fratris Jordani.* Paris:`Librairie Fischbacher, 1908. English translation: Placid Hermann, O.F.M. *XIIIth Century Chronicles; Jordan of Giano, Thomas of Eccleston, Salimbene degli Adami* . Chicago: Franciscan Herald Press, 1961.

Jørgensen-Sloane = Jørgensen, J. *Saint Francis of Assisi.* (New York, 1955).

Kardong, Terrence, O.S.B. *Commentaries on Benedict's Rule.* Wilmington: Michael Glazier, 1986.

LaChance, P., O.F.M. *The Spiritual Journey of the Blessed Angela of Foligno According to the Memorial of Frater A.* Roma: Pontificium Athenaeum Antonianum, 1984.

LAgA = Agnes of Assisi. *Letter to her sister Clare.*

Lainati, *Fonti* = C. A. Lainati, O.S.C. "Le fonti riguardanti il secondo ordine Francescano delle Sorelle Povere di Santa Chiara." *Forma Sororum* 23 (1986) 131-145, 196-220.

Lainati, *Regola* = C. A. Lainati, O.S.C. "La Regola Francescana e il II Ordine." *Vita Minorum* 44 (1973) 227-249.

Lambert, *Poverty* = M. D. Lambert. *Franciscan Poverty.* London: Church Historical Society, 1961.

Lapsanski = D. V. Lapsanski. *Evangelical Perfection: An His-torical Examination of the Concept in the Early Franciscan Sources.* St. Bonaventure, N.Y.: The Franciscan Institute, 1977.

Leclercq = J. Leclercq. "Il monachesimo femminile nei secoli XII e XIII." *MRFF,* 63-99.

Leclercq, J. "Does St. Bernard Have a Specific Message for Nuns?" *Distant Echoes,* 269-278.

Leclercq, J.—Vandenbroucke, F.—Bouyer, L. *A History of Christian Spirituality, Vol. II: The Spirituality of the Middle Ages.* Tunbridge Wells: Burns & Oates, 1968.

LegCl = F. Pennacchi, ed. *Legenda sanctae Clarae virginis.* Assisi: Società Internazionale di Studi Francescani, 1910.

LEr = Clare of Assisi. *Letter to Ermentrude.*

LG = *Lumen Gentium.*

LHug = Cardinal Hugolino. *Letter to Saint Clare.*

LM = S. Bonaventure. *Legenda Maior S. Francisci. AF* X, 555-652.

Lozano, *Discipleship* = J. M. Lozano, C.M.F. *Discipleship: Towards an Understanding of Religious Life.* Trans. Beatrice Wilczynski. Manila: Claret Center for Resources in Spirituality, 1980.

Lozano, *Foundresses* = J. M. Lozano, C.M.F. *Foundresses, Founders, and their Religious Families.* Trans. Joseph Daries, C.M.F. Chicago: Claret Center for Resources in Spirituality, 1983.

LP = R. B. Brooke, ed. and trans. *Scripta Leonis, Rufini et Angeli sociorum S. Francisci.* Oxford: Clarendon Press, 1970.

LRay = Cardinal Raynaldo. *Letter to the Poor Sisters.*

LTS = *Legenda Trium Sociorum.*

Mandelli, G., O.S.C. "Santa Chiara e profezia." *Vita Minorum* 56 (1985) 1-24.

Manselli, R. "La chiesa e il francescanesimo femminile." *MRFF,* 239-261.

Manselli, R. "La donna nella vita della chiesa tra duecento e trecento." *MRFU,* 243-255.

Manselli, R. *Nos qui cum eo fuimus: Contributo alla questione francescana.* Roma: Istituto Storico dei Cappuccini, 1980.

McDonnell, K., O.S.B. "Charismatic spirituality: one among many." *Theology Digest* 22 (1974) 211-216.

McNamara, J. A. "The Ordeal of Community : Hagiography and Discipline in Merovingian Convents." *Vox Benedictina* 3 (1986) 293-326.

MF = *Miscellanea Francescana.* Foligno/Assisi/Roma, 1886 ff.

Moorman, J. R. H. *A History of the Franciscan Order from its Origins to the Year 1517.* Oxford: Clarendon Press, 1968.

MRFF = *Movimento religioso femminile e francescanesimo nel secolo XIII.* Assisi: Società Internazionale di Studi Francescani, 1980.

MRFU = *Il Movimento religioso femminile in Umbria nei secoli XIII-XIV.* Regione dell'Umbria: "La Nuova Italia" Editrice, 1984.

Mühlen, H. "Sacrament and Charism: the Spirit and the Church," *Theology Digest* 15 (1977) 45-49. Extracted from the original: "El Spiritu y la Iglesia: relación entre sacramento y carisma," *Estudios Trinitarios* 3 (1975) 385-399.

Nimmo = D. Nimmo. *Reform and Division in the Medieval Franciscan Order.* Rome: Capuchin Historical Institute, 1986.

Oliger = L. Oliger, O.F.M. "De origine regularum ordinis sanctae Clarae." *AFH* 5 (1912) 181-209; 413-447.

Oliger, *Expositio* = L. Oliger, O.F.M., ed. *Expositio Quator Magistrorum Super Regulam Fratrum Minorum (1241-1242).* Roma: Edizioni di "Storia e Letteratura," 1950.

Omaechevarría, I., O.F.M. *Escritos de Santa Clara y Documentos complementarios.* Madrid: Biblioteca Autores Cristianos, 1982.

Omnibus = M. Habig, O.F.M., ed., *St. Francis of Assisi : Writings and Early Biographies (English Omnibus of the Sources for the Life of St. Francis).* 4th rev. ed. Chicago: Franciscan Herald Press, 1972.

Pásztor, E. "I papi del Duecento e Trecento di fronte alla vita religiosa femminile." *MRFF,* 29-65.

Pásztor, E. "The Sources of Francis' Biographies." Trans. Patrick Colbourne, O.F.M. Cap. *Greyfriars' Review* 1 (1987) 31-40.

Paul VI. "Ecclesiae Sanctae." *Acta Apostolicae Sedis* 57 (1966) 775-782.

Paul VI. "Evangelica Testificatio. On the Renewal of the Religious Life: Apostolic Exhortation." *Acta Apostolicae Sedis* 63 (1971) 497-526.

Pazzelli, R. *San Francesco e il Terz'Ordine.* Padova: Edizioni Messaggero Padova, 1982. English transl., Chicago: Franciscan Herald Press, 1989.

PC = *Perfectae Caritatis.*

Peaceweavers = L.T. Shank and J. A. Nichols, eds. *Medievel Religious Women Volume Two: Peaceweavers.* Kalamazoo: Cistercian Publications, Inc., 1987.

Pernoud, R. *I Santi nel Medioevo.* Milano: Rizzoli Editore, 1986.

Pisanu, L., O.F.M. *Innocenzo IV e i Francescani (1243-1254).* Studi e Testi Francescani, 41. Roma: Edizione Francescane, 1968.

Power, E. *Medieval Women,* Ed. M.M. Postan. London: Cambridge, 1975.

Proc = Z. Lazzeri, O.F.M. "Il processo di canonizzazione di santa Chiara d'Assisi." *AFH* XIII (1920) 403-507.

Quo elongati = ed. H. Grundmann. *AFH* 54 (1961) 20-25.

Raurell, F. *Lineamenti di Antropologia Biblica.* Casale Monferrato: Edizione Piemme, 1986.

RegB = Francis of Assisi. *Later Rule of the Friars Minor.*

RegCl = Clare of Assisi. *Rule of the Poor Sisters.*

RegErm = Francis of Assisi. *Rule for Hermitages.*

RegHug = *Rule* of Cardinal Hugolino.

RegInn = *Rule* of Innocent IV.

RegNB = Francis of Assisi. *Earlier Rule of the Friars Minor.*

Ruether and McLaughlin = R. Ruether and E. McLaughlin, eds. *Women of Spirit: Female Leadership in the Jewish and Christian Traditions.* New York: Simon and Schuster, 1979.

Rusconi, R. "L'espansione del francescanesimo femminile nel secolo XIII." *MRFF,* 279-285.

Schroeder, H.J. *Disciplinary Decrees of the Genereal Councils Text, Translation, and Commentary.* New York: Herder, 1937.

Schulenberg, "SAE" = J. T. Schulenberg. "Strict Active Enclosure and its Effects on the Female Monastic Experience (500-1100)." *Distant Echoes,* 51-86.

Schulenberg, "Patterns" = "Women's Monastic Communities, 500-1100: Patterns of Expansion and Decline," *Sisters and Workers in the Middle Ages.* Eds. Judith M.Bennett, Elizabeth A. Clark, Jean F. O'Barr, B. Anne Vilen, Sarah Wespahl-Wihl. Chicago: Chicago UP, 1989.

Scripture quotes from *New American Bible.* Ed. Confraternity of Christian Doctrine. Camden: Thomas Nelson Inc., 1971.

Sensi, *MRFU* = M. Sensi. "Incarcerate e Recluse in Umbria nei Secoli XIII e XIV: Un Bizzocaggio Centro-Italiano." *MRFU,* 87-121.

Seraphicae Legislationis Textus Originales. Quaracchi, 1897.

Shahar = S. Shahar. *The Fourth Estate: A History of Women in the Middle Ages.* London: Methuen, 1983.

Skinner, M. "Benedictine Life for Women in Central France, 850-1100: A Feminist Revival." *Distant Echoes,* 87-113.

Smith, J. "Robert of Arbrissel: *Procurator Mulierum."* Derek Baker, *Medieval Women,* 175-184.

SP = P. Sabatier, ed. *Speculum Perfectionis seu S. Francisci Assisiensis Legenda antiquissima autore fratre Leone.* Paris: Fischbacher, 1898.

TestCl = Clare of Assisi. *Testament.*

Thomas = A.G. Little. *Fratris Thomae vulgo dicti de Eccleston: Tractatus de Adventu Fratrum Minorum in Angliam.* Manchester: Manchester University Press, 1951.

Thompson, S. "The Problem of the Cistercian nuns in the twelfth and early thirteenth centuries." *Medieval Women*. 227-251.

Thomson, W. R. *Checklist of Papal Letters relating to the Orders of St. Francis: Innocent IV—Alexander IV.* Grottaferrata: Collegio S. Bonaventura, 1971.

Valerio, A. "La donna nella 'societas christiana' dei secoli X-XII." *Rassegna di teologia*. 3 (1983) 435-446.

Van Asseldonk, O., O.F.M. Cap. *La Lettera e lo Spirito.* 2 vol. Roma: Editrice Laurentianum, 1985.

Van Leeuwen, P., O.F.M. "Clare's Rule." *Greyfriars Review*. 1 (September, 1987) 65-76.

Vauchez, A. "L'Idéal de sainteté dans le mouvement féminin franciscain aux XIIIe et XIVe siècles." *MRFF,* 322-323.

Wade Labarge, M. *Women in Medieval Life: A Small Sound of the Trumpet*. London: Hamish Hamilton, 1986.

Waley, D. "Istituzioni comunali di Assisi." *Assisi nel tempo di San Francesco*. Assisi: Società Internazionale di Studi Francescani, 1978. 55-70.

Women in Medieval History and Historiography. Ed. Susan Mosher Stuard. Philadelphia: University of Pennsylvania Press, 1987.

Women in Medieval Society. Ed. Susan Mosher Stuard. Philadelphia: University of Pennsylvania Press, 1976.

Appendix

Comparison of the Rules

Rule of Hugolino	Rule of Innocent
I Form and manner of living	I Form of Life; enclosure; explanation of life
II Need for rules and laws	II Divine Office
III Gives Rule of St. Benedict	III Silence; the parlor
IV Obligation to remain enclosed; explanation of life prior to entrance	IV Fasting; care of the sick
V Divine Office	V Clothing; common dormitory
VI Silence; the parlor	VI Entrance into the monastery
VII Fasting	VII The Chaplain; the grill
VIII Care of the sick	VIII The Visitator
IX Clothing	IX Door; enclosure; the Portress
X Entrance into the monastery	X Extern Sisters
XI The Chaplain; the grill	XI Receive & retain possessions
XII The Visitator	
XIII The Portress; the key	
XIV Obligation of the Rule	XII Obligation of the Rule

Rule of Clare	Rule of 1223
I Form of Life of the Poor Sisters	I The Life of the Friars Minor
II Those who wish to accept this life & how they are to be received	II Those who wish to embrace this life & how they should be received
III The Divine Office & fasting; confession & communion	III The Divine Office & fasting, & the way the Brothers should go about the world
IV The election & office of the Abbess; the Chapter, & the officials and discreets	IV The Brothers are never to receive money
V Silence, the parlor, the grill	V The manner of working
VI The lack of possessions ***Forma Vitæ Last Will***	VI The Brothers shall not acquire anything as their own; begging alms; the sick Brothers
VII The manner of working	VII The penance to be imposed on the Brothers who sin
VIII The Sisters shall not acquire anything as their own; begging alms; the sick Sisters	VIII The election of the Minister general of this Fraternity & the Chapter of Pentecost
IX The penance to be imposed on the Sisters who sin; the Sisters who serve outside the monastery	IX The preachers
X The admonition & correction of the Sisters	X The admonition & correction of the Brothers
XI The custody of the enclosure	XI The Brothers are not to enter the monasteries of nuns
XII The Visitator, the Chaplain, and their Cardinal Protector	XII Those who go among the Saracens & other non-believers